ENDORSEMENTS DISCOVERING ROMANS

Those who had the privilege of meeting Dr. S. Lewis Johnson Jr. knew they were in the presence of "a scholar and a gentleman." He had clearly absorbed Paul's letter to the Romans into his soul and shared Luther's view that it is "the purest gospel." Today's commentaries sometimes seem to tell us more than the biblical authors themselves could have known and are in danger of losing the reader in a forest of technicalities. Here, by contrast, is an exposition of beautiful clarity and simplicity by a master craftsman who knew scholarship intimately but wore it lightly. *Discovering Romans* leads us carefully through the text and is a delight to read. Anyone who loves Romans—which we all should—will love this!

SINCLAIR B. FERGUSON, Professor of Systematic Theology, Redeemer Seminary, Dallas

S. Lewis Johnson was a premiere theologian and careful expositor of God's Word whose influence was widespread in the late twentieth century. His work on Romans is another example of the gift this man was to the church of the Lord Jesus Christ. You will find this book to be a valuable addition to your library.

DANNY AKIN, President, Southeastern Baptist Theological Seminary, Wake Forest, North Carolina

As I read the words of this commentary, I can't help but hear in my head the voice of S. Lewis Johnson Jr. I count it as an immeasurable blessing to have sat in the presence and under his influence as he preached through Paul's greatest epistle. His remarkable exegetical and theological insights, combined with a pastor's heart and a love for God's people, made that a genuinely life-changing experience. I am indescribably grateful for the efforts of Mike Abendroth in making this volume available. No one should undertake a study of Romans without Johnson at his side. Highly recommended!

SAM STORMS, PhD, Pastor, Bridgeway Church, Oklahoma City

S. Lewis Johnson is one of the great unsung theologians of the twentieth century. He had a brilliant mind and laid out a banquet of wit and wisdom in all his messages, both at Believers Chapel and Dallas Theological Seminary. As a professor at Dallas Seminary, Trinity Evangelical Divinity School, and other institutes, he taught Hebrew, Greek, and systematic theology—a true Renaissance man! His sermons were models that students at Dallas Seminary were required to listen to—an enjoyable homework assignment if ever there was one! Johnson was Reformed to the core. He was a perfectionist, not wishing to publish until he reached maturity in his views. Because of this, most of his sermons and class notes—all typed and in polished form—have never been published. I am delighted to see that Mike Abendroth has gotten permission from Johnson's heirs to publish this commentary. Just as Galatians was Luther's Katie von Bora, so Romans was Johnson's great love. In this commentary you will find clear, rich exposition of the greatest letter ever written. As Augustine was prompted to read Romans when he heard a child say, *Tolle lege!*, so too I commend you to take up and read this devotional yet scholarly commentary on Paul's letter to the Romans.

DANIEL B. WALLACE, Professor of New Testament Studies,
Dallas Theological Seminary

Anyone who sat in Dr. Johnson's classes or heard him preach knows that he brought to his teaching a dedication to understanding Scripture and honoring God. The opportunity for those who never had that privilege to get a glimpse of this in a book as significant as *Discovering Romans* is most precious. Here is a man of God handling God's Word with reverence and care. It is a wonderful combination as the power of God's message through Paul is explained by someone who walked through the Greek text and through life with listening ears.

DARRELL BOCK, Professor of New Testament Studies,
Dallas Theological Seminary

Having personally sat under the preaching of S. Lewis Johnson for five years at Believer's Chapel, I can strongly attest that he was a master of Scripture, a "Prince of Expositors." Few men have been so preeminent in the pulpit, so strongly committed to the biblical text, and so deeply steeped in sound doctrine. In my estimation, he is the least-known highly proficient and biblical preacher of the last half-century. All who love the truth will want to read the rich teaching of this gifted servant of the Lord.

STEVEN J. LAWSON, Senior Pastor, Christ Fellowship Baptist Church,
Mobile, Alabama; Teaching Fellow, Ligonier Ministries

S. Lewis Johnson possessed a superb theological mind and exquisite teaching gifts. He loved Scripture and was committed to its truth. His preaching was always powerful and profound, yet lucid and easily accessible. Bible teachers of his caliber are exceedingly rare, and his manner of blending biblical exposition with rich theological instruction is fast becoming a lost art. *Discovering Romans* will have a prominent place on my bookshelves.

PHIL JOHNSON, Executive Director, Grace To You

I am grateful that the writings of Dr. S. Lewis Johnson are being preserved and passed into the next generation. Dr. Johnson was committed to the exegetical and expositional preaching and teaching of God's inerrant Word. I am glad to recommend the project undertaken by my friend Mike Abendroth and am pleased that Dr. Johnson's family has encouraged this pursuit. May this commentary on Romans expand minds and hearts for God through the study of his Word.

MARK BAILEY, President, Dallas Theological Seminary

Dr. Johnson is at the top of my list of favorite expositors, and he is at his best in Romans. Reading this book offers a unique privilege to sit at the feet of a master teacher and theologian who exalts the sovereignty and glory of God. This book will fill your head for sure, but it will also fill your heart and your hands to gratefully serve the One who died for the many.

DR. MARK HITCHCOCK, Senior Pastor,
Faith Bible Church, Edmond, Oklahoma

S. Lewis Johnson Jr., my mentor and friend, was a gracious Christian gentleman, humble scholar, and lover of God's Word. His fondness for Romans was most evident in his teaching and preaching on the doctrine of imputation—the basis for substitutionary atonement; indeed for salvation itself! Much could be said about his sound, contextual exegesis, but I want to emphasize the clarion call he continued to trumpet for the vitally important doctrine of imputation, especially on the meaning of the final clause of Romans 5:12, "because all sinned." As Johnson has said, that single phrase "has been one of the major battlegrounds of the systems of theology." There are so many important truths pertaining to the representative headship of the first and last Adam and of God's justice, love, mercy, and grace in the messages propounded in this book that I can only say, "Read it! Ponder it! And embrace the truth! It is doctrinally sound, heart-warming, and spiritually nourishing."

GARY D. LONG, ThD, Faculty President,
Providence Theological Seminary, Colorado Springs

I am one of those privileged to have some history with Dr. S. Lewis Johnson. It began when I was a student at Dallas Seminary as well as a member of Believers Chapel, where he preached for many years. Later, I was blessed to be able to preach alongside him, under the giant shadow he cast. When we left Believers Chapel to start a new work (with the encouragement and assistance of the elders) our daughters were still young, so they never got to know Dr. Johnson. Years later, our whole family returned to Believers Chapel for the funeral of a good friend. As Dr. Johnson was delivering the message, one of my daughters leaned over and whispered in my ear, "I don't know who this guy is, but he's good!" I couldn't agree more. Like my daughter, you might not have been privileged to get to know Dr. Johnson personally, but as you read his brilliant treatment of Romans, I'm certain that you will agree that he is a marvelous teacher of the Word. And even more, I'm convinced that his teaching will fix your eyes on Jesus, who is infinitely better.

ROBERT DEFFINBAUGH, Pastor-Teacher,
Community Bible Chapel, Richardson, Texas

I first encountered Dr. S. Lewis Johnson Jr. in the beginning of my seminary education some twenty years back. Lost in the vast maze of my theological education, I was struggling to find the balance between scholarship and pastoral ministry—a balance that plagues so many of us who take up the task of preaching. Someone mercifully pointed me to the preaching ministry of Dr. Johnson. I recall the first moment I heard the stately southern gentlemen expound the Word of God. It was his exposition of Romans. It was at that moment that I first encountered what I did not think was possible. A deep and intensive exegesis of God's Word was combined with an equally deep compassion and love for God's people. I heard what it sounds like to study at the level of a scholar and communicate at the level of a friend. In my humble opinion, no modern preacher has proven to be his equal in the rare alchemy of knowledge and grace. The volume you hold in your hand was taken from the sermons that changed the course of that young preacher's life and ministry. I am beyond grateful it has been put into print.

BYRON YAWN, Pastor, Community Bible Church, Nashville

With that remarkable and admirable combination of a deeply and widely learned theological mind and an always keen exegetical eye, S. Lewis Johnson was known as a scholar of rare abilities. This was coupled with a heart warmly fervent for the gospel; he was always a treat to hear and to read, and I cherish every memory of him. He loved Paul's letter to the Romans, and he wrote, taught, and preached from it many times, always to distinct profit and blessing. Mike Abendroth, an avid student of Johnson, has done us a great service in collating Johnson's thoughts on this greatest of Paul's epistles.

FRED G. ZASPEL, Pastor, Reformed Baptist Church, Franconia, Pennsylvania;
Professor of Theology, Calvary Baptist Seminary

By the grace of God, S. Lewis Johnson played an instrumental role in the recovery of and concern for a solid biblical theology in the ranks of twentieth-century evangelicalism. I still treasure the memory of his teaching in this regard. It is a personal joy, then, to recommend *Discovering Romans*, which is of immense value in the ongoing struggle to maintain a truly evangelical theology that is deeply rooted in the Scriptures.

MICHAEL A. G. HAYKIN, Professor of Church History & Biblical Spirituality,
The Southern Baptist Theological Seminary, Louisville

For those privileged to hear Dr. Johnson teach the great book in the classroom and preach it from the pulpit, the publication of his work on Romans is a special delight. I think that few rival his ability as an expositor of Holy Scripture. His scholarship is impressive, grasp of theology profound, and pastoral insights deeply beneficial.

JOHN D. HANNAH, Distinguished Professor of Historical Theology, and Research
Professor of Theological Studies, Dallas Theological Seminary

It was my joy and privilege to sit under Dr. Johnson's preaching every Sunday for four years, as well as to learn from him in several courses at Dallas Seminary. For me, he has been a model of an excellent Bible expositor. I trust that his exposition of Romans will bless many.

THOMAS L. CONSTABLE, Senior Professor Emeritus of Bible Exposition,
Adjunct Professor in Bible Exposition, Dallas Theological Seminary

S. Lewis Johnson on Romans! What a delight it is to see the legacy of an exceptionally faithful Bible teacher helping us to behold the glories of Christ in Romans. Dr. Johnson's ministry is known for clarity, warm-hearted conviction, and a Christ-centeredness that resonates with pastors, scholars, and laypeople alike. Furthermore, the theological integrity of this work makes it a superb tool for discerning the difference between authentic gospel truths and vain speculations. If you are a pastor, the resource you recommend on Romans just became much easier. If you are a teacher, *Discovering Romans* can be your trustworthy "go to" guide. For Bible students, this book will be helpful in discovering the unfathomable riches of the gospel in Romans. I am thrilled to recommend *Discovering Romans*.

PATRICK ABENDROTH, Pastor, Omaha Bible Church

DISCOVERING
ROMANS

DISCOVERING
ROMANS

SPIRITUAL REVIVAL FOR THE SOUL

S. LEWIS JOHNSON JR.
ADAPTED BY MIKE ABENDROTH

ZONDERVAN

Discovering Romans
Copyright © 2014 by S. Lewis Johnson Jr. Family Trust and Mike Abendroth

This title is also available as a Zondervan ebook.
Visit www.zondervan.com/ebooks.

Requests for information should be addressed to:
Zondervan, 3900 *Sparks Dr. SE, Grand Rapids, Michigan* 49546

Library of Congress Cataloging-in-Publication Data

Johnson, S. Lewis Jr.
    Discovering Romans : spiritual revival for the soul / S. Lewis Johnson Jr.
        p.   cm.
    Includes bibliographical references.
    ISBN 978-0-310-51542-5
    1. Subject one. 2. Subject two. I. Title.
AA000.0.A00 2014
0000000 – dc23   2014000000

This book is published in association with The Benchmark Group Agency, Nashville, TN, benchmarkgroup1@aol.com.

Cover design: wdesigncompany.com
Cover photography: © Neil Beer / GettyImages.com
Interior design and composition: Greg Johnson/Textbook Perfect

Printed in the United States of America

HB 10.06.2023

To the two Gracies in my life.

Grace Johnson Monroe's commitment to see Jesus Christ exalted through her father's words inspires me.

Grace Abendroth joyfully reminds me just how important a godly father is in the life of his child.

CONTENTS

ACKNOWLEDGMENTS

I am especially thankful for Mark Newman, an elder at Believers Chapel. Without Mark this project never would have taken flight. I rejoice in our common love for Christ Jesus and for S. Lewis Johnson. Thanks for passing on my idea for this book to the Johnson family.

My agent, Patti Hummel, is simply the best. She knew exactly how this concept should be developed and how to walk me safely across the tightrope of contracts, estates, and a whole bevy of other factors that were beyond my grasp. Thank you for "thinking big."

The folks at Zondervan were a delight at every step of the process. Thanks especially belong to Paul Engle, Madison Trammel, Laura Weller, Verlyn Verbrugge, Stan Gundry, and Nathan Kroeze. I am indebted to your dedication to excellence. Thanks for working with a *soli deo gloria* attitude.

I am indebted to Ray Johnson and Tracy Johansen, who helped initiate the project, and to Erin Benziger, who rescued me near the end.

I thank John MacArthur for his faithful exposition of the full counsel of God, his humble servant's heart, and his ferocious determination to exalt Christ Jesus, and for introducing me to Lewis Johnson's preaching in 1991. My reasoning was simple: if S. Lewis was good enough for MacArthur to listen to, then I needed to stock up on cassette tapes from Believers Chapel.

A special note of appreciation goes to Martha Scogin Johnson for her hospitality and kind reception. To sit in her living room and listen to her recall stories about Lewis warmed my heart. When Martha brought me into Lewis's actual study, I was glad to see his computer (complete with a huge monitor), books, books, books, Bibles, and his classic typewriter. It was a profound joy simply to sit at his desk. I also relished peeking out at the backyard and gazing at the landscape that informed so many of Lewis's stories about grapes, vines, and fig trees!

It was my great privilege to travel to Texas to meet with Grace, the daughter of S. Lewis Johnson. The purpose of the meeting was to introduce myself and to get to know the family of a man whose passion for teaching the Bible had impacted my Christian life significantly. Dennis and Grace Johnson Monroe welcomed me with Christian love, and I left Dallas thinking, *My respect for*

Lewis has multiplied because of the fruit that Lewis as a father bore in his daughter (obviously through the Holy Spirit). Thank you, Grace!

My thanks to my bride, Kim, can never be fully articulated. I suppose I am no longer jealous that she starts her day with a cup of tea and an S. Lewis Johnson sermon. If my wife must have another man in her life, I am glad it is Lewis. Thank you for your enduring love and for your desire to serve the Lord Jesus with me. Your godliness humbles me. Thanks to Maddie, Hayley, and Luke for being patient with their father as he constantly mulled over the words of "SLJ."

I wish I could go to Dallas and present a copy of this book to Lewis, though he was such a meticulous scholar that I surely would be intimidated. For Lewis, ministry needed to be done with excellence and precision because such work was being done for the honor of the Lord. Christ Jesus was worth every effort for Lewis.

With that I offer the most important acknowledgment: I thank the Lord Jesus for his work in and through S. Lewis Johnson Jr. I am a pastor, and many congregants surely wonder, "If everyone needs a pastor, who is my pastor's pastor?" Lewis, along with John MacArthur, shepherd my soul through their audio and long-term ministries. I am humbled to be the instrument used to work with Lewis's biblical studies and to facilitate the production of this book. May it be a powerful tool for the Lord's work!

Mike Abendroth

FOREWORD

S Lewis Johnson possessed a rare combination of gifts and knowledge. He served more than forty years in pastoral ministry, and for thirty-one of those years, he simultaneously taught systematic theology at Dallas Theological Seminary. He was not only a beloved pastor, but also a first-class scholar, a highly esteemed theologian and professor, a superb Bible expositor, a committed churchman, and a tireless discipler of other men. From 1963 through 1993 he was the teaching pastor at Believers Chapel in Dallas. Each week he faithfully preached profound expository sermons—in an era when such preaching was widely deemed impracticable, ineffective, and unfashionable.

And his congregation thrived.

Dr. Johnson had come to faith in Christ in his twenties under the ministry of Donald Grey Barnhouse, pastor of Philadelphia's famous Tenth Presbyterian Church and speaker on a nationally-aired radio broadcast known as *The Bible Study Hour*. Barnhouse's distinctive style of verse-by-verse preaching (with an emphasis on clear, precise doctrine) left an indelible mark on Johnson. Personally, I am deeply indebted to both of them. The expository method they modeled set a pattern for me to follow, and both men exemplified the faithful persistence I still aspire to—preaching the Word of God in season and out of season.

Dr. Lewis Johnson pioneered the use of cassette tapes for recording and distributing sermons. With the help of generous labor and financial support from a team of devoted church members, Believers Chapel distributed tapes of the weekly messages without charge to anyone who wanted to listen. All those sermons are still available freely today on the internet, now reaching a wider audience than ever. They are timeless messages, full of edification and encouragement—a priceless resource I rely on frequently.

As prolific as he was, Lewis Johnson did not publish many written works. Preaching and teaching were his priorities. He prepared his sermons and classroom lectures with painstaking care, leaving little time for hobbies or extracurricular projects—including writing for publication. Until now, Bible students and pastors who wished to learn from him or glean his insights on key biblical texts were dependent mainly on the audio recordings. Mike Abendroth is doing us all a great favor by editing Dr. Johnson's sermon transcripts and compiling the content in book form. This is the inaugural volume in that project—the first in what I hope will become a long series. These books are an answer to many prayers and are worthy of a prominent place on every serious Bible student's bookshelf.

Dr. Johnson's famous expositions of Romans constitute some of his finest work. That's fitting, because Paul's epistle to the church at Rome epitomizes everything Dr. Johnson stood for. The epistle itself is a detailed, systematic exposition of gospel truth. The apostle Paul was the quintessential preacher, systematic theologian, and defender of truth—the archetype for the philosophy of ministry to which Dr. Johnson was committed. Furthermore, Romans is Paul's magnum opus—a profound but compact digest of doctrine, carefully outlined and skillfully presented.

The powerful truth of this inspired epistle, unpacked and examined in Lewis Johnson's ingenious teaching style, makes a wonderful resource. I love how this volume is both profoundly instructive and easily accessible, perfectly capturing all the strengths of Dr. Johnson's preaching. It is a superb overview of Paul's message, rich with insight at all the key points. It would be hard to find a more succinct, clear, and robust exposition of Romans.

Too many preachers today think key biblical terms like *imputation, propitiation, predestination*, and other crucial doctrinal expressions are just too academic or too advanced for laypeople. So they avoid not only the terminology but also the doctrines. Scripture also has a lot to say about certain topics that don't automatically inspire human enthusiasm or interest—matters like sin, judgment, and hell. Many preachers purposely try to sidestep or soft-pedal such themes.

As a result, the typical evangelical nowadays is untaught on significant doctrines like original sin, divine election, God's sovereignty, the vital distinction between justification and sanctification, and a host of other doctrines that are woven into the fabric of Pauline teaching (the book of Romans in particular).

Rather than avoiding these meatier points of doctrine, S. Lewis Johnson always took time to explain them carefully in simple, insightful, and compelling ways. This was perhaps his foremost skill: making hard theological concepts easily understandable while arousing his students' appetite for more. Johnson's ingenuity as a teacher shines through this book.

Whether you are a pastor teaching others or a layperson engaged in personal Bible study, I know you will find *Discovering Romans* highly readable, insightful, and spiritually edifying. May the Lord bless your study and open your eyes to behold wondrous truths in His Word (Psalm 119:18).

John MacArthur

INTRODUCTION

Who was S. Lewis Johnson?[1]

S. Lewis Johnson Jr. was born in Birmingham, Alabama, on September 13, 1915. When he was fourteen years old, his family moved to Charleston, South Carolina, where he completed high school and graduated from the College of Charleston in 1937. Lewis became a proficient golfer, participating in many amateur golf championships from 1933 to 1937. After graduating from college, he returned to Birmingham to join his father's insurance business and to wed Mary Sibley McCormack, who went to be with the Lord in 1979.

Lewis loved golf so much that he could not enroll in German language classes at college because they competed with his tee times. But the sovereignty of God ordained even this, as Lewis, who was not a believer at the time, registered for the only available morning class — Classical Greek. When the Lord later saved Lewis, he was instantly able to pick up the New Testament in Greek and read it fluently!

Lewis describes his conversion to Jesus Christ in the early 1940s:

> When we lived in Birmingham, Alabama, in the early forties, I was asked to go to a meeting, a tea. Now I didn't go to teas in the first place, but this one was with a preacher. Nevertheless, I was persuaded. I thought this was harmless, and after all, he was beginning a series of meetings this week and if I could go to the tea and escape the meetings then everything would be wonderful. So I went to the tea. During a discussion, I objected to the Bible as the Word of God and that I wouldn't listen to it because I didn't think it was the Word of God. Finally I spoke to Donald Grey Barnhouse and said, "How can we know that the Bible is the Word of God?" His answer showed me that I hadn't thought a great deal about the matter.
>
> When the tea was finished, we walked out into the hall, and there was an evening service. I never intended to go to the service. I'd only promised to attend the tea and even that was a sacrifice because I probably would have played golf that afternoon. When Dr. Barnhouse turned around to this crowd of people and said, "Who's taking me to the church?" my wife said, "We will." Now I was very frustrated over this. I felt exactly like Simon the Cyrene did. I had been requisitioned. I had been commandeered. I found myself sitting in

about the third row, listening to the great preacher preach on God's plan of the ages. For the first time in my life I heard someone speak with authority about Jesus Christ. But I didn't want to admit that I was touched.

Mary went to the meeting the next day by herself. When she came home I asked her a lot of questions. The next morning as I got up to go to work, I just blurted out to Mary, "You've got to get a babysitter for every night this week, I'm going to hear every one of those messages." That week I came face to face with Jesus Christ and was saved. God saved me. Have you ever been brought face to face with Jesus Christ who loved you and gave himself for you?[2]

Lewis earned a Master of Theology degree in 1946 and a Doctor of Theology in 1949, both at Dallas Theological Seminary. He then taught Greek, Hebrew, and Systematic Theology at DTS for thirty-one years (Professor of New Testament, 1950–1972, and Professor of Systematic Theology, 1972–1977). Later, Lewis became the Professor of Biblical and Systematic Theology at Trinity Evangelical Divinity School in Deerfield, Illinois, from 1980 to 1985, as well as a visiting Professor of New Testament at Grace Theological Seminary in Winona Lake, Indiana. From 1985 to 1993, he served as a visiting Professor of Systematic Theology at Tyndale Theological Seminary in Badhoevedorp, Amsterdam, Netherlands.

S. Lewis Johnson's years in the pastorate began in 1951 at Independent Presbyterian Church, where he served until 1954. From 1954 to 1958, he was the pastor of Grace Bible Church, and later he became a teaching elder and minister at Believers Chapel, serving there from 1980–1993.

Lewis met his Savior face-to-face on January 28, 2004. He was eighty-eight years old. He is survived by his second wife, Martha Scogin Mayo, and his two children: his son, Samuel L. Johnson III, and his daughter, Grace Johnson Monroe.

Those who listen to Lewis will notice the relentless preaching of Jesus Christ through a southern gentleman. One cannot help but be struck by his clear and forceful exposition of the Scriptures. In a time when the pomp and circumstance of oratorical delivery is celebrated even above content, the preaching of Lewis is without show, as he simply let God speak through the biblical text. Contrived pastoral panache was absent from Lewis's preaching, but Christ and the Word were preeminent.

My description of Lewis's expository preaching would be "deliberately biblical and intentionally Christ-centered." His material withstands time because he remained so close to the trans-chronological truths of Scripture. While many in pulpits today employ a variety of man-made solutions, human wisdom, and worldly methods so that they might be perceived as "relevant" and be received by the masses, Lewis knew that both God and his Word were always relevant. If God, the Creator, Sustainer, Judge, and Savior, is not germane or pertinent to people, who or what would be? Lewis's words about Romans from the early 1980s ring just as true today as when they first were spoken nearly thirty-five years ago.

The impact of S. Lewis Johnson is especially evident in the lives of those who knew him best. His daughter, Grace, will say things such as, "I will always remember Daddy praying on his knees in his room." An encounter with any one of Lewis's thousands of seminary students would find their faces beaming with appreciation and gratitude to the Lord for such a wonderful gift to the church body. Martha speaks of her husband's godliness in both the classroom and in the living room. As Fred Zaspel said of his friend,

> He was in so many ways a man to emulate. He was a true gentleman. He was always personable and a great delight in conversation. His humor was always good, and his wit was always quick. He was a careful student of the Scriptures with unusually superior abilities as an exegete and theologian. His abilities with the original languages were clearly superior, and when discussion began he would always lead from his Greek and Hebrew text. He was a man of conviction, willing to step down from a noted career rather than surrender his beliefs. He was passionate for the gospel, and his heart was always hot for Christ. He was a humble and godly man. I have said many times that if God would allow me to grow old as gracefully and as saintly as Dr. Johnson I would become proud and ruin it. He was a model scholar, a model teacher, a model preacher, a model friend, and a model Christian. He was that rare combination of so many abilities and virtues. I thank God for him and feel much the poorer without him.[3]

In total, Dr. Johnson served the Lord Jesus Christ and his church for approximately forty-five years. In a day filled with evangelical impropriety, Lewis's life was above reproach. There were no shameful scandals, no disqualifying blemishes, and no breaches of integrity. Lewis did not force himself into the limelight nor did he use manipulation to claim a stake to a reputation. S. Lewis Johnson was faithful, not flashy; he was Christ-centered, not self-focused.

Lewis's southern demeanor was perfectly complemented by his southern accent. To quote Lewis, his way of speaking was "English in its pure form." But there was one thing that Lewis was never heard saying with or without an accent. Ascribing to George Mueller's philosophy that the Lord would provide for his work, S. Lewis Johnson was never heard asking or begging for money. Instead, his favorite subject was the redeeming work of Jesus Christ. Lewis regularly found ways to incorporate into his sermons the great truth of the Lord's substitutionary death. For Lewis, Christ's death accomplished salvation. If Spurgeon was known for preaching a biblical passage and making a beeline to Christ Jesus, Lewis was known for heading straight toward the penal substitution of Jesus the Messiah. He loved to talk about Jesus as both mankind's representative and the substitutionary Lamb of God. To listen to Lewis is to understand quickly the three great imputations described in Romans 5. He knew and loved the gospel and preached it without compromise.

Understanding what commentaries were available to him when he studied Romans might best reveal Lewis's true exegetical prowess. While he utilized the best scholarship available at the time (C. E. B. Cranfield, John Murray, Charles Hodge, John R. W. Stott, et. al.), he did not have access to some of the most valuable Romans resources ever written (Douglas Moo, *The Epistle to the Romans*, New International Commentary on the New Testament, 1996; Thomas Schreiner, *Romans*, Baker Exegetical Commentary on the New Testament, 1998; Leon Morris, *The Epistle to the Romans*, Pillar New Testament Commentary, 1988). This limitation of resources thus makes Lewis's contribution to the study of Romans all the more impressive.

Aristotle, speaking of proficiency in sciences, admitted, "Every systematic science … seems to admit of two distinct kinds of proficiency; one of which may be properly called scientific knowledge of the subject, while the other is a kind of educational acquaintance with it."[4] Lewis did not simply know the Word academically; his heart desired to be known by the Word on a deep level. Rarely can one man preach passionately, pastor, and excel in the classroom. Lewis's academic aptitude was unquestioned, and his preaching through the ministry at Believers Chapel continues to have worldwide effects. What a gift the Lord gave to his church in Lewis.

ORIGIN OF *DISCOVERING ROMANS*

The aim of this book, *Discovering Romans*, is to expound, in simple fashion, Paul's most wonderful epistle to the Romans. Lewis taught Romans more than forty times, each time from the original Greek language. In some ways, Lewis was "known" for teaching this book. I think the reader soon will see why.

All of my great ideas seem to materialize on a bicycle, weather permitting. There is nothing like straddling a carbon-fiber bike and pedaling for hours at ninety revolutions per minute. To refresh my soul while riding, I *always* listen to Samuel Lewis Johnson Jr. Three years ago, on a long and winding Massachusetts road, I heard through my headphones Lewis discussing the federal headship of Jesus Christ from Romans 5. My mind was riveted to the eternal truths about Jesus Christ. I could barely contain myself with joy. A thought flashed through my mind as fast as an eighteen-wheeler zooming past me: "Every person at the church I am privileged to pastor needs exposure to this life-changing truth. I want them to read an S. Lewis Johnson book on the topic of Romans 5!" While the theological output of Lewis was staggering, he only published one formal book in his lifetime.[5] Yet I wanted everyone I knew to listen to these words about the righteousness of the Lord God. I also desired to see these truths placed in a book so that as many people as possible could benefit from the Lord's servant Lewis.

Almost without hesitation, I blurted out in prayer, "Lord, I would be willing to put that book on Romans together." The idea was etched in my mind. Mile after mile, sermon after sermon, I could not shake the idea of a Johnson book. After more prayer, I phoned Believers Chapel and inquired generally about the possibility of such a publication. Even though I suspected that I was not the first one to conceive such an idea, the kind receptionist forwarded my information to an elder at Believers, namely, Mark Newman. Once Mark and I talked about my plans for a book, he graciously encouraged me to move forward and gave my contact information to Lewis's daughter, Grace.

I never will forget the first time Grace and I spoke over the phone. The gospel's truths, taught by her father and her mother, Mary, peppered the conversation. The Lord Jesus' glory was preeminent as Grace walked me through her father's life and ministry. I thought to myself, "What an amazing legacy the Lord can grant through a life of faithful ministry." Six months later, my wife and I traveled to Dallas to meet with Grace and her husband, Dennis. It was a blessing to listen to Grace lovingly talk about her father and his admiration for Jesus Christ. I only wish I had brought along a tape recorder! The most moving recollection was listening to Grace describe her knowledge, even at a young age, of the special things the Lord was doing through her human father.

Grace took us to meet Lewis's wife, Martha, whom he married on March 22, 1980. Martha also reflected on the grace of God in the life of Lewis, and my estimation of her husband only increased as the fond stories flowed. I told the Johnson family about my desire to see Christ Jesus magnified through the publication of Lewis's work. Ministry centered on biblical exegesis with Christ-centered exposition is always needed. If the Lord still is using the sermons of J. Vernon McGee, the work of S. Lewis Johnson certainly could also exceed the bounds of his earthly life and stretch to serve another generation of Christians. Martha and Grace said they would read some of my other books to properly vet me (my words, not theirs). Yikes. I am humbled and honored that they agreed to let me pursue this great project. It has been a delight to my soul, and I pray that those who read *Discovering Romans* will experience the same enrichment.

THE FORMAT

It generally is acknowledged that there are three basic types of biblical commentaries. The first is known as *exegetical*, and it is the most scholarly and detailed, filled with Greek words, syntax, and interpretative dilemmas and their proposed solutions. On the opposite end of the spectrum resides the *devotional* commentary. This type highlights application and personal response to the truth in Scripture. Devotional commentaries may pass over large swaths of material, but they do so to focus on passages that lend themselves to the worship and "devotion" of the Lord God. The *expositional* commentary finds itself comfortably situated between the other two. Skilled preachers exposit the Word and point the listener to the intent of the author of Scripture. These commentaries, then, are essentially sermons that have been reworked, edited, and put into written form. They seek to "expose" the reader to the biblical passage in a way that a pastor should on a Sunday morning, showing authorial intent and highlighting Christ.

If I had to categorize *Discovering Romans*, it would be under the heading of *expositional*, but the reader quickly will see Lewis's exegetical expertise perfectly combined with a warm, fervent zeal for Jesus Christ. When reading the insights on Romans 5:12, Lewis's exegetical mastery cannot be ignored. At the same time, his material discussing Romans 8 undoubtedly will leave the reader appreciative of its comforting, devotional emphasis, written for even the newest Christian. Since Lewis was not a man caught up in the new and novel, I must resist promoting this book as a new category of commentary ("expo-votional"), but it is valuable to recognize that *Discovering Romans* would be perfect for home groups, small Bible studies, Bible teachers, and seminary professors.

Lewis put it this way, "If one reads the Epistle to the Romans, he, or she, immediately discovers that the apostle wrote for the common people. The many names that are mentioned in chapter 16 are just the names of ordinary people such as you and I. The apostle wrote for common people, he wrote for freed men, he wrote for slaves, he wrote for men, and he wrote for women." In other words, Paul wrote Romans for you. So, whether you are a seminary professor or stay-at-home mother, God has a message for you in the book of Romans, and consequently in this book, *Discovering Romans*. I originally conceived of this volume as being the ideal book to give to every person at the church I pastor — a church that is home to engineering students, people with PhDs in theology, grandmothers, doctors, and seemingly every occupation and life stage in between. After its completion, I still agree with my initial instinct.

WHAT I DID TO THE MATERIAL

What does "adapted by Mike Abendroth" mean? One online dictionary describes "adapt" as "to make suitable to or fit for a specific use or situation."[6] My adaptive work on the project consisted of gathering over 160,000 words of Lewis's sermon transcripts from Romans (delivered from July 13, 1980, to September 20, 1981, at Believers Chapel in Dallas, Texas) and making them suitable for a book of approximately 90,000 words.

After preaching each sermon, Lewis would type his messages on his typewriter. He then gave his manuscript to his secretary, Emily Ray, and she typed it on her IBM Selectric. To make the titles bold, she even used rub-on letters! Emily then sent the copy she had typed to the printer, and they later delivered the printed copies to Believers Chapel. The finished product was called the "Believers Bible Bulletin."

I gathered all of these Believers Bible Bulletins from Romans. Thankfully, Lewis also produced a series of nine articles for *Bibliotheca Sacra* spanning Romans 1:1 – 3:20. These articles, published between 1971 and 1974, have proved invaluable in the preparation of the section discussing Romans 1 – 3.[7] I am thankful for Roy Zuck's permission to use this material.

Discovering Romans collates and further refines Lewis's magisterial work for print. Sermon collections rarely make easy-to-use commentaries because the auditory nature of a sermon does not always translate into print. This case proves to be an exception because the reader is helped by Lewis's detailed exegetical work, clear delivery, and theological acumen. Many technical notes are listed in the footnotes.

My overriding goal as adapter is to let Lewis speak. When studying the Bible one should strive to understand authorial intent ("What did Paul mean when he said...?"). This commentary utilizes the same philosophy as it seeks to convey the authorial intent of S. Lewis Johnson. "What did Lewis mean when he said...?" I am quite confident that you will "hear" the voice of Lewis in the volume you hold even though his southern accent (I love the way he pronounces, "viticulture" and "lion") will be muffled. While I might have changed some flow or transitions and condensed some sentences, most every word you read was spoken or written by Johnson. I claim any and all of the mistakes in this volume. I have deleted almost every reference to the Dallas Cowboys. But for the sake of those who appreciate Dr. Johnson's wonderful sense of humor, here is one of his actual benedictions: "I invite you to come to Christ and trust in him. Time is up, the Cowboys have started playing. Let's stand for the benediction."

My theology almost exactly mirrors Dr. Johnson's. There are two reasons for the similarity. First, I listen to about three hundred S. Lewis Johnson sermons on my bicycle every year. Second, many of my theological professors were taught directly by Lewis. In this commentary, not one theological position of Lewis has been altered or changed. In fact, I received a supreme compliment when Grace Johnson read some of my other books and said to me, "You quote all the men my daddy quoted." Now I quote her daddy.

CLOSING WORDS FROM LEWIS

No one needs more books to clutter shelves and collect dust, but there is a need for books that offer truth, passion for the gospel, and hope for eternity by a man who served Christ with commitment in humble adoration. After reading this book, I know you will agree and come to a deep appreciation for Dr. S. Lewis Johnson Jr. If you are already acquainted with Lewis's ministry, you will rejoice knowing his material is now in book form. If you are not familiar with him, you will say to yourself, "Why did it take me so long to learn about this man?"

If you were to ask Dr. Johnson how you could become a better Bible student, he would instantly respond by saying, "Read more Calvin!" When my seminary students ask me the same question, I reply, "Listen to S. Lewis Johnson." Now, thanks to Zondervan, I can say, "Read *Discovering Romans* by S. Lewis Johnson."

I leave you with some wisdom from Lewis. I hope you will hear his heartbeat and grasp the importance of the epistle of Romans in these words:

> As I was sitting in the airport, waiting for my plane to take off to Chicago, a young man walked by and said, "Good morning, Dr. Johnson." We had a very interesting conversation and he then gave me his personal card. On the back of the card were these words, "Thank you for bringing the light of Jesus to my heart. I, of all people, needed Romans." Well, we all need Romans.

Mike Abendroth
Lancaster, Massachusetts
January 2014

CHAPTER 1

THE CHRIST
PAUL PREACHED

ROMANS 1:1–17

In countless instances, Romans has been the means of arousing individuals and churches out of spiritual lethargy. Augustine, the learned municipal teacher of rhetoric in the city of Milan, was vexed over the condition of his soul. With a "mighty rain of tears" pouring from his eyes, he threw himself on the ground under a fig tree. He kept crying out, "And Thou, O Lord, how long? How long, O Lord, wilt Thou be angry unto the end? Remember not our former iniquities." There he heard from a neighboring residence the voice of a child chanting repetitiously, *Tolle, lege! Tolle, lege!* What "Take it, read it! Take it, read it!" meant to the child, Augustine does not say. To him, however, it meant that he should open a book and read the first passage he found. He took up a copy of Romans he had left there. Snatching it up, he opened it and read the first passage on which his eyes fell: "Let us behave decently, as in the daytime, not in orgies and drunkenness, not in sexual immorality and debauchery, not in dissension and jealousy. Rather, clothe yourselves with the Lord Jesus Christ, and do not think about how to gratify the desires of the sinful nature." With the end of this sentence from Romans 13:13–14 the darkness was dispelled, and his heart was flooded with light.[1] The epistle to the Romans has warmed the heart of countless others who have pondered its message, for in it is the sum and substance of the voice of God to humans.

"The Epistle to the Romans," C. H. Dodd said in the opening sentence of his commentary on the book, "is the first great work of Christian theology."[2]

It is the only part of Scripture in which there is found a detailed and systematic presentation of the main features of Christian doctrine. Since the apostle's thought is founded on and drawn from the Old Testament primarily, Romans is also an excellent introduction to the theology of the Old Testament. The epistle is calculated to provide its reader with an incisive insight into the riches of the Old Testament and with a sterling handbook to the theology by which Christian believers are to live. Therefore, it should come as no surprise that Paul's letter to the Romans is one of the most influential letters ever written.

THE INTRODUCTION

The introduction to Romans is no ordinary salutation. Embedded within it is one of the apostle's classic statements of the person and work of the Redeemer he preached. He calls Jesus the Son of God, and it is evident that Paul knows no distinction in dignity between his Lord and his God.

THE AUTHOR

> [1]*Paul, a servant of Christ Jesus, called to be an apostle and set apart for the gospel of God —* [3]

It was winter of the years AD 54 – 55 in the city of Corinth, the vanity fair of the ancient world. Two quiet and dignified men, guests in the house of Gaius, a Christian businessman of Corinth, sat down to engage in the work of correspondence. Paul, a man who appeared to be in his late fifties, prepared to dictate a letter to a man named Tertius (cf. Rom. 16:22). That papyrus scroll that flowed from the hand of Tertius would be sufficient to change the course of the history of the Western world.

The letter began insignificantly enough, being composed in accordance with the common formula of salutation, which was in the form of, "A to B, greeting." But once that is acknowledged, everything changes, and Christian expansions enter. The author expands the description of himself, the description of the addressees, and the greeting. Further, in the midst of the salutation there appears a lengthy aside on the nature of the Christian message, resulting in an almost unique epistolary introduction.

The author in his opening words relates himself to three things: his Master, his spiritual gift, and his work. With regard to his Master, Paul describes himself as "a servant of Christ Jesus." The word "servant,"[4] used here for the first time in Romans, is a familiar term from the Old Testament. It is used of the relationship of the Old Testament believers to Yahweh, such as Abraham (cf. Ps. 105:6, 42), Moses (cf. Num. 12:7 – 8), and David (2 Sam. 7:5, 8). The prophets too were accorded this dignity (cf. Amos 3:7; Zech. 1:6). Although a Jew and steeped in the thought of the Old Testament, Paul is proud to call himself a slave of Christ Jesus. To him it is evident that to be the servant of Yahweh and the servant of Jesus Christ is one and the same thing. In his opening words, then, we are given a hint of the lofty majesty of the Jesus whom Paul preached.

The noble phrase "servant of Christ Jesus" is undoubtedly intended to refer to a position Paul holds in the Lord's service. He calls himself a servant simply to indicate his official status.

Paul refers to himself as an apostle by calling (*klētos*, "called to be"). He is an apostle by a divinely initiated calling, not by human seeking.[5] Paul, therefore, has not gained his position by arrogant, ambitious, and presumptuous self-efforts. His call, as Abraham's, was an invitation that came from heaven.

The word "apostle" is a word that comes into importance in Christian circles. Among the spiritual gifts of the New Testament church apostleship stands first (cf. 1 Cor. 12:28; Eph. 4:11).[6] An apostle had seen the risen Messiah and had been appointed by him to plant the flag of faith in every community to which his Master led him. He was his emissary and spoke with his authority. Thus, in Paul's words there is the implicit claim that he is the authoritative representative of Jesus Christ, divinely called to his task.

Finally, Paul relates himself to his work. He has been "set apart for the gospel of God,"[7] a statement that must have been written out of the context of his experience on the road to Damascus. That left an indelible impression on Paul; he was forever and fully dedicated to the ministry of God's gospel.

THE SUBJECT

>[2]*the gospel he promised beforehand through his prophets in the Holy Scriptures* [3]*regarding his Son, who as to his human nature was a descendant of David,* [4]*and who through the Spirit of holiness was declared with power to be the Son of God by his resurrection from the dead: Jesus Christ our Lord.* [5]*Through him and for his name's sake, we received grace and apostleship to call people from among all the Gentiles to the obedience that comes from faith.* [6]*And you also are among those who are called to belong to Jesus Christ.*

The mention of the good news of the gospel leads Paul into an illustration of a peculiarity of his style, the tendency to take off into an expansion of one or more of the essential elements of his address to his readers. This one consumes five verses. Often these asides provide the reader with a key to the theme of the epistle, as is the case in the opening sentences of 1 Corinthians (cf. 1:2). The theme of Romans is simply "the gospel of God" (cf. vv. 1, 16 – 17).

The Roots of the Gospel (1:2)

The first thing said of God's gospel is that, while it is good news, it is not new news. Its roots lie firmly embedded in the Old Testament. It is not without reason that this epistle has been called a theology of the Old Testament, because Paul's words "promised beforehand" are ultimately written out of the background of Isaiah 40 – 66 (cf. 40:9; 52:7; 61:1) and Habakkuk 2:4 (cf. Rom. 1:17; 3:21; 4:3, 6 – 8; et al.). "The gospel represents," Franz Leenhardt says, "not a break with the past, but a consummation of it."[8] It is, therefore, exegetical suicide to attempt to interpret the New Testament apart from the voice of its predecessor, the Old Testament. Gerhard von Rad is right: "Christ is given to us only through the double witness of the choir of those who await and those who remember."[9]

The fact that Paul uses the words "promised beforehand" points also to the element of divine foreordination in the gospel. As Martin Luther in his characteristically rugged way said, "Christianity did not originate by accident or in the fate of the stars (as many empty-headed people presume)," but "it became what it was to be by the certain counsel and premeditated ordination of God."[10]

The Content of the Gospel (1:3 – 4)

Otto Kuss has said that verses 2 – 4 contain a concise but full paraphrase of the gospel preached by Paul.[11] The apostle adds the claim that it concerns God's Son, referring to the *theanthropic*[12] person, the Son clothed with man's nature. He is the Son of God because he is consubstantial with the Father, equal with him in power and glory. "The term," Charles Hodge adds, "expresses the relation of the second to the first person in the Trinity, as it exists from eternity.... He was and is the Eternal Son."[13] Thus, Paul's theology is theocentric in that God is the ultimate source of salvation, but it is Christocentric in that its executive is the unique Son of God, who cut the covenant with his blood on the cross. This sonship, then, is the foundation of all that follows.

At this point, the reader is brought face-to-face with a passage that surely would rank with Paul's greatest christological passages, were it not for its difficulty of interpretation. Students of verses 3 and 4, and the description of the Son they contain, are agreed on one thing: the clauses are arranged in an obvious antithesis to one another.

First, then, what does Paul mean by the verb "declared"? A search of a concordance and a consideration of New Testament usage of "declared" leads to the conviction that the Greek word means *to appoint*.[14] The first antithesis, then, between the words "who as to his human nature" and "appointed" suggests that the Son entered the human stage of his existence by birth, and that this was followed by an appointment to a further status. The details of these two facets of his life and ministry are developed in the second of the antitheses.

Second, the antithesis between "a descendant of David" and "the Son of God" is not difficult. The former phrase is a clear reference to the Davidic descent of our Lord, and it is evident, not only from this reference but from others also,[15] that this was an essential part of the Pauline gospel. Davidic sonship, with all its messianic meaning, is therefore to be added to divine sonship as a fundamental feature of the Jesus Paul preached.

The other side of the antithesis spells out the significance of the Son's appointment. It seems best to take the phrase "with power" with "the Son of God" and not with "declared." His sonship in power refers, then, to the authority he possesses by virtue of his exaltation. Almost imperceptibly sonship begins to merge into lordship.

The resurrection is the great event that reveals the true meaning of the saving work of the cross. It is the evidence that the redeeming work has been accomplished with the full approval of the Father (cf. Rom. 4:25).

The third antithesis is between "as to his human nature" and "through the Spirit of holiness." The first phrase clearly refers to the human nature of the Lord in its entirety (cf. 9:5; John 1:14; Eph. 2:15; 1 Tim. 3:16; Heb. 5:7). With respect to his human nature, he was born of the seed of David. What, however, does "through the Spirit of holiness" mean? Earlier commentators, due to the clear reference to the human nature in the opposite side of the antithesis, referred the phrase to his divine nature (cf. Rom. 9:5).[16] If, as seems certain from usage, "declared" means "appointed," then in what sense could it ever be said that Jesus Christ was appointed Son of God according to his divine nature? He was eternally the divine Son by virtue of his own inherent right to the title.

We may take the phrase "through the Spirit of holiness" to characterize Christ spiritually, just as "according to the flesh" characterizes him physically. It expresses the spirit of holiness that dominated all his thoughts and actions. It was the holy obedience, the complete consecration by which he did the will of God, seen most clearly in the obedience of the cross. It is no wonder, then, that Paul added, "Therefore God exalted him to the highest place and gave him the name that is above every name" (Phil. 2:9).[17] The Messiah's life is characterized by two stages, the stage of humiliation and the stage of exaltation, and the former gave way to the latter.[18] He who was Son of David according to his physical being was appointed God's powerful Son according to his spiritual consecration following the resurrection.

Paul, instead of contrasting the human and divine natures of the Son in verses 3 and 4, contrasts the two stages in the historical process of his first coming, the incarnate and the glorified stages. The clauses, then, move from messiahship to lordship, the resurrection being the point of division between the state of humiliation and weakness and the state of exaltation and power.

The final words of verse 4, "Jesus Christ our Lord," effectively summarize the points of the interpretation. The Son is, first, "Jesus Christ," the historical messianic figure who will fulfill the covenant promises to Israel. He is, second, "our Lord," the exalted sovereign who is Judge over all. Thus, the historical and the official, the humiliation and the exaltation, unite in a thrilling affirmation of his supreme glory.

The Aim of the Gospel (1:5 – 6)

Here is Paul's first use of the word "grace" in the letter, a word that J. H. Jowett once defined as "holy love on the move."[19] At this place in Romans it is the particular grace of apostleship, and its aim is to win believing obedience among all the nations (cf. 11:13; 15:16, 18). The last expression of verse 5 in the Greek text, "for his name's sake," stresses that the glory of Jesus Christ is the ultimate goal of God in the proclamation of the gospel.

THE ADDRESSEES

> [7]To all in Rome who are loved by God and called to be saints:
> Grace and peace to you from God our Father and from the Lord Jesus Christ.

The apostle closes the monumental introduction by expressing his desire that God's favor, his "grace," and confident access after alienation,[20] his "peace," may be the experience of the Romans. It is to come "from God our Father and from the Lord Jesus Christ." He links his "Lord" with "God our Father,"[21] viewing the two persons together as the common source of the supernatural gifts of grace and peace. Paul could not do this if he did not believe that the two stand on the same ground, equal in power and wisdom and authority.

THE GOSPEL PAUL PREACHED

Since the great truth of justification by faith alone is at the heart of Paul's letter to the Roman church, the epistle may come as something of a surprise to modern ecclesiastics. We might have expected the apostle to address believers at Rome, a city crammed with social problems, with a social manifesto or, at the least, a recitation of the primary truths of Christianity in their application to the social problems of the imperial city. Rome was a city of slaves, but Paul did not preach against slavery. It was a city of lust and vice, but he did not aim his mightiest guns at these evils. It was a city of gross economic injustice, but he did not thrust the sword of the Spirit into the vitals of that plague. It was a city that had been erected on and that had fed on and prospered by the violence and rapacity of war, but the apostle did not expatiate on its immorality. Apparently, if we are to judge the matter from a strictly biblical standpoint, Paul did not think that social reform in Rome was "an evangelical imperative."[22] The proclamation of the gospel of Jesus Christ solved the crucial and urgent need for the society as a whole and for people in particular. It is still the imperative of the Christian church, and the Christian church will advance only to the extent that its gospel advances.

Romans 1:16 – 17 is a concise summary of the content of the letter. Professor C. K. Barrett has written, "Most commentators recognize in them the 'text' of the epistle; it is not wrong to see in them a summary of Paul's theology as a whole."[23] It has been said that the whole law, according to the Jews, was given to Moses in 613 precepts, that David reduced them in Psalm 15 to 11, that Isaiah further diminished them to 6, Micah to 3, Isaiah in a later passage to 2, but Habakkuk 2:4 condensed all 613 into 1: "The just shall live by faith" (KJV).

THE POWER OF THE PAULINE GOSPEL

[8]First, I thank my God through Jesus Christ for all of you, because your faith is being reported all over the world. [9]God, whom I serve with my whole heart in preaching the gospel of his Son, is my witness how constantly I remember you [10]in my prayers at all times; and I pray that now at last by God's will the way may be opened for me to come to you.

[11]I long to see you so that I may impart to you some spiritual gift to make you strong — [12]that is, that you and I may be mutually encouraged by each other's faith. [13]I do not want you to be unaware, brothers, that I planned many times to come to you (but have been prevented from doing so until now) in order that I might have a harvest among you, just as I have had among the other Gentiles.

[1]I am obligated both to Greeks and non-Greeks, both to the wise and the foolish. [15]That is why I am so eager to preach the gospel also to you who are at Rome.

[16]I am not ashamed of the gospel, because it is the power of God for the salvation of everyone who believes: first for the Jew, then for the Gentile.

Explanation (cf. 1:8 – 15)

The Romans, living in the world's most important city, might have wondered why the apostle to the Gentiles had not visited them. It is to this implied question that Paul addresses himself in the paragraph that follows his introduction (1:1 – 7). He explains that it was not from lack of desire to see them. He was "prevented" (cf. 1:13), a probable reference to satanic forces. Contrary to what the Romans might have been thinking, the apostle feels a great burden of debt to all types of people, whether Greeks or barbarians, and so he is ready to preach the good news to the Romans also (cf. 1:14 – 15).

The Gospel's Effect on Paul (1:16a)

The Greek includes a "for,"[24] introducing the reason for the apostle's readiness to preach the gospel in Rome. Paul felt no need to apologize for his message. We might have suspected that at the seat of the empire among the wise and contemptuous the apostle would have been tempted to shrink from the incongruous message of a crucified carpenter, of a murdered Galilean. But opinion, society, convention, custom, and other forms of the world's scorn were never of concern to Paul.

The term *gospel*[25] means "good tidings, good news," and it carried with it a note of excitement. "Good news" was, and is, the type of message we might shout across the street to a friend or neighbor. "The war's over!" "It's a boy!"[26] The Christian message has that same note of exhilaration. "The atonement's accomplished!" "God welcomes sinners because of Christ's work!"

The Gospel's Effect on Others (1:16b – c)

If the gospel buoyed up the apostle's spirit with supernatural boldness, it does even greater things for lost people, such as saving their souls, for its power is divine.[27] The word translated "power" is the Greek word *dynamis*, which refers to intrinsic power transforming human lives.

The prepositional phrase "for the salvation" expresses the goal of the operation of the divine power. Salvation is spiritual deliverance from the penalty of sin (cf. Eph. 2:5, 8; Phil. 1:28; 2 Thess. 2:13), from the power of sin in the believer's life (cf. 2 Cor. 1:6; 7:10; Phil. 2:12), and of future deliverance from the presence of sin at glorification (cf. Rom. 13:11; 1 Thess. 5:8 – 9).

We are reminded of the famous story of an Anglican bishop and a young Salvation Army lassie. At an evangelistic meeting in England, a young girl spied among the gathered people an Anglican bishop. Thinking that he was surely a likely prospect for the Lord's salvation, she approached him with the friendly question, "Sir, are you saved?" The bishop replied, "Young lady, do you mean *esōthan* (aorist, for the past event), *sesōsmai* (perfect, for the past fact with continuing results), *sōzomai* (present, for the present deliverance from the power of sin), or *sōthēsomai* (future, for the future consummating deliverance from the presence of sin)?" The young lady was completely taken aback, and no wonder, for the bishop was the renowned Brooke Foss Westcott.

The remaining phrases of verse 16 stress the universal offer of God's salvation. As John Murray says, "There is no discrimination arising from race or culture and there is no obstacle arising from the degradations of sin."[28] The last phrase, "first for the Jew, then for the Gentile," does not express Paul's preference, but simple historical precedence.[29] The gospel came to the Jews before it came to the Gentiles, as the Scriptures required (cf. 15:8–13; Luke 24:47; Acts 13:46).

THE RIGHTEOUSNESS OF THE PAULINE GOSPEL

[17]*For in the gospel a righteousness from God is revealed, a righteousness that is by faith from first to last, just as it is written: "The righteous will live by faith."*

The Source of the Righteousness (1:17a)

Verse 17, as verse 16, is introduced by the particle "for,"[30] showing that the chain of reasoning continues. Paul is ready to preach in Rome, *for* he is not ashamed of the gospel. He is not ashamed of the gospel, *for* it is God's power unto salvation. It is God's power unto salvation, not because it contains a beautiful code of ethics, but because in it there is contained the righteousness from God.[31] To possess the righteousness of God is to be saved, and vice versa.

What, then, is the meaning of the phrase "a righteousness from God"?[32] The term must be understood forensically,[33] which is found in its Old Testament Hebrew counterpart[34] and in the Septuagint.[35] The forensic sense is that of being *in the right* in relation to God, God being regarded as the judge, before whose court all people must stand and be examined. To be justified is to be *declared righteous* by God, not to be *made righteous* by God. This force is clearly demanded by the Old Testament (cf. Deut. 25:1) and the New Testament (cf. Rom. 3:4; 5:17, "gift"; 10:3). To possess the righteousness of God, then, is to possess a righteousness that God provides (cf. 5:17) and thus approves (cf. 2:13). It is not done by people, nor is it done in people; it is done for people.[36] It can be a person's only by imputation. "A righteousness of God," revealed and offered in the gospel, is the work of God in Christ, that which the Mediator did and suffered to satisfy the demands of divine justice (cf. 3:24 – 25).

The phrase "a righteousness from God" was the phrase that led Martin Luther into the light of the truth that produced the Protestant Reformation. Luther confessed later that he had always hated the expression "the righteousness of God," for it suggested to him a stern judge, waiting to hurl thunderbolts of judgment down on helpless, disobedient men. Through his study of the Psalms in 1514 he learned that the righteousness of God was related to man's deliverance, not man's condemnation. Commenting on his experience years later in 1545, Luther said, "As violently as I had formerly hated the expression 'righteousness of God,' so I was now as violently compelled to embrace the new conception of grace and, for me, the expression of the Apostle really opened the Gates of Paradise."[37] The righteousness of God, then, is the key to salvation. Those who have it know the power of God in personal salvation, and they know that they are "right before God."[38] Those who do not have it are lost and are not right before him. Scholar William Cunningham used to say, "The righteousness of God is that righteousness which his righteousness requires him to require."[39]

The Manifestation of the Righteousness (1:17a)

Paul's word describing the manifestation of this divine righteousness is "revealed."[40] The apostle does not mean that God's righteousness is simply to be observed in the gospel; rather, he means that it is seen in the gospel to be a saving power. It is, as John Murray points out, "manifest in its saving efficacy."[41] It is active in the sphere of human sin, saving and delivering the sinner.

The Source (or Means) and Design of the Righteousness (1:17b)

How are the words "by faith from first to last"[42] to be understood? C. K. Barrett, agreeing with the New International Version, has suggested taking the words in a rhetorical sense, namely, "faith from start to finish."[43] James Stifler thought the first phrase indicated the source of righteousness[44] and the second indicated the goal[45] for which God's provision of righteousness was designed. The divine righteousness is *out of* faith, that is, it has its origin in the believing heart. It is also *provided for* a believing heart.[46] The apostle's aim is simply to stress that the righteousness comes to man by faith, not works.[47] The quotation he now introduces from the Old Testament Scriptures makes that self-evident.

THE ORTHODOXY OF THE PAULINE GOSPEL

Paul cites Habakkuk 2:4 in verse 17: "The righteous will live by faith." He does this to stress that the righteousness of God is received by faith and that the doctrine he is teaching is not new.

The New Testament Usage of the Citation (1:17c)

Paul has used the Habakkuk passage analogically. The principle of justification by faith alone in the promises of God and not in human endeavor, initially set forth so clearly in the story of Abraham, is found also in Habakkuk. Romans 1:16 – 17 is simply another statement of that great truth.

For Paul there was no other hope for people than that found in his gospel. Good works, such as the works of the law, will not deliver ruined people. Even Christian works — baptism, confirmation, attendance at the Table of the Lord, church membership, and all other Adamic fig leaves — cannot avail. It was, and is, the good news of Christ's sacrificial work in blood and cross, received by faith, that liberates from sin, for it alone is the power of God unto salvation.

DISCUSSION QUESTIONS

1. Since Paul proclaims Jesus as the divine Son and Davidic Messiah, why is the modern portrayal of Jesus (simply a good teacher or moral religious leader) different than Paul's depiction?

2. Paul considers the doctrine of the Son of God as critical. Why do so many today have a negative concept of doctrine? How important is doctrine for Christian living?

3. What is the gospel?

4. In what ways are Christians tempted to be ashamed of the gospel? How can Christians become bolder in evangelism?

5. In light of the many social ills in the urban environment of Rome, what explains Paul's silence regarding social action for the church?

CHAPTER 2

THE REVELATION OF GOD'S WRATH

ROMANS 1:18–32

Some messages are pleasant to deliver, and others are unpleasant. Both, how-ever, may be necessary for the well-being of the recipients. Paul must have found Romans 1:18–32 difficult to deliver, but in spite of its unpleasantness, Paul did deliver the message, and humankind is the better for it. It is doubtful if there is a more perceptive analysis of human nature, its sin, guilt, and judgment.

This section teaches that perversion in life stems from perversion in faith. "Our moral perversion," Walter Lüthi claims, "is not the cause but the result of wickedness, the consequence of a more deep-seated evil. However justifiable they may be, sermons on morals are therefore of little value, because they do not get to the root of the matter."[1] This is one of the great burdens of the first chapter of the book, and it is suggested by the first words of Romans 1:18.

> [18]*The wrath of God is being revealed from heaven against all the godlessness and wickedness of men who suppress the truth by their wickedness,*

In developing the great theme of justification, it is to be expected that the biblical teaching on the sin of people and the consequent condemnation be set forth first, for it is necessary for people to see their need before the remedy is offered. Therefore, from 1:18 to 3:20 the apostle develops the case history of human sin and condemnation, starting with the declaration of Gentile sin (1:18–32).

Verse 18 was called by Melanchthon "an exordium terrible as lightning," because it is a terrible indictment of humankind, a divine denunciation that expresses the revulsion of a holy God against human unbelief and rebellion. This is why the preaching of the gospel is urgent.

The Greek, utilizing the word "for," makes the connection with the preceding section. The connective sense has been caught by Frédéric Godet, who writes, "There is a revelation of righteousness by the gospel, because there is a revelation of wrath on the whole world."[2] "Wrath"[3] is a term generally repugnant to the modern mind, which would much prefer to have a God without wrath. G. C. Berkouwer put it well: "Attempts to tone down the wrath of God are powerless in the face of the strong and frequent biblical words of threat and judgment."[4] The God of the Bible is a God whose holy being is revolted by that which is a contradiction of his holiness, and he expresses his wrath in punitive justice. He loves enough to hate evil; in fact, his wrath is just that, the antagonism of holy love to evil.[5] It is not a vindictive rage, nor is it an emotional reaction to irritated self-concern.

But what is the precise force of "revealed"?[6] The present tense verb, in the light of the parallel with its occurrence in the preceding verse, must refer to a continuing revelation. Some have suggested that this revelation is to be found in nature, with its laws of health and suffering, or in conscience, with its laws of right and wrong.[7] Paul himself has given the reader the solution to its meaning in verses 24–32. The threefold "God gave them over" (*paredōken* in vv. 24, 26, 28) introduces the judicial infliction of the abandonment of people to the intensified cultivation of unnatural sexual atrocities and other debasing and degrading vices. Friedrich von Schiller once said, "The world's history is the world's judgment."[8]

The object of God's wrath is the ungodliness and unrighteousness of people who are suppressing the truth in unrighteousness. The two words "godlessness" and "wickedness," in the order in which they appear in the text, express the basic truth that immorality in life proceeds from apostasy in doctrine. The basic responsibility of humans is first Godward, then manward. It is, in this order, " 'Love the Lord your God with all your heart and with all your soul and with all your mind.' This is the first and greatest commandment. And the second is like it: 'Love your neighbor as yourself.' All the Law and the Prophets hang on these two commandments" (Matt. 22:37–40).

The world has neglected the truth and is reaping the harvest of the product — violence, crime, and immorality of the lewdest type. It claims an interest in morality, but having weighed anchor from the port of biblical truth, it has launched itself on the sea of ethics alone and is now foundering on the rocks of the laws of God. The priority of morality is an insult to God, for he is to be worshiped because he is the high and holy God who inhabits eternity. He is not a means to an end.

The meaning of the word "suppress"[9] is debatable. It may mean to possess, grasp (cf. 1 Cor. 11:2; 15:2; 2 Cor. 6:10); or the word may mean "to hold down, restrain, or suppress" (cf. 2 Thess. 2:6 – 7).[10] This second meaning is well suited to express the reaction that unrighteous people offer to the manifested truth,[11] also implying that people have some knowledge of the truth but nevertheless stifle it.

THE DIVINE RATIONALE OF MAN'S WICKEDNESS

[19]*since what may be known about God is plain to them, because God has made it plain to them.* [20]*For since the creation of the world God's invisible qualities — his eternal power and divine nature — have been clearly seen, being understood from what has been made, so that men are without excuse.*

The causal "since"[12] introduces verses 19 and 20 and gives the reason Paul is justified in saying that men suppress the truth.[13] They have willfully rejected the light of the revelation of God shown in his works. The expressions "plain to them" and "made it plain to them" imply that the revelation has entered the minds and consciences of people. John Calvin comments, "By saying that God has made it manifest, he means that man was created to be a spectator of this formed world, and that eyes were given him that he might, by looking on so beautiful a picture, be led up to the Author himself."[14]

Verse 20, introduced by an explanatory "For," confirms and amplifies the statement that God has manifested himself to people. People are, therefore, without excuse, for they have been exposed to far more than "the dim light of nature" (although invisible attributes, his eternal power and deity are clearly apprehended in intelligent mental conception). The verb "clearly seen"[15] is intensive, meaning to discern clearly and is, therefore, a further rebuke to humankind.[16]

That which is revealed is called "his eternal power and divine nature." Eternal power is specific and suggests his omnipotence, as well as implying his eternity. The words "divine nature"[17] are generic and refer to the sum of the divine attributes, or his Godhood, suggesting a full revelation of the majesty and the glory of God.

The last clause of verse 20 presents a purpose clause.[18] The apostasy of humanity is deliberate, and man's continued unbelief is the act of a determined will. What, then, is the purpose of God's revelation in creation? It serves the negative purpose and function of preserving man's responsibility before God because it heightens the conviction of sin and brings to consciousness the state of inexcusability.[19] Humankind must come to the revelation of Christ in the Scriptures for salvation.

THE HUMAN RATIONALE OF MAN'S WICKEDNESS

[21]*For although they knew God, they neither glorified him as God nor gave thanks to him, but their thinking became futile and their foolish hearts were darkened.* [22]*Although they claimed to be wise, they became fools* [23]*and exchanged the glory of the immortal God for images made to look like mortal man and birds and animals and reptiles.*

In verse 21 the apostle turns to a more detailed consideration of the human response to the divine revelation in nature. Paul gives further reason for people's culpability, namely, they resisted the light of the knowledge they received, snubbing its directive and refusing to honor God as God or give him thanks. We might ask, "How can Paul say men *knew* God?" The Greek participle translated "knew" makes the question more imperative, because it refers to experiential knowledge. The answer of Frédéric Godet is appropriate. "Paganism itself," he says, "is the proof that the human mind had really conceived the notion of God; for this notion appears at the root of all the varied forms of paganism."[20]

With the verb "became futile,"[21] Paul begins his description of man's regression, for he could not remain stationary. The tenses of the verbs in this verse, all aorists referring to the past in contrast to the preponderance of presents up to this point in the paragraph, suggest that the apostle is writing of historical events and interpreting the story of man after the fall of Adam. Two things emerge. First, it is not a story of evolution but of devolution, of retrogression, not progression. Second, it is not the tale of man's climb from animism through magic, ancestor worship, and polytheism, to monotheism. It is the reverse. Heathenism's "faith" is the result of apostasy.

In the final two verses of the paragraph, Paul concludes the description of the passage of unbelief from futility to folly. The fruit of depravity is idolatry, and that is the dismal and miserable end to which the unbelief and ungodliness of man comes. The creature is worshiped instead of the Creator, the corruptible instead of the incorruptible, the temporal instead of the eternal, the earthly, fleshly animal instead of the heavenly spiritual being!

God designed nature to be a source of knowledge to humankind.[22] Nature's glorious theater of the majesty and splendor of God should lead men and women to an unmistakable sense of his eternal power and divinity. The entrance of sin and man's inability to respond to the revelation of God in nature do not, however, render man excusable. This failure is no trivial thing and, since man's deficiency arises from his own fault, he is inexcusable (cf. v. 20). The "Bible of nature" is insufficient to save sinners.

A STUDY IN DIVINE RETRIBUTION

> [24]*Therefore God gave them over in the sinful desires of their hearts to sexual impurity for the degrading of their bodies with one another.* [25]*They exchanged the truth of God for a lie, and worshiped and served created things rather than the Creator — who is forever praised. Amen.*
>
> [26]*Because of this, God gave them over to shameful lusts. Even their women exchanged natural relations for unnatural ones.* [27]*In the same way the men also abandoned natural relations with women and were inflamed with lust for one another. Men committed indecent acts with other men, and received in themselves the due penalty for their perversion.*
>
> [28]*Furthermore, since they did not think it worthwhile to retain the knowledge of God, he gave them over to a depraved mind, to do what ought not to be done.* [29]*They have become filled with every kind of wickedness, evil, greed and depravity. They are full of envy, murder, strife, deceit and malice. They are gossips,* [30]*slanderers, God-haters, insolent, arrogant and boastful; they invent ways of doing evil; they disobey their parents;* [31]*they are senseless, faithless, heartless, ruthless.* [32]*Although they know God's righteous decree that those who do such things deserve death, they not only continue to do these very things but also approve of those who practice them.*

Preaching to his Sunday congregation in Bern, Switzerland, from Romans 1:18 – 32, Walter Lüthi said, "In the words that we have just read, we are told the whole truth about our condition. There may well be people among us who cannot bear to hear the truth, and would like to creep quietly away out of this church. Let them do so if they wish."[23] Paul's canvas on which he has painted his picture — dark, foreboding, threatening, flashing with lightning, and crashing with thunder — is crammed with forms and figures, sights and shadows, of sin, wrath, and judgment. The revelation of wrath is total and complete, encompassing all and rendering all without excuse and under condemnation, both individually and collectively.

Here God's retributive justice, one of his essential properties, comes to the center of the stage. In the threefold "gave them over" (vv. 24, 26, 28)[24] the problem is plainly before the reader. There remains, therefore, only one alternative for God and man, divine retribution, and it is this that the apostle so solemnly, and yet vigorously,[25] proclaims in the final section of chapter 1 (vv. 24 – 32). "Therefore" makes the connection that sin justly brings judgment,[26] a judgment expressed clearly in the final section of chapter 1.

"GAVE THEM OVER"

The threefold "gave them over" (vv. 24, 26, 28) is repeated as a terrifying refrain. It is a term over which has raged considerable debate.

Perhaps the favorite interpretation has prevailed since the time of Origen and Chrysostom, in which the "gave them over" is taken in the permissive sense. According to this view God passively permitted people to fall into the retributive consequences of their infidelity and apostasy. But it is not that God permitted rebellious people to fall into uncleanness and bodily dishonor; he actively, although justly in view of their sin, consigned them to the consequences of their acts. It is his divine arrangement that people by their apostasy should fall into moral impurity, sin being punished by further sin, and he himself maintains the moral connection between apostasy and impurity by carrying out the judgment himself.

Another popular view, which became popular after the time of Augustine, takes the "gave them over" in the privative sense. According to this interpretation God deprived man of an aspect of his work of common grace. He withdrew his hand that had restrained people from evil. Godet has asked, "Wherein did His action consist?" And the answer follows, "He positively withdrew His hand; He ceased to hold the boat as it was dragged by the current of the river."[27] Practically, this view is equivalent to the permissive view, but the Pauline language is stronger than this.

It becomes clear that the term must be given a judicial sense.[28] The meaning is not simply that God withdrew from the wicked the restraining force of his providence and common grace, although that privative sense is included in the judicial sense, but that he positively gave people over to the judgment of "more intensified and aggravated cultivation of the lusts of their own hearts with the result that they reap for themselves a correspondingly greater toll of retributive vengeance."[29] The usage of the word in both this epistle (4:25; 6:17; 8:32) and in the other Pauline epistles (cf. 1 Cor. 5:5; 1 Tim. 1:20) supports this force.[30] The interpretation is also in harmony with the occurrence of the precisely identical form in Acts 7:42, where, in speaking of Israel's apostasy in the days of Moses, Stephen says, "But God turned away and *gave them over* to the worship of the heavenly bodies." The expression "God gave them over to shameful lusts" describes a "judicial abandonment."[31]

In the midst of the retributive action of God, there is no coercion of humanity. God does not entice or compel to evil.[32] Men and women remain responsible and can even be said to be giving themselves over to uncleanness while God gives them up to the judgment of their sin.

GIVEN UP TO VILE PASSIONS

The apostle turns to the theme of homosexuality. As a result of apostasy from the faith, humanity was given over to the judgment of unnatural sexual practices, both among the women and the men. The words "because of this" (cf. v. 26) make the connection with the preceding, that is, verse 25. The words that Paul uses to describe the women and the men are words that mean essentially females and males, stressing the sexuality of individuals. He looks derogatorily at them as sex-animals.

The theme of homosexuality and its judgment begins with the women. The emphasis on the women's involvement points to the degradation of human sin in the divine judgment. William Shedd is right: "The sex which is naturally most shamefaced is in this instance the most shameless."[33] In speaking of "natural relations" Paul makes it plain that the propriety of the sex act is grounded in the natural constitution of males and females established by God. Homosexuality is, therefore, an offense against God and his order. Rampant homosexuality is further evidence of the judgment of God on our society.

GIVEN UP TO A REPROBATE MIND

The final section of chapter 1 lays stress on the mental sins of people rather than the sensual. It concludes with one of the most damning texts in the Bible: "Although they know God's righteous decree that those who do such things deserve death, they not only continue to do these very things but also approve of those who practice them" (v. 32). There are absolute standards that come down to us from heaven, and one of them is the wrath of God on human sin.

CONCLUSION

Paul is emphatically teaching that moral depravity is the result of the judgment of God. What is the real significance of the spread of immorality, crime, and violence in Western civilization? Sexual rebellion, license, and anarchy *are* the retributive judgment of God. Civilizations do not die because of violence, crime, immorality, and anarchy. Charles Hodge's diagnosis is telling, "Religion is the only true foundation, and the only effectual safeguard for morality. People who abandon God, he abandons. Irreligion and immorality, therefore, have ever been found inseparably connected."[34]

It should be carefully noted that the apostle is not speaking of eternal punishment in these verses. What he has specifically in mind is a judgment that pertains to this life, not to the life to come. But it is also plain that Paul's words lead on to the doctrine of everlasting torment (cf. v. 32).[35] The vindicatory judgment inflicted by God is continued in the life to come in a more terrible and permanent form if the escape through the gospel of the cross is neglected.

To the question "Can God really give man up to judgment?" this passage provides a resounding "yes." But, in fact, it is not the final and convincing answer to the question. That comes from the cross of Jesus Christ, which in the cry it elicits from our Lord, "My God, my God, why have you forsaken me?" (Matt. 27:45), unmistakably affirms that God can give people up to judgment. It was there that the sinless Man bore the judgment of God on sin, and it forever proclaims the true nature of sin — it is worthy of the penalty of spiritual and physical death — and God's hatred of it with his necessary condemnation of it.

DISCUSSION QUESTIONS

1. Do verses 18 – 32 describe the world we live in today? What remedy would Paul give to our society today? Why?

2. What explains the modern concept of the natural goodness of humankind? Discuss the reasons people trace their predicaments to every conceivable alternative except sin.

3. Vile passions are the results of God's judgment. True or False? Why or why not?

4. Harvard sociologist Pitirim Sorokin, in *The American Sex Revolution* (Boston: Porter Sargent, 1956), points out that sexual anarchy leads to mental breakdowns. Would Pitirim's idea reflect the truth in Romans 1? Why or why not?

5. In light of judicial abandonment ("God gave them up"), does God really care for sinners? If so, how?

6. Why do some doubt God's love when the greatest evidence of God's concern comes from the cross, where he gave his Son as the vicarious sacrifice and initiated the remedy for sinners?

CHAPTER 3

THE JUDGMENT OF GOD

ROMANS 2:1–29

The reality and inescapability of the justice and judgment of God are elementary truths of Holy Scripture. There are several possibilities of escape for the person who offends against human laws. In the first place, it is possible that the person's offense will not become known. Second, there is always the chance that the guilty person may be able to escape the bounds of the legal jurisdiction under which the crime was committed. Further, there may occur, after apprehension by the authorities, a breakdown in the legal processes. And, finally, the ultimate hope of the criminal is that he may escape from detention and live in a measure of freedom.[1]

There are no such possibilities with God. It is unthinkable that a crime may escape the attention of the one of whom it is said, "You discern my going out and my lying down; you are familiar with all my ways" (Ps. 139:3). The roadside sign that pointedly warns, "Prepare to meet God," is surely justifiable. The divine judgment is not only real and inescapable, but it is also just. The words *judgment* and *justice* are closely related. *Justice* is the quality of being righteous or impartial, while *judgment* is the activity of rendering a decision.

Romans 2:1–16 particularly deals with God's distributive justice, whereby he executes the law, distributing justly the rewards and penalties (cf. 2:6).[2] This distributive justice, therefore, is of two kinds, remunerative and retributive. Remunerative justice has to do with the distribution of rewards to both humans and angels (cf. 2:7). It proceeds on the ground of relative merit only, for we have no absolute merit. Retributive justice is made necessary by reason of sin and perdition. It refers to the infliction of penalties. Remunerative justice is the expression of the divine love; retributive justice is the expression of the divine wrath (cf. 2:8). While man does not merit his reward, he does merit his penalty.

The apostle has demonstrated the guilt of the Gentile in chapter 1, and now he turns to deal with the person who, standing by, is vociferously agreeing with Paul's assessment. Paul addresses the pious religious hypocrite, identified as the Jew in verse 17 (cf. Gal. 2:15). Even though he possesses all the privileges and advantages of being a member of the chosen community, he cannot escape divine judgment for his unbelief.

There are three sections in the larger division of Romans 2:1 – 3:8, which sets forth the guilt of the Jew. In 2:1 – 16 the principles of divine judgment are propounded. In 2:17 – 29 the application of them is made to the Jew (vv. 17 – 24) and their covenant status (vv. 25 – 29). Finally, in 3:1 – 8 the apostle answers Jewish counterclaims. His style, as often in the letter, is similar to the Stoic *diatribe*. Questions or objections are put into the mouth of an imagined critic and answered.[3]

It has been said that visitors to the labyrinths of certain catacombs used to take hold of a silk thread by which they could retrace their steps if they became fearful of becoming lost. In this section of Romans, there are also abundant opportunities of losing our way. It is necessary, then, to keep in mind the purpose of Paul in these verses. Paul's purpose is expressed plainly in 3:9; it is to accuse both Gentiles and Jews of the guilt of sin. The theme of this immediate section, 2:1 – 16, may be put simply: God's judgment is righteous, and by this standard the Jew too is guilty.

GOD'S JUDGMENT IS ACCORDING TO REALITY

[1]You, therefore, have no excuse, you who pass judgment on someone else, for at whatever point you judge the other, you are condemning yourself, because you who pass judgment do the same things. [2]Now we know that God's judgment against those who do such things is based on truth. [3]So when you, a mere man, pass judgment on them and yet do the same things, do you think you will escape God's judgment? [4]Or do you show contempt for the riches of his kindness, tolerance and patience, not realizing that God's kindness leads you toward repentance?

The particle "therefore"[4] is a strong word, introducing an inference drawn from 1:32a-b. People know that those who sin are worthy of death, and in his act of judging others, the Jew admits that he knows also. So he too is without excuse, even though he contents himself with applying it to others.[5]

In verse 2 the apostle introduces the first variation of the principle of righteous judgment. God's judgment is "based on truth" in the sense of reality. James Stifler comments, "When gold is assayed, the test considers only the metal which is under it; it does not ask whence it came, whose it is, but what it is."[6] The judgment of God concerns itself with the reality of a matter (cf. 1 Sam. 16:7).

In spite of this axiomatic truth, there are always those who think they can escape the inescapable. It is these whom Paul addresses in verse 3. The stress rests on the second "you" of the verse.[7] Do you think that *you*, because you are a Jew, will escape?[8] Surely not.

Verse 4 introduces the alternative. Is it that you have such a poor estimate of God's goodness that you think it gives you license to sin? The ignorance of the Jew is the reason for the defiance of God's goodness, and it is his ignorance of the fact that his goodness is ever active in the pursuit of Jewish repentance (cf. 3:2; 9:4 – 5). The verb "leads" is in the present tense, expressing God's continuing activity in producing repentance. The primary reference of the goodness is to the messianic promises given with a view to Jewish repentance.

GOD'S JUDGMENT IS ACCORDING TO WORKS

[5]But because of your stubbornness and your unrepentant heart, you are storing up wrath against yourself for the day of God's wrath, when his righteous judgment will be revealed. [6]God "will give to each person according to what he has done." [7]To those who by persistence in doing good seek glory, honor and immortality, he will give eternal life. [8]But for those who are self-seeking and who reject the truth and follow evil, there will be wrath and anger. [9]There will be trouble and distress for every human being who does evil: first for the Jew, then for the Gentile; [10]but glory, honor and peace for everyone who does good: first for the Jew, then for the Gentile. [11]For God does not show favoritism.

The relative clause in verse 6 states the principle precisely; he "will give to each person according to what he has done." But a doctrinal question is sometimes raised at this point: How can we reconcile judgment according to works and justification apart from works? Paul is not here expounding the gospel. He is expounding the law. According to the law, judgment is according to works, and life is according to works (cf. Gal. 3:10 – 12). Thus, the law can only condemn (cf. Rom. 3:20). If we, then, are to obtain justification, it must be apart from law or human works (3:21). All will be judged by works and will be found guilty. But those who have sought another way, the way of faith, will find righteousness. He is particularly addressing the legal sin of the Jew. He had in mind the kind of self-righteousness and pride of privilege that brought forth such statements as "Abraham will sit at the gate of Gehenna and will not permit a circumcised Israelite to go down there."[9]

Verses 7 – 11 amplify this condemnation of the Jewish attitude of claiming exemption from divine judgment because of their special place in election and revelation. God's judgment is not according to one's special privileges, but according to one's deeds, as the Mosaic law teaches.

GOD'S JUDGMENT IS ACCORDING TO IMPARTIALITY

> [12]*All who sin apart from the law will also perish apart from the law, and all who sin under the law will be judged by the law.* [13]*For it is not those who hear the law who are righteous in God's sight, but it is those who obey the law who will be declared righteous.* [14]*(Indeed, when Gentiles, who do not have the law, do by nature things required by the law, they are a law for themselves, even though they do not have the law,* [15]*since they show that the requirements of the law are written on their hearts, their consciences also bearing witness, and their thoughts now accusing, now even defending them.)* [16]*This will take place on the day when God will judge men's secrets through Jesus Christ, as my gospel declares.*

God's judgment is just, dealing with Jews and Gentiles in the same manner. And, further, each is judged by the light possessed by each, whether the light of the Mosaic law (cf. vv. 12 – 13), the moral law (cf. vv. 14 – 15), or conscience (cf. v. 15).

Verse 12 introduces the explanation of the principle. There is no respect of persons with God, no partiality, for he will judge people according to the knowledge of his will that they have. Religious connections will not avail in that day.

The "for" of verse 13 looks at the last clause of verse 12 and explains why the Jews will be judged by law. Mere knowledge will not satisfy divine justice, for it is not the hearers but the doers that are justified. As James Stifler points out, "For the only virtue in hearing the law lies in hearing to do.... A child might hear his parent's command, might admire the clearness of his voice and the perspicuity of his words, but what of this approval if he did not obey and do as told."[10] Paul's usage of the verb "declared righteous" demands a forensic sense. "Those who obey the law" are just by definition and in reality; they need no justification. Thus, if doers of the law are justified, it can only mean that they are pronounced "just" by a legal authority.[11] Romans 3:4, confirming this interpretation, says, "Not at all! Let God be true, and every man a liar. As it is written: 'So that you may be *proved right* when you speak and prevail when you judge.' "[12]

The "for," included in the Greek text of verse 14, looks not at verse 13 but back to verse 12. The Gentiles too have a law by which they are to be judged.

The apostle uses the anarthrous "Gentiles,"[13] which points to the character of the ones under discussion. They are such persons as Gentiles, and they have a rule of duty in their hearts, written in their very constitutions. The words "by nature" refer to one's basic constitution. By nature, not by an external law such as the Mosaic law, the Gentiles do perform moral acts, but only partially. Paul is referring to such things as honoring one's parents, paying one's debts, and being kind to the poor; thus they betray the fact that there is written in their constitutions a moral law. That law, however, they do not keep perfectly, so that they are without excuse (cf. 1:20).

Verse 15 demonstrates the evidence that the Gentiles do have a law from God, although not the Mosaic law, in that they show the law's work written in their hearts. It has left its stamp on their minds and consciences.[14] To this prescript of the law, conscience also testifies. Thus, the conscience, which Calvin called the "guardian appointed for man,"[15] an "inner witness and monitor,"[16] combines with the divine law for a double witness to moral truth. The effects of the fall on the conscience make natural revelation in creation less than an infallible guide.

Verse 16 is to be connected with verse 12, the intervening words forming a parenthesis. The judgment is a future judgment. Paul has just made the point that people are to be judged by the light that they have, and it is patently clear that not all people have the gospel. Paul means that this just judgment is a part of the message he preaches. God will indeed judge the secrets of people through Jesus Christ in that future day, and that is according to the gospel Paul preaches.

The final phrase in the Greek, "through Jesus Christ," bears some stress by reason of its position in the verse, emphasizing that the judgment is *through Jesus Christ*. It is he who is the Judge, and Jews must reckon with that fact (cf. John 5:22, 27–28; Acts 17:31; 1 Cor. 4:5). If Jesus Christ sits in judgment on the secrets of people, he must have infinite knowledge and, therefore, be God himself!

RITE VERSUS RIGHTEOUSNESS

Throughout the remainder of chapter 2, Paul expatiates on the peril of Jews. Guilty of thinking too highly of themselves and too poorly of others, they stand in great jeopardy. While they possess enormous privileges (cf. vv. 17–20), their practices do not at all conform to their privileges (vv. 21–24). Finally, should they seek to stand on their ultimate trust, their special covenantal relationship, the apostle overthrows that bastion by reminding them that God honors inward spirituality, not outward religion (vv. 25–29). The apostle masterfully states the case for personal and spiritual righteousness as over against its deadly enemy, the mechanical and sanctimonious practice of religious rites.

THE PRIVILEGES OF THE JEWS

> [17]*Now you, if you call yourself a Jew; if you rely on the law and brag about your relationship to God;* [18]*if you know his will and approve of what is superior because you are instructed by the law;* [19]*if you are convinced that you are a guide for the blind, a light for those who are in the dark,* [20]*an instructor of the foolish, a teacher of infants, because you have in the law the embodiment of knowledge and truth —*

Five Privileges Relative to Themselves (2:17 – 18)

The peril in which Jews stand becomes more visible when we ponder the unusual privileges the Jews claim for themselves. The first claim was that they were "Jews," that honorable name that suggests the special relationship that Abraham and his descendants bore to God.

The second claim has to do with the Jewish confidence in the law. The Mosaic law was given to them and not to the Gentiles. They rest in it, confident that simply the possession of it, not the doing of it, is life.

The third claim is that God is their God, not the God of others. This claim also has a measure of truth in it, for of them and for them the Messiah will come (cf. 9:5). But the claim obscures a broader truth. The special relationship to God was to be the means for the ingathering of the Gentile world. Thus, as Paul says later in the epistle, "Is God the God of Jews only? Is he not the God of Gentiles too? Yes, of Gentiles too" (3:29).

The fourth claim is that they know God's will, an understandable one in the light of the claim to possess the law. The Greek expression in verse 18, "if you know his will,"[17] contains the article, which may suggest *the one perfect* will. The claim, of course, further accentuates the guilt.

The final claim relative to themselves is that they have the capacity, because of their knowledge of the law, to appreciate moral distinctions. How difficult it is for humanity to see itself as it really is, especially because of the curse of the fall in Eden! It is just as easy for the evangelical to fall into the trap of spiritual unreality and hypocrisy as it was for the chosen people. Beware!

Five Privileges Relative to Others (2:19 – 20)

There follow five privileges that relate to others. The terms that refer to the others give a telling description of the opinion the Jews had of the Gentiles.

The latter were "blind," "in the dark," "foolish," and "infants," bereft of true knowledge, which could be found only in the law of the Jews.

THE PRACTICES OF THE JEWS

[21]you, then, who teach others, do you not teach yourself? You who preach against stealing, do you steal? [22]You who say that people should not commit adultery, do you commit adultery? You who abhor idols, do you rob temples? [23]You who brag about the law, do you dishonor God by breaking the law? [24]As it is written: "God's name is blasphemed among the Gentiles because of you."

The apostle, speaking in the tones of a Nathan with his "thou art the man" sternness, directs his attention to the activities of the Jews. Paul centers his remarks on five practices, but they all, in effect, teach the same lesson. No person may expect God's blessing simply because the light of divine revelation shines brightly around him or her. Just because truth has come through the instrumentality of great teaching or teachers, it does not necessarily follow that the hearer appropriates it. The brightness and clarity of divine revelation does not itself create its converts.

The "then" of verse 21 introduces an inference from the preceding words of Paul. Since the Jews possess such privileges, is it not, therefore, reasonable to expect that they should live up to them?[18]

The climax of the apostle's condemnatory critique is reached in verse 24. There, in words derived freely from Isaiah 52:5 and Ezekiel 36:20, he charges Jews with responsibility for Gentile blasphemy of the true God. By their pretensions and hypocrisy they have caused Gentiles to speak slanderously of their God. It is only natural that the Gentiles should reason that a people reflect their God. The Gentiles, reasoning perceptively from the farce of Jewish claims without corresponding conduct, speak critically of a God who, seen by them only through the Jews, apparently countenances such charades. Paul feels the Jews are responsible to a considerable degree for the unpleasant picture of Gentile blasphemy of the Holy One of Israel.

THE POSITION OF THE JEWS

[25]Circumcision has value if you observe the law, but if you break the law, you have become as though you had not been circumcised. [26]If those who are not circumcised keep the law's requirements, will they not be regarded as though they were circumcised? [27]The one who is not circumcised physically and yet obeys

*the law will condemn you who, even though you have the written code and
circumcision, are a lawbreaker.*

*[28]A man is not a Jew if he is only one outwardly, nor is circumcision merely
outward and physical. [29]No, a man is a Jew if he is one inwardly; and circumcision is circumcision of the heart, by the Spirit, not by the written code. Such a
man's praise is not from men, but from God.*

In these last verses of the chapter, the apostle pursues the Jew into his last
stronghold, his membership in the covenant nation through the sign of circumcision. The Old Testament taught that circumcision was a sign of reality, and if
there was no reality present, its force was invalidated and was actually uncircumcision (cf. Deut. 10:16; Jer. 4:4; 9:25 – 26; Ezek. 44:7; Acts 7:51).

The Rite without the Reality Is Unrighteousness (2:25)

The apostle acknowledges that circumcision is of profit if it is accompanied by
a keeping of the law. The present tense of the verb "observe"[19] stresses that persistent adherence to the precepts of the law is in view (cf. vv. 17 – 24). Paul is not
speaking of Old Testament times, for to neglect circumcision then was a grievous
omission. He speaks of New Testament times when the church is a Gentile and
Jewish church. The ordinance has become incidental. It may be practiced (cf.
Acts 16:3); it does not have to be (cf. Gal. 2:3).

Next, the apostle stresses the other side of the truth. To be a transgressor of
the law is, in effect, to make circumcision uncircumcision, for there is no difference between Jew and Gentile in this case. The sign or seal of righteousness (cf.
4:11) is of value only so long as the covenant is kept (cf. Deut. 30:6).

The Reality without the Rite Is Righteousness (2:26 – 27)

If breaking the law makes circumcision uncircumcision before God, it follows
that the keeping of the law renders uncircumcision circumcision and constitutes
the uncircumcised as the judge of the circumcised. The label on a can is not
as important as the contents of the can. Jews, on the contrary, had ripped off
the label from the container of righteousness by faith and were boasting in the
meaningless imprint.

The Reality Is Praised by God, the Rite by People (2:28 – 29)

God always desires worship that has its source and motivating power in a heart
in right relationship to him through the Spirit. The causes of external worship
alone, aside from the fundamental and basic one of the wickedness and perver-
sity of the human heart, lie in the fact that people tend to become dominated

by their senses and that rites may be performed without any renunciation of the pleasures of sin.

In the last verse, there is a telling play on the word "praise." The word *Jew* comes from a Hebrew word[20] that means *to praise* (cf. Gen. 29:35; 49:8). It is as if Paul closes the section by saying that the true Jew is the inward one whose circumcision is also the inward one of the heart; that is, the true Jew is the Jew whose Judaism (lit., *praise*) is not from people but from God. As the Old Testament teaches, circumcision of the heart is not something a man may perform on himself or on others; it is God's work alone. Moses' word encloses a great theological truth, "The LORD your God will circumcise your hearts" (Deut. 30:6). To God's grace belongs the final praise.

The importance of the possession of truth, not merely the profession of truth, is the thrust of chapter 2. Both Jews and Gentiles, as over against the empty practice of the religious rite, require genuine righteousness.

DISCUSSION QUESTIONS

1. Does baptism have any value for the person who does not believe the gospel? Explain.

2. Does a change in the inward person inevitably lead to a change in the person's actions? How does the outward reformation of the flesh differ from the inward regeneration of the human heart?

3. How does the inward regeneration of the human heart cure mere externalism?

4. How can believers guard themselves from thinking too highly of themselves and too poorly of others?

5. Since Jesus Christ sits in judgment on the secrets of men and women, he must have infinite knowledge. In what way does this commend Christ's deity?

CHAPTER 4

THE JEWS, THE ORACLES OF GOD, AND THE UNIVERSALITY OF SIN

ROMANS 3:1–20

Are the promises of God to the nation Israel still valid? What effect on them has the national rejection of Jesus by Israel had? Paul now answers Jewish counterclaims, seeking to convince them of their sin and exposure to divine wrath. Walter Lüthi has written, "Like a herdsman carefully and skillfully driving his unruly sheep and cattle and horses towards the narrow door of the stable, Paul has led us up to the narrow door of Heaven."[1] How happy is the person who has had the divine light fall on the darkness of their sin; they are as blessed as a person whose doctor has been able to diagnose their illness. In both cases, it is the first step to recovery and healing.

WHAT, THEN, IS THE ADVANTAGE OF THE JEW?

> [1]*What advantage, then, is there in being a Jew, or what value is there in circumcision?* [2]*Much in every way! First of all, they have been entrusted with the very words of God.*

The Question (3:1)

The first question arises, as we might expect of Paul, directly from the context. The apostle has just proved that the Jew may expect to be judged on the same principles as the Gentile, for he too is a sinner and in peril just as his hated adversary. Does this Jewish Christian, Paul, think that the God-originated distinction between Jew and Gentile has been obliterated? Is the Old Testament, so full of the promises of earthly spiritual blessing for Israel and so beautifully expressed that it often appears that the psalmists and the prophets dipped their pens in a rainbow to proclaim them, really a gigantic collection of false hopes?

Paul's methodology and style, as Bruce Metzger points out, "was like a homily or sermon, and characterized by a lively and vivid semi-conversational style."[2] The "then," inferential as usual, makes the connection with the preceding context, opening the window and letting in the light on the apostle's thought and argument. "But Paul," the objector expostulates, "your theology is thoroughly inconsistent with the admitted privileges and superiorities of our nation. What, then, is the advantage of the Jew, or what is the benefit of circumcision?" Does national origin and covenant relationship bear on the standing of Israel before Yahweh (cf. 2:26 – 29)?

The word "advantage" suggests literally that which exceeds the usual number or size. There is a comparative sense and a sense of superiority that cannot be overlooked. The practice of circumcision was so distinctive to the Jewish nation that it became practically a name. This very fact, however, also indicates that the rite, the sign and seal of the Abrahamic covenant, was always in the foreground when Israel was under consideration. Paul is thinking of the promises of that covenant as the plus that Israel had. The questions of verse 1 essentially mean this: Is the Abrahamic covenant still in force?

How will Paul answer this question? Israel has turned against the promised Messiah, denounced him, and crucified him, and is persecuting his followers with deadly venom. Further, Christian churches are rising throughout the world, composed not only of believing members of the ancient theocracy but also of believing Gentiles, and the latter have equal standing in the new fellowship of the one body, the church.

The Answer (3:2)

There is no vacillation in Paul's reply. The very brevity of its four words, "Much in every way,"[3] adds tremendous force to the answer. What is that advantage? Preeminently,[4] Israel has been entrusted with "the very words of God." What are the words, or oracles, of God? "The words of God" are probably not the Old Testament in general, but more specifically the special and particular truths connected with the passages of the Old Testament that are fulfilled in the ministry of Jesus Christ the Son.

In the next verse of the present context (3:3), there is a statement that is the last piece of evidence for the fact that Paul had the Old Testament promises chiefly before him in using the expression "the very words of God." The apostle, introducing an objector's argument, asks, "What if some did not have faith?" Now, the reference to unbelief is far more appropriate when directed to specific promises than to the whole Bible, or to the entire Old Testament. William Shedd agrees: "The Jews, previous to the Advent, had misinterpreted the Messianic prophecies, and had desired a merely temporal prince and savior; and since the Advent, they had positively rejected Jesus Christ."[5] We may paraphrase Paul's answer, then, as follows: "Much in every way, because, first and foremost to them was granted the Word of God, in which more particularly is the messianic revelation of covenants, law, promises, and, above all, the Messiah himself."

If the oracles were committed, or entrusted, to Israel, how can it be said that they belong to Israel in any way? Committal implies a commission, but it says nothing concerning possession. The promises given to Israel were promises that ultimately terminated upon the world. World blessing is the aim and goal of the divine program, and it is so set forth in both Testaments (cf. Isa. 42:1 – 7; 49:5 – 6; Acts 15:13 – 18; Rom. 11:11 – 15). Israel is the divinely appointed steward of the promises, the instrumentality by her reception and propagation of them for the blessing of the world in the kingdom of God on the earth. They are God's promises, his oracles, for they originate with him, and he guarantees their victorious fulfillment in world blessing. They are only Israel's as trustee and as beneficiary.

BUT WILL NOT JEWISH UNBELIEF ANNUL THE PROMISES?

[3]*What if some did not have faith? Will their lack of faith nullify God's faithfulness?* [4]*Not at all! Let God be true, and every man a liar. As it is written:*

"So that you may be proved right when you speak
and prevail when you judge."

The Question (3:3)

Again the apostle suggests an objection to his own conclusions. "It is true that to Israel were extended the oracles of God," the imaginary objector might admit, "but, Paul, Israel has fallen into disobedience and has rejected the promises. Does not their own unwillingness to receive the promises effectively annul them?" Paul's reply is something like this: "Her unbelief does not affect the validity of the promises. For (to amplify) what if some have not believed? Their unbelief will not make void the faithfulness of God, will it?"[6] The objection is a direct challenge to the character of God and an attack on his veracity and faithfulness. Paul's imaginary objection is, paraphrased, "The unbelief of the nation Israel will not render inoperative and powerless the faithfulness of God to his promises, will it?"

The Answer (3:4)

Paul's answer is simple: God will keep his word and will fulfill the Abrahamic promises. The answer, in its form, is threefold. First, the question is rejected as abhorrent. The expression "Not at all" (*mē genoito*)[7] is equivalent to English, "Impossible!" or "Good heavens, no!" or "Are you crazy?"

Second, Paul adds that the faithfulness of God is to be maintained even if, when people contend with him in court, the maintaining of it demands that in every case a guilty verdict be returned against man. If it is necessary to affirm that all people are liars, still God is true.

Finally, Paul appeals to Scripture to support his case. The text is Psalm 51:4, a passage in which David pictures himself in a heavenly tribunal before the divine Judge. David is unfaithful, but his Judge is proven righteous and clear of guilt.[8] The same is true with God and his promises to Israel; he is faithful to them, though at the moment Israel stands guilty of unbelief and is under judgment.

DIVINE FAITHFULNESS, DIVINE JUDGMENT, AND THE PROBLEM OF ANTINOMIANISM

The brief paragraph of verses 5–8 is structured around the two questions of verse 5, which are answered by another question in verse 6, and the two questions of verses 7 and 8, which are answered in verse 8 by a simple, vigorous, and emphatic concluding statement, "Their condemnation is deserved." C. K. Barrett has commented, "It is easier to bring such complaints against a profound view of the mysterious divine government of the universe than to answer them; this time Paul makes no fresh attempt to answer."[9] The apostle's method is, at least at this point, to reject the thought of his opponents as impious. At a later time, he will deal with the principle in greater detail, giving it full treatment (cf. 6:1–23). Paul might, however, have pointed out this simple fact: that man's sin may be the instrument of divine glorification is no credit to *man*. It is *God* who brings this to pass. The fact that he makes the wrath of people to praise him is no cause for man to boast in the matter; only God alone deserves the glory.

IS GOD UNJUST TO PUNISH THE UNJUST?

> [5]*But if our unrighteousness brings out God's righteousness more clearly, what shall we say? That God is unjust in bringing his wrath on us? (I am using a human argument.)* [6]*Certainly not! If that were so, how could God judge the world?*

The Godward Question (3:5)

The "but" is adversative and introduces an objection that comes from a self-confessed objector.[10] The expression "our unrighteousness" refers to the sin of Israel in failing to believe and rest in the Old Testament messianic promises, promises destined to be fulfilled in spite of the nation's present unbelief. The expression "God's righteousness" is not a reference to the righteousness of God that is given in justification to people who believe (cf. 1:17; 3:21, 22; 10:3), but to the divine attribute of righteousness in its comprehensive sense, inclusive of his faithfulness (cf. v. 3) and truth (cf. vv. 4, 7). John Murray calls it "the inherent equity of God."[11]

The apparently plausible and logical question, "But if our unrighteousness brings out God's righteousness more clearly, what shall we say?" is answered with another question phrased negatively. "That God is unjust in bringing his wrath on us?"[12] It is obvious that God's justice cannot be questioned. Only human thinking and speaking would attempt that. The last clause of verse 5 is an implicit insight into Paul's attitude toward human reason. The work of human reason, as John Calvin pointed out, is "ever to bark against the wisdom of God,"[13] always railing against the truth of God (cf. 1 Cor. 2:14). Only when we submit our reason to the Spirit of God and the Word of God are we able to understand his mysteries.

The Apostolic Answer (3:6)

Paul now speaks as a Christian apostle. It might seem to some that he begs the question in his additional words, "If that were so, how could God judge the world?" As John Murray says, "For of what avail is it to affirm that God will judge the world if the question is: how can God be just in executing judgment if his righteousness is commended by our unrighteousness? Categorical assertion of the thing to be proved is no argument!"[14] In this case, however, the apostle's argument is sound because it rests on what is to his mind an unquestioned truth, universal judgment (cf. Acts 17:31; Heb. 6:2).

We might, however, still ask the question, "Granting that the objector's apparently plausible reasoning is wrong because it contradicts the plain teaching that God will judge the ungodly for their sin, even if it is turned by divine activity into the commendation of his righteousness, *where* is the fallacy in the reasoning?" There are two helpful suggestions. In the first place, as E. H. Gifford points out, "God's righteousness is established not by sin *in itself,* but by sin as dealt with by God, punished by His holy vengeance, pardoned by His grace, or overruled to good effect by His wisdom."[15] A second suggestion is better, since the sinner does not intend to commend God's righteousness by his sin, he can claim no merit for the fact that God turns his sin to his own glory.

IS IT RIGHT TO JUDGE SINNERS WHO GLORIFY GOD?

[7]Someone might argue, "If my falsehood enhances God's truthfulness and so increases his glory, why am I still condemned as a sinner?" [8]Why not say — as we are being slanderously reported as saying and as some claim that we say — "Let us do evil that good may result"? Their condemnation is deserved.

The Manward Questions (3:7–8a)

Putting words in the sinner's mouth, Paul essentially asks, "If God's truth is increased and God's glory advanced by means of my lying, then why am I brought to judgment; why may I not just do evil that good may come?" The apostle has inserted a parenthesis in the last question, asserting that this is the very charge brought against him and his followers, namely, that they practiced this very doctrine, "Let us do evil that good may come." "The slogan," John Murray adds, "pointedly sets forth the underlying assumption with which Paul is dealing from verse 5 onwards."[16]

The apostle has the last judgment primarily in mind, as the future tense of "judge" in verse 6 indicates.

The Apostolic Answer (3:8b)

The logically absurd conclusion of his opponents, that sin enhances the glory of God and, therefore, precludes judgment, is not only inconsistent with the future judgment, but also destructive of all morality. Paul in one cutting stroke, as short as the question is long, rejects the thought and those who propound it. Evil is evil, no matter what God may bring from it. Speaking of these who object to divine judgment on their sin, John Calvin wrote, "And their perverseness was, on two accounts, to be condemned — first, because this impiety had gained the assent of their minds; and secondly, because in traducing the gospel, they dared to draw from it their calumny."[17] Paul concludes his charges against those who object to *judgment* as sinners by saying, "Their condemnation is deserved." This final word is directed to the Jews particularly, as the context indicates. They thought they were excused from divine judgment and free to judge the Gentiles, but they overlooked the justice of God. Paul has skillfully returned to the charge with which he began the section on the sin of the Jews in Romans 2:1.

THE UNIVERSALITY OF SIN

John Calvin, just like Martin Luther,[18] spoke of the law of Moses as the mirror of sin. "The law is like a mirror," he wrote in the *Institutes*; "in it we contemplate our weakness, then the iniquity arising from this, and finally the curse coming from both — just as a mirror shows us the spots on our face."[19] Paul now lifts up the mirror of the Old Testament before the faces of all people and proves that all people, whether Jew or Gentile, are under sin.

THE INDICTMENT OF ALL PEOPLE

⁹What shall we conclude then? Are we any better? Not at all! We have already made the charge that Jews and Gentiles alike are all under sin.

Verse 9 contains Paul's indictment of the human race, both Jew and Greek. Paul teaches that the Jews excelled the Gentiles only in the limited sense expressed in 3:1 – 4, where he had pointed out that the Old Testament promises of a Messiah and a kingdom belonged to them, and they were the guarantee that Israel as a nation could look forward to a grand future. In this sense it could be said that Israel "excelled." In the sense of individuals before God, the members of the nation, just as individual Gentiles, stand guilty and condemned before God.

In the verb "conclude," we have Paul's own interpretation of the preceding context (1:18 – 3:8). It was Paul's intention in the opening chapters to charge the Jews and Gentiles with guilt. The proof is to be found in "the verdict of Scripture."[20] The phrase "under sin" suggests the idea of divine condemnation in view of the context, and Otto Michel has caught the force of it well in giving it the sense of under the wrath of God, or under the power of sin.[21]

THE EVIDENCE FOR THE INDICTMENT

¹⁰As it is written:

"There is no one righteous, not even one;
    ¹¹there is no one who understands,
        no one who seeks God.

> [12] *All have turned away,*
> *they have together become worthless;*
> *there is no one who does good,*
> *not even one."*
> [13] *"Their throats are open graves;*
> *their tongues practice deceit."*
> *"The poison of vipers is on their lips."*
> [14] *"Their mouths are full of cursing and bitterness."*
> [15] *"Their feet are swift to shed blood;*
> [16] *ruin and misery mark their ways,*
> [17] *and the way of peace they do not know."*
> [18] *"There is no fear of God before their eyes."*

After the accusation comes the demonstration. The catena, or patchwork of Old Testament passages, may have come from the apostle's memory, for sometimes it is exact, and sometimes it is not.[22] The collection of citations shows two great emphases. In the first place, there is a clear testimony here to the universality of sin. All are under its power and condemnation, and the inclusiveness of this judgment is strongly stressed, for over and over again he comments that not even one person is excluded from the indictment (cf. vv. 10–12). A second emphasis in the catena of quotations is on the intensity of sin; there is a total depravity manifested. All aspects of human life, both words and works, are affected by sin. Human beings are wholly touched by sin.

The apostle concludes the section with a clue to the cause of it all in the citation from Psalm 36:1, "There is no fear of God before his eyes." People tend to see themselves only in relation to other people, but Paul brings man to God so that he may see himself in the divine light. And the damning indictment is that there is "no fear" before the throne. The word "fear" is a word of unbelief, and Paul's charge is in remarkable harmony with the biblical teaching on the nature of sin. Sin is unbelief, which surfaces in rebellion and leads on to immorality (cf. John 16:8–9).

THE APPLICATION TO THE WORLD

> [19] *Now we know that whatever the law says, it says to those who are under the law, so that every mouth may be silenced and the whole world held accountable to God.* [20] *Therefore no one will be declared righteous in his sight by observing the law; rather, through the law we become conscious of sin.*

The "now"[23] is transitional, and with it Paul moves to the conclusion of the section, the application of the truth of the Old Testament teaching regarding the guilt and power of sin to the whole world. The word *law* often refers to the Mosaic law, but here it refers to the entire Old Testament, especially in the light of the fact that the apostle has just cited from the Psalms and Isaiah. The application of the passages, however, is surprisingly broad. It involves "the whole world." C. K. Barrett is on the right track when he writes, "The Old Testament proves that the Jews, and *a fortiori* all other men, are guilty before God."[24]

It is as if the nation Israel were a sample of the human race and, after testing, has been found wanting. Since a choice section of the human race has been taken as a testable unit and has had the benefit of every conceivable divine blessing, far beyond that of the race as a whole, and has been found guilty, it is only reasonable to conclude that "the whole world" has been brought under the judgment of God (cf. Acts 17:26).

In verse 19 the law, when seen in its rightful office as representative of the holiness of God, brings to the enlightened human heart such a sense of sin and guilt that the mouth is stopped and all hope of human righteousness flees.

The "therefore" in 3:20 means "because" or "since." [25] The apostle is seeking to destroy the last stronghold of the Jew, his law. The law's office is not to save but to give the knowledge of sin. As far as the Jew, then, is concerned, "his death warrant is, as it were, written into his own birth certificate."[26] That which was thought by many to be a means of salvation is really the means of condemnation, and not of the Jew alone, but also of the Gentile.

Righteousness, then, can never come from self-effort. Jesus, speaking of the self-righteousness, declared, "It is not the healthy who need a doctor, but the sick. I have not come to call the righteous, but sinners to repentance" (Luke 5:31 – 32). By this he hoped to point his listeners to an examination of their hearts and, by that examination, to a sense of their need. Paul, more bluntly, simply blurts out that there are no righteous people. All are sick, all are sinners, and all need the Great Physician. Righteousness must come from God, for there is no bath that can take away a single stain, but that "fountain filled with blood, drawn from Immanuel's veins."

DISCUSSION QUESTIONS

1. Would Paul concur with the modern self-esteem philosophy?

2. Society views the human race as inherently good. Is such a view based on God's revelation or rationalism? What drives such thinking?

3. Why is our culture biased toward universal salvation and not universal judgment? Is it cultural? Is it rebellion? Explain.

4. Have you come to the point in your life where you have recognized your own lack of righteousness and your need for forgiveness?

5. What can Paul teach us about evangelism insofar as he starts with "bad news?"

CHAPTER 5

HOW SHOULD MAN BE JUST WITH GOD?

ROMANS 3:21–31

Paul has challenged human pride with its peacock's feathers in Romans 1 and 2. He has shown convincingly the fatal disease of sin, both original and total. And that which makes man so pitiful in his state is that he is for the most part blind to his sin. When there is no recognition of sin, there is no perceived need of the saving cross of Christ.

This section of Romans gives the solution to the problem of sin and contains the normative passage on the great Protestant doctrine of justification by faith alone. Concerning the last two verses of the section, Frédéric Godet wrote:

> It is not without reason that these two verses have been called "the marrow of theology." Calvin declared "that there is not probably in the whole Bible a passage which sets forth more profoundly the righteousness of God in Christ." And yet it is so short that the statement seems scarcely to have begun when all is said, within so few lines are the most decisive thoughts concentrated! It is really, as Vitringa has said, "the brief summary of divine wisdom."[1]

Martyn Lloyd-Jones's words support the claim, "It is a foolish thing to say, perhaps, but I was going to say that if I were asked which in my opinion is the most important and crucial passage in the whole of Scripture, I would have to include Romans 3:21 – 31."[2]

THE MANIFESTATION OF JUSTIFICATION

> [21]*But now a righteousness from God, apart from law, has been made known, to which the Law and the Prophets testify.* [22]*This righteousness from God comes through faith in Jesus Christ to all who believe. There is no difference,* [23]*for all have sinned and fall short of the glory of God,*

Its Relationships (Romans 3:21)

"In the opening words of Romans 3:21, 'But now ...' you can almost hear a sigh of relief," Ray Stedman comments, adding, "Now, after God's appraisal of man's efforts to achieve some standing before him, come God's words of relief. God's total answer to man's total failure."[3] "But now" makes the turn in the argument. The righteousness of God "revealed" (cf. 1:17) is now "manifested."

It was Martin Luther who, in dealing with man's sin and hopelessness, referred to Horace's rule of dramatic art that a god must not be introduced into the action unless the plot has gotten into such a tangle that only a god could unravel it. That is the state of the story line in Romans at this point. The righteousness of God is said to be "apart from law, has been made known, to which the Law and the Prophets testify." Righteousness is not gained by legal effort or by the works of the law. It is not contrary to the law, for the law did not teach that man gained life by good works. Instead, the law brought by its demands, which man could not meet, the knowledge of sin (cf. 3:20).

The Old Testament witnessed to the righteousness that was apart from legal works. It taught that righteousness came by the merits of a Redeemer who justified people by faith (cf. Gen. 15:6; Ps. 32:1 – 2; Isa. 8:14; 28:16; 59:20 – 21; Hab. 2:4; all these texts are used by Paul in Romans). The Old Testament sacrifices, by a kind of Pavlovian conditioned reflex, impressed on the minds of the Israelites that God was to be approached only on the ground of sacrifice, and that forgiveness was received only on the ground of the blood that was shed (cf. Heb. 9:22).

Its Rationale (Romans 3:22)

Paul gives further explanation as he sets forth the rationale of the righteousness. It is a righteousness (cf. 1:17) given by the instrumentality of faith in Jesus Christ to all believers. This is necessary, namely, that it be through faith and not by works, because there is no difference in the sinner-hood of all people.

Its Reason (Romans 3:23)

All people fail, for both Jews and Gentiles are sinners. The apostle's statement that "all have sinned" may be taken as a reference to the sin of Adam in the garden of Eden, where all people fell in their federal representative (cf. 5:12). The majority of commentators, however, take the reference to be to personal sins,[4] suggested by the context of 1:18 – 3:20.

The Greek verb translated "fall short" is in the present tense and refers to the present situation. People are constantly coming short of the glory of God. Paul does not say that all come equally short of the standard. The standard is nothing less than perfection, and nothing less can pass. That means that the lack of an inch is as fatal as the lack of a foot. Thus, in the light of God's standard (cf. Matt. 5:20; 22:37), religion, culture, education, good works, and religious ordinances cannot save. Man is lost; his mouth is "silenced" before the demands of a just and holy Sovereign. Paul's necessary and inevitable note concerning man's state is that he is a sinner, under divine judgment. His fate is death (cf. 6:23).

THE DESCRIPTION OF JUSTIFICATION

[24]and are justified freely by his grace through the redemption that came by Christ Jesus. [25]God presented him as a sacrifice of atonement, through faith in his blood. He did this to demonstrate his justice, because in his forbearance he had left the sins committed beforehand unpunished— [26]he did it to demonstrate his justice at the present time, so as to be just and the one who justifies those who have faith in Jesus.

The Manner, or Principle (Romans 3:24, "freely")

Two words demand definition if we are to understand the apostle here. To "justify" must be given the forensic, or legal, sense of "to declare righteous" (cf. Deut. 25:1; 1 Kings 8:32; Isa. 5:23; Rom. 2:13; 3:4; 4:3 – 25; 5:17) by virtue of the imputation of the merits of the crucified Savior, Jesus Christ. The other word, "propitiation" (3:25), may be loosely paraphrased by the word "satisfaction" or, as in the NIV, "sacrifice of atonement." It may mean "mercy seat," for it is doubtful that a Jew could fail to make the connection, since the root was commonly used in the Old Testament for that part of the furniture of the tabernacle where the blood was sprinkled in the Most Holy Place. Since the article is lacking from the word in Paul's usage here, the emphasis rests on the mercifulness of the mercy seat. It, the cross, is a *mercy* seat.

The apostle speaks of the manner, or principle, of justification in the use of the adverb, "freely." It is rendered by the phrase "without reason" in John 15:25 and by "without paying" in 2 Thessalonians 3:8 (cf. Rev. 22:17). It is clear that the word here underscores the grace that underlies God's dealings with man in justification. It is what R. C. H. Lenski calls "pure, abounding, astounding grace."[5]

The Method (Romans 3:24–25a)

In the course of the exposition of the method of justification, Paul refers to the instrumentality of redemption. The word Paul uses is a beautifully intensive word. He might have used the simple "ransoming"[6] (NIV "redemption"), but he used the Greek word that means a "ransoming *away*."[7] As Adolf Deissmann points out, justification is not through the ransoming, but the ransoming away, which is in Christ Jesus. It suggests that we will never again come into the same slavery to sin (cf. Lev. 16:22).[8] The Father provided that which was the satisfaction of his holiness and justice in their claims against man. That satisfaction was secured by the substitutionary death of the Lord Jesus Christ. It was the satisfaction of the divine holiness and its claims on man in judgment through the death of the Representative of his people that secured the redemption from the bondage of sin.

The Means of Appropriation (Romans 3:25)

The means of appropriation of the benefits of the death of Christ is through faith and faith alone.

THE INTENTION OF JUSTIFICATION

Righteousness for the Past (Romans 3:25b)

In a sense, we have the motive in the heart of God in the provision of righteousness. There is a manifestation of God's righteousness in the past: "He did this to demonstrate his justice, because in his forbearance he had left the sins committed beforehand unpunished" (v. 25b). It is clear that God has first place in the cross, not man. It is for his propitiation due to the past sins of man that Christ must die. The reference here is not to the sins committed by believers before they came to Christ, but to the sins done under the old economy, before Christ came (cf. Heb. 1:3; 9:15). The question "Where are the wages of sin?" no doubt constantly on the lips of the Old Testament men and women, is answered here. Godet writes:

> For four thousand years the spectacle presented by mankind to the whole moral universe (comp. 1 Cor. iv 9) was, so to speak, a continual scandal. With the exception of some great examples of judgments, divine righteousness seemed to be asleep; one might even have asked if it existed. Men sinned here below, and yet they lived. They sinned on, and yet reached in safety a hoary old age.... Where were the wages of sin? It was this relative impunity which rendered a solemn manifestation necessary.[9]

The cross silences the question forever.

Righteousness for the Present (Romans 3:26a)

Jesus was also set forth for the manifestation of God's righteousness in the present season. He died for the sins of people who live in the present age.

Righteousness for the Believer (Romans 3:26b)

The final intention of the Father is that he might be seen to be both just and the justifier of the one who believes in Jesus. The great problem, not of how to get people to God, but of how to get God to people, is righteously solved (cf. 5:21). In the cross of Christ, he is seen to be both righteous in his judgment and loving in his mercy (cf. Ps. 85:10). God has been propitiated, and it is not necessary to coax, cajole, or wheedle mercy from him. God *is* propitious by reason of the death of Christ. Just believe him and thank him, receiving the gift of eternal life.

All barriers are removed in the cross, which exhibits his righteousness and yet also broadcasts his love. His redemption is not "a pity that agrees to ignore sin; but a power that cancels it and sets free from its dominion," as a famous Bible teacher has put it. In the light of this, we can only exclaim with the hymn writer Edward Mote:

> My hope is built on nothing less
> Than Jesus' blood and righteousness;
> I dare not trust the sweetest frame,
> But wholly lean on Jesus' Name,
> On Christ, the solid Rock, I stand,
> All other ground is sinking sand.
> All other ground is sinking sand.[10]

BOASTING EXCLUDED, DISTINCTIONS REJECTED, THE LAW ESTABLISHED

The apostle now draws out the implications of the teaching that humans are justified by grace alone, through faith alone, in Jesus, who has been set forth as a propitiation, alone. The fact that consequences are before the reader is evident from the conjunctions the apostle writes, "Where, then, is boasting?" The "then"[11] indicates that the question is derived from the preceding exposition of justification by faith alone.

The apostle continues his reasoning by pointing out what would necessarily follow if a person were not justified by faith. If the law were the means of justification, that would strongly suggest that God was desirous of the salvation of Jews alone, since the law was given to them.

THE EXCLUSION OF BOASTING

> [27]*Where, then, is boasting? It is excluded. On what principle? On that of observing the law? No, but on that of faith.* [28]*For we maintain that a man is justified by faith apart from observing the law.*

The Interrogation (Romans 3:27)

We might ask, "Why does Paul come back to the question of boasting? He has already dealt with that in the previous chapter" (cf. 2:17). It is useful to state truth negatively, for it serves to delimit the positives. Notice that throughout the section Paul argues his case not only convincingly but also polemically.

"Where, then, is boasting?" is Paul's question. Boasting, to put it somewhat awkwardly, is self-announcing, while faith is self-renouncing. Boasting is introspective, while faith is extraspective. Boasting looks inward to the man himself, while faith looks outward and upward to God. It is clear from these simple considerations that faith must be a gift of God (cf. 1 Cor. 4:7; Eph. 2:8–9). The apostle answers his first question with a simple statement, "It is excluded" or "shut out." The reason the apostle feels it necessary to bring up the subject with his reader is that boasting was one of the essential problems of the Jew (cf. Rom. 2:17; Phil. 3:4–6; Luke 18:9–14).

A second question follows in the interrogation: "On what principle?" The apostle quickly answers his own question with another, "On that of observing the law?" and then points to the true source of the exclusion of boasting, "on that of faith." The expression "that of faith" is generally thought to mean the principle of faith in general, but in the light of the context it may refer to the Old Testament law, regarded as teaching that people are to be justified by faith (cf. 9:31–32; 10:6–8). The Jews had misunderstood it, thinking that the law taught people to seek justification as a reward for law-keeping, or for good works.[12] The reference in verse 21 to "the Law and the Prophets" confirms this interpretation.

The Explanation (Romans 3:28)

It is important to note that the apostle does not say that a person is justified *because* of faith, because that might suggest that it is faith that saves. Faith is not the cause of justification; it is the means of it. It is not ultimately faith that saves.

It is Christ who saves through faith, the source being his perfect vicarious work on Calvary's cross. Faith was neither crucified nor resurrected.

It is a well-known fact that Luther, in his rendering of the verse, inserted a word not found in Paul's text. He translated, "Therefore, we conclude that a man is justified by faith alone apart from the works of the law."[13] His translation is fully justified in light of the phrase "apart from observing the law." C. K. Barrett was right: "If anything other than faith could be the means of justification, then works done in obedience to the law, which was set forth by God himself, and is holy, righteous, good, and spiritual (vii. 12, 14) could justify. If these are excluded, everything is excluded, and faith alone remains."[14]

THE REJECTION OF DISTINCTIONS

> [29]*Is God the God of Jews only? Is he not the God of Gentiles too? Yes, of Gentiles too,* [30]*since there is only one God, who will justify the circumcised by faith and the uncircumcised through that same faith.*

The Interrogation (Romans 3:29a-b)

The second consequence is introduced here. God's way of justification by faith alone on the principle of grace alone rejects all distinctions between Jews and Gentiles. Paul writes, "Is God the God of Jews only? Is he not the God of Gentiles too?" All Jews would grant that God is the God of all people in the sense that he is their Creator, Ruler, and Judge. The apostle goes a bit further, writing that he is also a merciful and gracious God to all people. That was not a common view among the Jews, as the comment of Rabbi Simeon ben Jochai on Exodus 20:2 indicates: "God spake to the Israelites: 'I am God over all who enter the world, but my name have I associated only with you; I have not called myself the God of the nations of the world, but the God of Israel.'"[15]

The Explanation (Romans 3:29c – 30)

The apostle's answer to his own questions is a simple, "Yes, of Gentiles too." The divine purpose includes mercy and grace for all people (that is, "all kinds of men," as the usage of "all" often demands; cf. 3:22; 10:12).

In support of the fact that God is also the God of the Gentiles, the apostle appeals to the doctrine taught in the great Shema[16] of Deuteronomy 6:4, the creed of Judaism. "Since there is only one God" is perhaps clearer rendered "If, as is indeed true, God is one," giving clear expression to the nature of the conditional clause. The relative clause that follows, "who will justify the circumcised by faith and the uncircumcised through that same faith," gives the corollary that should be drawn from the confession of the oneness of God, namely, that he will justify Jew and Gentile in the same way (by faith on the principle of grace).

Thus, the fact that God is one means for Paul that there is not a number of different ways of saving people. Paul's statement here makes indubitably clear that salvation is for Jews and for Gentiles by the same method.

There have been many attempts to explain why Paul says that the Jews are justified "by faith"[17] and the Gentiles "through faith."[18] Augustine explained the variation as a purely rhetorical one. I am inclined to think that Augustine is right, as a careful study of Galatians 2:16 and 3:8 will show. In the former passage, the apostle says that the Jews are justified through faith, and in the latter, he says that the Gentiles are justified by faith, the same Greek expressions being used for the other race of people.

THE ESTABLISHMENT OF THE LAW

> [31]*Do we, then, nullify the law by this faith? Not at all! Rather, we uphold the law.*

The Interrogation (Romans 3:31a)

The final question of the section is the conclusion of the section, and it introduces the third consequence of the Pauline doctrine of justification by faith. The "then" infers a false conclusion that Paul realizes might be drawn from what he has been saying. Someone might contend that the law was a means of salvation and that Paul's teaching nullifies it, for the law is not of faith but the doer of it will live by it (cf. Gal. 3:12).

The Explanation (Romans 3:31b-c)

Two questions must be settled if we are to arrive at the meaning of Paul's explanation, "Not at all! Rather, we uphold the law." The first has to do with the meaning of the term "law," and the second concerns the meaning of the expression "uphold the law."

The term "law" has been taken to mean the whole of the Old Testament, a meaning it appears to have in 3:19, since Paul has cited from a wide spectrum of the Old Testament in 3:9–18. Alternatively, it has been taken to refer to the Pentateuch only, a meaning that the term "law" has in 3:21, since there it is clear that the Prophets are excluded from its meaning. The most common meaning of the term in the epistle is the Mosaic law, the Ten Commandments, a meaning the term has in 3:20, 27, and 28. Paul has this meaning in mind here.

Second, in what sense does his teaching "uphold" the law? Some believe that Paul's teaching establishes, or upholds, the law in the sense that Christ has fulfilled it; that is, by living and dying as he did, he honored its righteous requirements, paying the penalty of the broken law for those whom he represented. The Lord Jesus honored the Mosaic law by his active obedience in his life, from his earliest actions to his final ones (cf. Matt. 3:13 – 17; 8:4; 26:17 – 29; Gal. 4:6; et al.). Furthermore, he honored the law by his passive obedience of submitting to the judgment of the law on the failure of those whom he represented to keep the law. In fact, there is no greater honoring of the law of God and of the moral undergirding of God's creation than that accomplished in the voluntary death of the Redeemer. His work confirmed the holiness of God, the wrath of God, and the sinfulness of humans.

That Christ has fulfilled the law in that sense I do not doubt. I am not at all sure, however, that that is what Paul has in mind here. In 3:20 the apostle wrote, "Through the law we become conscious of sin." That is, it is the office of the law, not to save, but to convince of sin (cf. 4:15; 7:7 – 13). Thus, Paul's method of salvation by faith alone is in perfect harmony with the intent of the Mosaic law. The law convinces of sin and thus prepares for salvation by grace through faith. The doctrine of justification by faith alone establishes the law in its rightful office of revealer of sin and preparation for justification.

The threefold consequence of justification is plain. All boasting is excluded, except that genuine and allowable boasting in the Lord. All distinctions are abolished between Jew and Gentile in the doctrine of the one God. False Jewish concepts of salvation through the law, which were given only to the Jew, are rejected.

It may seem to some that it is tautologous or repetitious to continually speak of justification by grace alone through faith alone. "Can we not go on to something new?" is the cry of many. It is not monotonous, however, to look at the sea and enjoy the abiding sameness of its deep blue surface, its fresh and rolling undulation, and the whiteness of its billows. It is not hard to stand by the sea for hours on end and enjoy its repetitious sameness, being thrilled by the call of its nature. We have never complained of the sun in its lack of variety, every morning rising in the east and setting in the west without fail. Nor do we complain of the monotony of the bread that we continually, day by day, eat. Thus is it with the doctrine of justification by faith alone through the principle of grace alone. It is as fresh as God's supernatural manna was to the Israelites every day.

DISCUSSION QUESTIONS

1. What advice would you give a Christian who was searching for something more than the doctrine of justification by faith alone? Could a Christian become bored with Christ's work on Calvary?

2. Is justification by faith alone practical? If so, how?

3. Would a thorough understanding of the Old Testament positively contribute to a personal grasp of the righteousness of God and justification? What explains the lack of familiarity with the Old Testament?

4. In light of Ephesian 2:8 – 9, why do most evangelicals believe that faith causes their salvation (instead of seeing faith as the nonmeritorious instrument of salvation)?

CHAPTER 6

ABRAHAM'S SALVATION

ROMANS 4:1–25

Paul's teaching on the plan of salvation in Romans 4 is crystal clear. He is continuing his discourse on justification by faith alone on the principle of grace alone. The ultimate question, the way of salvation, is his theme. The able Swiss pastor Walter Lüthi commented on the importance and difficulty of Romans 4, "The argument continues to revolve round the question of how man can enter Heaven, if at all; and if so, under what conditions. This question is undoubtedly important enough for us to make an honest effort to answer it."[1] We must have no uncertainty about the divine plan of salvation, and this section of Romans is an aid to that assurance.

The apostle uses Abraham's life to demonstrate the grace of God in salvation. One of the errors of Jewish thinking in the understanding of the Old Testament is the view that Moses was the greatest Jew who ever lived. This has oriented Jewish thinking to legal righteousness rather than faith righteousness, the fundamental teaching of both true Judaism and Christianity.

From belief in Nannar, the moon god, to Yahweh, the true God, is the spiritual pilgrimage Abraham traveled. In Ur of the Chaldees, he had been a pagan idolater. Then came the epiphany of the true God, and Abraham left home and most of his family for an unknown destination. The idol worshiper finally found his destined place as a devotee of the God of mercy and grace, the Lord God of creation and redemption. Outside of references to the Lord Jesus Christ, and excluding also such references as "Moses said" or "Moses wrote," the names most frequently mentioned in the New Testament are these (in order): (1) Paul, (2) Peter, (3) John the Baptist, and (4) Abraham. We might have thought that one of the other apostles, such as John or James, or even the Virgin Mary would have been mentioned more often than the Old Testament patriarch, but not so.

In chapter 4 Paul makes four important points: First, the Old Testament ("the Scriptures" to him and to his readers) teaches justification through faith on the principle of grace (cf. vv. 1 – 8). Second, the Old Testament teaches justification apart from any ordinances, even divinely given ones (cf. vv. 9 – 12). Third, the Old Testament teaches justification apart from legal works of any kind (cf. vv. 13 – 17). Fourth, the Old Testament teaches that the faith that justifies is a faith that is in essence like the faith that Abraham exercised (cf. vv. 18 – 25).

THE PROBLEM OF ABRAHAM

¹What then shall we say that Abraham, our forefather, discovered in this matter? ²If, in fact, Abraham was justified by works, he had something to boast about — but not before God.

The Problem (Romans 4:1)

This chapter turns to the consideration of a natural question that might have been posed by a reader of Scripture, particularly a Jewish reader. "Paul," one might have said, "you have eliminated the law and works as a means of salvation and, therefore, boasting, but what about the teaching of the Scriptures, the teaching of the Old Testament? Were not the people of the Old Testament (the Scriptures to the Hebrew) justified by keeping the law of Moses?" The purpose of the apostle in this chapter is to answer just such a question, that is, to show that God's method of dealing with people in old covenant days is the same as his method of dealing with people in new covenant days. There is only one way of justification before God, and it excludes any boasting by saved people (cf. Eph. 2:8 – 9).

The Partial Answer (Romans 4:2)

The answer is a partial one to the problem raised in the opening question of the chapter. As a word of explanation, Paul points out that if works justified Abraham, he might have cause for boasting. That boasting, however, would not be valid before God. Paul's words "but not before God" reject the boasting, which necessarily carries with it the denial that works justified Abraham.

   Paul's aim in chapter 4 is to show that what he is teaching is in complete harmony with the teaching of the Scriptures, that is, the Old Testament. The relevance of mentioning Abraham and justification by works is indicated by the comments of C. E. B. Cranfield, "That Abraham was justified on the ground of his works was indeed what Paul's Jewish contemporaries were accustomed to assume. According to Jub. 23.10, 'Abraham was perfect in all his deeds with the Lord, and well-pleasing in righteousness all the days of his life.' ... On such a view Abraham clearly has ground for glorying."[2]

THE PLAIN TEACHING OF SCRIPTURE

   3What does the Scripture say? "Abraham believed God, and it was credited to him as righteousness."

   4Now when a man works, his wages are not credited to him as a gift, but as an obligation. 5However, to the man who does not work but trusts God who justifies the wicked, his faith is credited as righteousness.

The Citation of Scripture (Romans 4:3)

The apostle now supports his point by an appeal to the Word of God, in this case an appeal to Genesis 15:6. The point of the citation is simply this: The Bible does not support Abraham glorying in himself, for Abraham believed, not achieved. If any Jewish man was well known for his obedience, it was Abraham. It was he who responded to the command of God to emigrate to a strange land and gathered his possessions and family, and he went out, not knowing where he was going. That is remarkable faith-obedience, as the epistle to the Hebrews points out (see Heb. 11:8 – 19). We might think, and the religious people of Paul's day generally concurred, that Abraham had a great deal to boast about. He certainly was an exceptional man.

   Before God, however, even Abraham had nothing of which to boast. Boasting before people and boasting before God are two entirely different matters. Before God, Abraham was as ungodly as any man in Ur of the Chaldees, so far as his position before Yahweh was concerned. He was a lost sinner until God intervened in his life of sin and called him by grace into salvation and righteousness. Abraham's boasting could only be in the Lord who saved him. In the citation from the Old Testament, the apostle Paul quoted from the Greek version of Genesis, but he varied the wording a bit to emphasize that Abraham *believed*. In Paul's Greek letter, he threw forward the word "believed" in order to underscore it.

The Exposition of the Scripture (Romans 4:4 – 5)

Verses 4 and 5 expound the point of the citation, the gracious character of humankind's salvation, by pointing out the nature of grace and work. The apostle begins by pointing out that when a man works, his pay is not reckoned to be a gift. It is something he has earned; it is owed him. If it were possible to produce a character acceptable to God or do works that God would accept, then humans could come to the gate of heaven with confidence in themselves, in their ability to meet God's standards. They would have the same kind of boldness with which laborers stand in the line before a company's cashier to receive their pay.

In the case of salvation, however, it is different, Paul says. There we have a man not working but simply believing. We should notice the use of the term *logizomai*, rendered by the words "credited" and "counts"[3] in verses 3 – 8. It means "to put to one's account." Eight times the verb *logizomai* occurs in verses 3 – 11. Paul lays great stress on the fact that righteousness is imputed to the believer in grace (cf. Philem. 18). That righteousness is the product of the merits of the sacrifice of our representative sufferer, the Lord Jesus Christ. He has both earned righteousness for us and paid our debt.

Martin Lloyd-Jones illustrates "credited" this way:

> For instance; you remember what Paul says in writing to Philemon about Onesimus. He says, "If he has defrauded you and if he owes you anything, put that down to my account, I will repay it." The Apostle did not owe Philemon anything; but he tells Philemon to put it down to his account as if he did owe something. That is "imputing."... When we have nothing at all, God puts in the righteousness of Jesus Christ. He imputes it to us ... as it were in our account, and thereby clears our guilt and debt. He does not make us righteous in so doing, we are left, in this matter of justification, exactly where we were; but God puts this to our account and thereby clears our debt. He pronounces that all His claims against us are satisfied.[4]

Abraham is singled out because he did not work for his salvation.

THE PARALLEL OF DAVID

[6]*David says the same thing when he speaks of the blessedness of the man to whom God credits righteousness apart from works:*

[7] *"Blessed are they*
   whose transgressions are forgiven,
   whose sins are covered.

> *[8]Blessed is the man*
>   *whose sin the Lord will never count against him."*

In verses 6 – 8, the final verses of the section, David is brought in as being in agreement with Abraham insofar as the method of salvation is concerned. It is not another illustration on a level with the illustration of the patriarch, as the words "says the same thing" might suggest. Rather, the rest of the chapter continues the exposition of the meaning of Abraham's experiences. He, Abraham, is Paul's subject, but David's words are in harmony with the principles of God's dealings with Abraham.

The connection between the two passages Genesis 15 and Psalm 32 lies in the use of the term *logizomai* ("to credit" or "count"), which is found in both of them. Psalm 32:1, however, deals with the negative side of the matter, that is, the nonimputation of sin, or forgiveness. It is evident, then, that forgiveness somehow involves the imputation of righteousness. The key is that sins are sins of both commission and omission. It follows that, if sin cannot be imputed to a man, he has neither omitted one commandment required nor committed one breach of God's law. Thus, the nonimputation of sin does not leave him neutral, so far as righteousness is concerned; it really means that he is viewed as righteous, as not having omitted any positive act of good work.

JUSTIFICATION APART FROM RITES OR ORDINANCES

> *[9]Is this blessedness only for the circumcised, or also for the uncircumcised? We have been saying that Abraham's faith was credited to him as righteousness. [10]Under what circumstances was it credited? Was it after he was circumcised, or before? It was not after, but before! [11]And he received the sign of circumcision, a seal of the righteousness that he had by faith while he was still uncircumcised. So then, he is the father of all who believe but have not been circumcised, in order that righteousness might be credited to them. [12]And he is also the father of the circumcised who not only are circumcised but who also walk in the footsteps of the faith that our father Abraham had before he was circumcised.*

The Objector's Question (Romans 4:9 – 10b)

The imaginary objector's question indicates that he too is familiar with the Old Testament. His question is basically, "But Paul, have you not forgotten that Abraham was circumcised? Is that not the rite that brings us a righteous standing before God?"

The Apostle's Answer (Romans 4:10c)

The apostolic answer is simple, "Not in circumcision, but in uncircumcision." True, Abraham was circumcised, but that event took place long after he had been pronounced righteous by the Lord in those words cited above, "Abraham believed God, and it was credited to him as righteousness" (4:3; cf. Gen. 15:6). Twenty-four years after Abraham's migration from Ur, fourteen years after the covenant was ratified by sacrifice in Genesis 15, and thirteen years after Ishmael's birth, when Abraham was now ninety-nine years old, well past the age of begetting children, the Lord appeared to him. God demands him, "I am God Almighty; walk before me and be blameless" (cf. Gen. 17:1). At the same time, he confirms, by promises, the ancient covenant (cf. 17:2). The covenant was to have a sign, the sign of circumcision, suggesting the removal of the body of the flesh, or the putting away of the sins of the old life. In this timeline, long before Abraham was circumcised, he had been justified. In simple terms, the objector has forgotten that Genesis 15 comes before Genesis 17 in the Scriptures!

The Apostle's Elaboration (Romans 4:11 – 12)

Circumcision did not save; rather, it was simply a "'token," a sign, of faith-righteousness, because the patriarch had already been justified (cf. Gen. 15:6). The Jews in Paul's day, by transferring the instrument of justification from faith to the sign of faith had erred grievously. As James Stifler so aptly puts it,

> Circumcision attested the validity of Abraham's faith-righteousness in uncircumcision. In no dispensation do rites bestow anything; they are the shadow, not the substance; they are a seal. But the seal is worthless apart from the matter or from the document that it attests. The Jew had torn off the seal from the covenant and then vainly boasted of this meaningless imprint.[5]

The intent of the rite is given in the remainder of the section. Without the rite of circumcision, the patriarch would have been the father of the Gentiles alone, but with it he became the father of the Jewish people also. Being the head of the clan of faith, he is their father. The Gentiles are mentioned first, since the plan of God to save the world antedates his plan to save Israel. "Israel," as Stifler points out, "was the means to the universal end."[6] Unbelieving people of both the Gentiles and the Jews are excluded. By his solid exposition of the Scriptures, the Jews' glorying has been overthrown. In fact, it is not the Gentiles who must come to the Jews for salvation; ultimately, it is the Jews who must come to the faith of uncircumcised Abraham.

JUSTIFICATION APART FROM LAW WORKS

> *¹³It was not through law that Abraham and his offspring received the promise that he would be heir of the world, but through the righteousness that comes by faith. ¹⁴For if those who live by law are heirs, faith has no value and the promise is worthless, ¹⁵because law brings wrath. And where there is no law there is no transgression.*
>
> *¹⁶Therefore, the promise comes by faith, so that it may be by grace and may be guaranteed to all Abraham's offspring — not only to those who are of the law but also to those who are of the faith of Abraham. He is the father of us all. ¹⁷As it is written: "I have made you a father of many nations." He is our father in the sight of God, in whom he believed — the God who gives life to the dead and calls things that are not as though they were.*

The Argumentation (Romans 4:13 – 15)

The apostle, further arguing that salvation is by grace, turns to the consideration of the terms on which the promises were made to Abraham. In the opening verse of this section, Paul says that they came to the patriarch through faith, not by law works. This is plain, because the law annuls faith and the promises. The law, being the means by which sin is known, works wrath. Where there is no law, there is no transgression. Faith and the law are opposites. Bring in the one and the other must go, just as God banishes night by bringing in the day.

The Conclusion (Romans 4:16 – 17)

In verse 16 we have one of Paul's most meaningful sentences, clearly stressing that the dominant goal is that the promise might be sure to the elect seed. For this to happen, the principle on which the promise is to come to them must be a gracious one, for they, being sinners, could never earn the reward. Thus, the promise is according to grace.

But what means, or instrumentality, is compatible with grace? For the human means of receiving the promise must be set out. Paul's answer is that faith is the only means that is harmonious with the principle of grace, for in faith humans do nothing but believe, or receive, the gifts of God.

The divine intent is seen by looking at the last of the key words in the statement, "guaranteed." To be sure, it must be by grace. And to be by grace it must be of faith. The Mosaic law, and other forms of legalistic salvation, can only produce doubt and tension and despair, while grace and faith lead to safety, certainty, and enjoyment of the promises of God. That is why all plans of salvation, even among professing Christians, that confuse the principles of grace and works, even unconsciously, can only lead to loss of assurance of salvation.

Verse 17 confirms the fatherhood of Abraham over both Jews and Gentiles, in support of which the text from Genesis 17:5 is cited. The final words of the verse underline the creative power of God that is exemplified in the justifying of both Jews and Gentiles (cf. 2 Cor. 4:6), the creation *ex nihilo* being in the background of the statement.

THE NATURE OF ABRAHAM'S FAITH

> [18]*Against all hope, Abraham in hope believed and so became the father of many nations, just as it had been said to him, "So shall your offspring be."* [19]*Without weakening in his faith, he faced the fact that his body was as good as dead — since he was about a hundred years old — and that Sarah's womb was also dead.* [20]*Yet he did not waver through unbelief regarding the promise of God, but was strengthened in his faith and gave glory to God,* [21]*being fully persuaded that God had power to do what he had promised.*

Its Impediments (Romans 4:18 – 19)

Having cogently made his point that Old Testament people were justified in the same way that New Testament people are, it would be expected that someone should say to him, "But, Paul, just exactly what is saving faith? You say a man is justified by faith, not by the works of the law. But what do you mean by 'faith'? Just what is the kind of faith that justifies?" His answer is that faith is unswerving trust in the God of the resurrection. That too was the essence of Abraham's trust (cf. v. 17; Acts 27:25).

When Abraham was ninety-nine, the Lord appeared again to him, renewed the covenantal promises, and gave him the sign of the covenant, the rite of circumcision. At the same time, he told Abram that the promised seed would come from the womb of Sarah. In token of the situation, Abram was given a new name, Abraham, meaning father of a multitude. The impediments to Abraham's faith were large and imposing. It was as Chrysostom put it, "against human hope, in the hope which is of God." Abraham was beyond human expectations of being a father through Sarah. Cranfield aptly cites Wesley's lines:

> In hope, against all human hope, Self-desperate, I believe;
> Faith, mighty faith, the promise sees, And looks to that alone;
> Laughs at impossibilities, And cries: It shall be done![7]

The expression "and so became the father of many nations" (cf. Gen. 17:4 – 5) may express the content of Abraham's faith, the result of his faith, or the purpose of his faith. The last named is the most common use of the grammatical construction. Abraham considered fully the state of his body and yet believed. What we have is Paul's exposition of the sense of Genesis 17:17. He thinks that Abraham's laughter over the idea of Sarah and him having a son is the laughter of faith.

Its Encouragements (Romans 4:20 – 21)

The encouragement to faith found in verse 20 is the promise of God, which in this case includes the promises of Genesis 12:1 – 3 and the reference to them in 15:5 – 6. By the grace of God (cf. Eph. 2:8 – 9), Abraham was enabled to believe the promises given to him, and the result was that he gave glory to God. The heart of the validity of justification by faith leads to the glorification of the triune God. That is why a plan involving the free will of man cannot be in harmony with distinguishing grace.

In verse 21 the second of the encouragements to faith is mentioned. It is the character of God. As Paul puts it, it is "being fully persuaded that God had power to do what he had promised." We might expand this second encouragement to both the power and faithfulness of God. His promises are the ground of our hope, and his powerful faithfulness to his Word provide additional support (cf. Heb. 6:13 – 20).

The best biblical definition of faith is found in Acts 27:25, where Paul said, "So keep up your courage, men, for I have faith in God that it will happen just as he told me." That is faith: simply believing that things are and will be just as God says they are. Faith, then, is simply taking the Word of God at face value. It is not delusion, nor is it the presumption of rationalism, nor is it credulity, akin to which is the mumbo jumbo of witch doctors, the Latin of the priests, and the ritual of the churches. It is the reception of the Word of God as truth. Do you believe?

THE DIVINE RESPONSE TO ABRAHAM'S FAITH

[22]*This is why "it was credited to him as righteousness."*

The faith of Abraham was not merely in the promise of God, but it was also a faith in the God who had promised, as the preceding verses indicated. Now we have the divine response to the faith of the patriarch. With the "this is why" (lit., "wherefore") the apostle points out that the resultant imputation of righteousness is the result of the expression of saving faith on the part of the patriarch.

THE PAULINE APPLICATION TO US

²³The words "it was credited to him" were written not for him alone, ²⁴but also for us, to whom God will credit righteousness — for us who believe in him who raised Jesus our Lord from the dead. ²⁵He was delivered over to death for our sins and was raised to life for our justification.

The Twofold Application of the Old Testament (Romans 4:23 – 24a)

The apostle here makes the point that the story of Abraham is not written for the sake of Abraham alone, that is, as a memorial of him, or that he might live on in the memory of people. It is written for others and for us, since the manner in which the patriarch was justified is the same method by which we, too, are justified by a just God and a Savior. The imputation of righteousness is secured by us in the same way, faith in the God of Abraham and in his promises concerning the Redeemer.

The Essence of Saving Faith (Romans 4:24b)

The essence of saving faith, Paul says, is found in believing in him who raised up Jesus, our Lord, from the dead. It is no vague, indefinite, amorphous feeling, but it is the firm conviction that a set of facts concerning Christ are true. The expression "who raised Jesus our Lord from the dead," points to the essence of every Christian's faith. It is in the God of the resurrection, or in the God, in this context, "who gives life to the dead and calls things that are not as though they were" (cf. 4:17, 19). There is a harmony of essence between the begetting of Isaac and the resurrection of Isaac's seed, the Lord Jesus Christ.

The Rationale of the Saving Acts (Romans 4:25)

In this expression, which by its balance suggests that it was used often by Paul and became something like a formula, and which seems to clearly recall Isaiah 52:13 – 53:12 (cf. 53:11 – 12, 5, 6; et al.), the apostle expounds the meaning of the cross and the resurrection. Christ's death took place because of offenses, while his resurrection took place because justification had been completed.

The word translated by "for" in the last verse has been taken in different senses. Some have taken the first occurrence in a causal sense, and the second one in a final (purpose) sense. It is best to take the two prepositions in their normal causal sense. Thus, in God's sight the death of Jesus justified, and the resurrection is his receipt for the satisfaction of every claim of holiness against those for whom Christ died. It is God's "Amen" to Christ's "It is finished." Looking at the cross, we see justification completed, and looking at the open tomb, we see it accepted.

DISCUSSION QUESTIONS

1. Do you know the Old Testament well enough to preach the gospel from it? What steps can you take to be more proficient in the Old Testament?

2. Does God deal with the salvation of Abraham in the same way he deals with people today? If so, in what way or ways?

3. How does Romans 4 help people realize that keeping the Ten Commandments does not save them?

4. In what ways are water baptism and circumcision parallel? In what ways are they dissimilar?

5. Paul clearly teaches that circumcision is a work. What does that imply regarding baptism and its role in salvation?

6. Since people are justified before God on the principle of grace, and salvation is received through the instrumentality of faith, what do you say to someone who thinks faith is meritorious?

7. Why does Acts 27:25 give a good definition of faith?

8. The New Testament emphasizes the Father's role of raising Jesus from the dead. Why?

CHAPTER 7

SAFETY, CERTAINTY, AND ENJOYMENT

ROMANS 5:1–11

Peace with God," what a wonderful expression! What could be more satisfying than the enjoyment of reconciliation with him? What could be more rewarding than the truth that our relationship with the Creator and Ruler of the universe is harmonious? In one of Paul's other writings, he says Jesus Christ wins peace "through his blood, shed on the cross" (Col. 1:20). In Paul's mind, peace with God is the result of reconciliation with God and justification before God. It is the consummation of the process by which we are tried before God and given the judgment of acquittal from the exalted Judge.

The apostle Paul, having set out his doctrine of justification by faith alone, now turns to the certainty and the enjoyment of the peace that believers have through faith in the Redeemer, the Lord Jesus Christ. Every believer is safe.

THE TRIBULATIONS OF GOD

¹Therefore, since we have been justified through faith, we have peace with God through our Lord Jesus Christ, ²through whom we have gained access by faith into this grace in which we now stand. And we rejoice in the hope of the glory of God. ³Not only so, but we also rejoice in our sufferings, because we know that suffering produces perseverance; ⁴perseverance, character; and character, hope. ⁵And hope does not disappoint us, because God has poured out his love into our hearts by the Holy Spirit, whom he has given us.

What We Have (Romans 5:1 – 2)

It would have been a natural thing for a doubter, or questioner, to ask in objecting to the faith way of salvation, "Is this method safe? Will it enable us to hold out to the end? After all, faith is a tenuous thing. Can it stand up when the trials of life come to us?" Paul answered in the aggressive affirmative.

A question exists over the correct reading of the original text in verse 1. Many of the ancient manuscripts have the finite verb of verse 1 in a Greek form rendered "let us have." It does seem more in harmony with Paul's thought here to prefer the NIV rendering, "we have."[1]

In setting forth what we have, Paul mentions "peace," which was obtained in the past, "access," which is our present possession, and "hope," which stretches out into the future (cf. Col. 3:4). The peace is possible because of the work of justification that the apostle has just expounded. It is obtainable by those who meet God at the appointed meeting place of Calvary.

What We Should Do (Romans 5:1, 3)

The apostle has said that we should go on enjoying the peace we have, and he adds in verse 3 that we should also glory in sufferings or tribulations. That seems a strange thing to say, does it not? It fairly cries out for explanation, and that is what Paul gives in the following verses.

Why We Should Do It (Romans 5:3 – 5)

The word "know" introduces the ground on which we should boast in our sufferings. Knowledge is the ground of faith in Paul's mind, and in this case it is the knowledge of a spiritual process. Suffering introduces a pattern of growth in the believer's life that concludes with the possession of an approved character. Tribulations strengthen us, contrary to what we might think.

The first thing Paul says is that tribulations work perseverance. Trials come from God (cf. 8:35 – 39), and they give occasion for the exhibition of his power and grace (cf. 2 Cor. 12:9). Otherwise, there might be impatience in his saints. There is an old story about a young man who found himself very impatient. That man asked Robert Chapman, the well-known Brethren Bible teacher, to pray for him that he might learn patience. He was rather surprised to hear Mr. Chapman immediately turn to the Lord in prayer and say, "Oh Lord, send this young man tribulation!" The young man expostulated that he had not asked him to pray that prayer, but the older, experienced man of God answered, "But young man, it is tribulation that worketh patience" (KJV).

The apostle goes on to say that patience does its work too. It produces an approved character (cf. 2 Cor. 2:9; 8:2; 9:13; 13:3; Phil. 2:22). And finally, character works hope. As C. E. B. Cranfield said, "To have one's faith proved by God in the fires of tribulation and sustained by him so as to stand the test is to have one's hope in him and in the fulfillment of his promises, one's hope of his glory (v. 2), strengthened and confirmed."[2]

The final step in the process is expressed in verse 5, "And hope does not disappoint us, because God has poured out his love into our hearts by the Holy Spirit, whom he has given us." We have what we began with when the tribulations came, that is, hope, plus the approved character given through the trials. Hope never disappoints by proving to be a false and illusory thing, because the love of God for us is the pledge that the hope it promises is valid through the indwelling Spirit (cf. 8:16). The verb "poured out" expresses the unstinting lavishness of the giving of the third person of the Trinity. The extravagant nature of the giving is spelled out in verses 6 – 8.

THE LOVE OF GOD

> [6]*You see, at just the right time, when we were still powerless, Christ died for the ungodly.* [7]*Very rarely will anyone die for a righteous man, though for a good man someone might possibly dare to die.* [8]*But God demonstrates his own love for us in this: While we were still sinners, Christ died for us.*

What We Were (Romans 5:6, 8, 10)

Verses 6 – 8 describe the nature of the divine love referred to in verse 5. If we were to ask, "Paul, how do we know God's love?" the answer would come, "by his death." That is the theme the apostle expounds in verses 6, 8, and 10. Four descriptions of sinners are given in these verses. In verse 6 they are said to be "powerless" and "ungodly." In verse 8 they are referred to by the word "sinners," and in verse 10 they are described by the term "enemies." To sum up what Paul says about the terms, we could say those who are powerless Christ died for, the ungodly he justified, the sinner he saved, and the enemy he reconciled to himself.

What He Did (Romans 5:8)

The work of Christ, expressed here, is one of the most touching and beautiful passages the apostle ever wrote: "But God demonstrates his own love for us in this: While we were still sinners, Christ died for us." The apostle's use of the present tense "demonstrates" should be noted. While the act of dying on the cross is an event of the past, the fact that it did occur remains as a present proof and encouragement of the love of God for his saints. That the apostle has believers in mind is clear from the use of the first person plural pronoun, "us." Paul makes much of the fact that he died for us when we were yet "sinners." He is contrasting the love of man and the love of God. We are able on occasion to die for those who are dear to us, or good, or perhaps for a righteous person, but God's love is distinguished from human love by the truth that it is exercised for his enemies.

THE RECONCILIATION OF GOD

> [9]*Since we have now been justified by his blood, how much more shall we be saved from God's wrath through him!* [10]*For if, when we were God's enemies, we were reconciled to him through the death of his Son, how much more, having been reconciled, shall we be saved through his life!* [11]*Not only is this so, but we also rejoice in God through our Lord Jesus Christ, through whom we have now received reconciliation.*

It Guarantees Our Future Salvation (Romans 5:9 – 10)

Cranfield comments, "Having described in vv. 6 – 8 the nature of God's love for us, to the reality of which (brought home to our hearts by the Holy Spirit) he had appealed in v. 5 as proof that our hope will not disappoint us, he now returns to the subject of our hope's not disappointing and affirms the certainty of our hope's fulfillment, of our final salvation, in two parallel statements (vv. 9, 10)."[3] This is a marvelous *a fortiori* argument, and it contains one of the most convincing arguments for the security of the believer and for the definiteness of the atonement also.

It is a brilliant climax to the section as Paul reasons from the death of Christ to the certainty of final salvation. The "for if" introduces the inference from the preceding statement concerning his death. The key verse is verse 10, which contains the second of the *argumenta a minori ad maius*.[4] In this case, the argument already accepted is the reconciliation of enemies to God by the death of his Son, Jesus Christ. If that is accepted, then with even greater logical necessity it follows that God will save his former enemies by the sharing of his Son's life.

In verse 10 there is a triple antithesis, with an advance in the last phrase rendered, "through his life." The first antithesis is that of "enemies" and "reconciled." The second is that of "having been reconciled" and "shall we be saved." The third is that of "through the death of his Son" and "through his life."

What, then, is the resulting sense of the apostle's argument? If God has done the most for us, giving us a crucified Savior for our reconciliation when we were enemies, he surely will give us the least, save us through to the end, now that we have become friends, reconciled to him. Or, surely if he has done the best for us, he will do the rest. Verse 9 defines salvation as defined by the statement "saved from God's wrath." Paul is thinking of the deliverance of the believer from the wrath and condemnation of sin, not from its dominion in the believer's life.[5] If, when we were enemies, God reconciled us to himself by giving his Son as a penal, substitutionary sacrifice for sin, he will surely do that which is less, now that we are friends, especially since we now share in the life of our representative through the union consummated with him. The logic is inescapable.

If Christ did the greatest thing by dying for certain persons, he surely will do the lesser thing and give the Holy Spirit in convicting and converting ministry to them, will he not? If that is so, then he must have died for the purpose of saving only his elect. Otherwise, we would have to conclude that universalism is a biblical doctrine, which, of course, it is not. The personal pronouns, then, refer to the people of God.

From the verse, therefore, we derive the greatest assurance of the certainty of the salvation that is given by grace through faith. As an Irish convert once said, "I often trimble on the Rock, but the Rock never trimbles under me."[6]

It Guarantees Our Future Exultation (Romans 5:11)

A question exists over the rendering of the participle *kauchomenoi* as "we rejoice." It may be construed as an indicative.[7] It may also be taken as an imperative, being translated, then, "And not only so, but joy in God." That is less likely, since the construction is not frequent in the New Testament. The antithetical "now," opposed to the future sense of the verb in verse 9, "we shall be saved," supports the taking of the participle as modifying the subject, "we." We would then interpretatively render verse 11, "And not only so, but we shall be saved, boasting in our Lord Jesus Christ, by whom we have now received the reconciliation." The meaning of Paul, then, would be simply this: We will be not only saved by sharing in his life, but we will be saved, or carried right on through to heaven, boasting in our Lord Jesus Christ. A triumphant, abundant entrance into glory is assured the saints for whom he has died. We will not enter the glorious presence of the Lord with morose and lugubrious countenances, woe-be-gone and sorrowful, but we will enter his presence exulting in him and his work of grace for us!

DISCUSSION QUESTIONS

1. In what ways do the truths in Romans 5:1 – 11 make you want to break out singing, "Amazing grace! how sweet the sound, That saved a wretch like me! I once was lost, but now am found, was blind, but now I see"?

2. How does theology lead to doxology and praise? In what way would healthy doctrine stimulate worship?

3. Has the Christian church lost the sense of the importance of theology? If so, how is the church the weaker for it?

4. When people say that salvation can be lost, what is your response? Would it be fair to frame the eternal security question this way: "Can God lose a Christian?" Why or why not?

CHAPTER 8

IMPUTATION AND TWO REPRESENTATIVE MEN[1]

ROMANS 5:12 – 21

Imputation is one of the greatest theological words in Holy Writ. There are three great acts of imputation in the Bible. First, Scripture teaches the imputation of Adam's sin to his posterity, or to the whole human race (cf. 1 Cor. 15:21 – 22). Second, there is the imputation of the sin of the elect to Jesus Christ, who bore that sin's penalty in his death on the cross (cf. 2 Cor. 5:21; Gal. 3:13). Third, there is the imputation of the righteousness of God to the elect (cf. Rom. 3:24 – 26; 4:1 – 8). It is to the first of these imputations that the passage in Romans 5:12 refers. In it Paul offers an important interpretation of the sin of Adam, one that is fundamental for every aspect of theology.

THE ORIGINATION OF HUMAN SIN AND DEATH

12Therefore, just as sin entered the world through one man, and death through sin, and in this way death came to all men, because all sinned —

The Source (Romans 5:12a)

The first question the reader should have is, "What is the connection between verses 1 – 11 and 12 – 21?" Paul's connecting phrase, "Therefore,"[2] is causal, which means "for this cause" — that is, we now have a sure salvation by one man, Jesus Christ. As the first Adam introduced the world to sin and death, so the last

Adam has introduced it to righteousness and life. Sin, condemnation, and death are by our human progenitor, Adam, just as righteousness, justification, and life are by our spiritual progenitor, Jesus Christ.

So if we should ask, "How by the well-doing of one man, Jesus Christ, are the many saved?" it may be said in reply, "How by the disobedience of one man, Adam, were the many condemned?" The picture is that of contrastive solidarity.[3] There is a direct comparison to the work of Adam and the work of Jesus, the last Adam.

The apostle writes that the origination of human sin is to be traced to "one man." Paul alludes to the fall in the garden of Eden. There, after the creation of Adam and Eve, God placed them and gave the terms of the probation to Adam, "And the LORD God commanded the man, 'You are free to eat from any tree in the garden; but you must not eat from the tree of the knowledge of good and evil, for when you eat of it you will surely die'" (Gen. 2:16 – 17). The tree was a test of man's creaturehood, for the condition hinged on man's belief in the word of God.[4] Nevertheless, sin came and man fell. Adam became the instrumental cause by which sin entered the world.

The Fact (Romans 5:12a)

The apostle writes, "sin entered." The sin of Adam in one sense was an irrational act, for no explanation of sin can be given that makes it reasonable. At the moment the inclination to take the fruit began, Adam sinned. The action that followed is the completion of the inclination. Adam wanted the one thing that was forbidden him.

The apostle's use of the word "entered" should be noted. The word, which looks at the fall by its tense, suggests that sin was in existence in the universe before the fall (cf. 1 Tim. 2:14). Paul gives us no details of that fact, although there are some hints in other parts of the Scripture that seem to say that sin began in heaven with the sin of Lucifer (cf. Isa. 14:12 – 17; Ezek. 28:11 – 19; John 8:44). Adam's sin was the original human sin, so far as the devastating results for the human race are concerned.

The Result (Romans 5:12a)

The catastrophic result of the first human sin is stated in the words "and death through sin." The fact that sin is said to be the basis of universal death strongly implies that Adam's sin has produced universal sin. The clause "and death through sin" clearly teaches that death is a penal evil and, as Charles Hodge points out, "not a consequence of the original constitution of man." That which was implied in 1 Corinthians 15:21 – 22[5] is here stated plainly. While Chrysostom, Augustine, and F. B. Meyer regarded the death here as physical, the greater number of commentators regard it as both physical (cf. Rom. 5:14; Gen. 3:9) and spiritual (cf. Rom. 5:18, 21; 6:23: here the death is contrasted with spiritual life, for Paul writes, "eternal life").

There are three aspects to the death that is the result of sin, although the penalty is really one penalty. The first aspect has to do with spiritual death. It is clear from the fact that Adam was told, "when you eat of it you will surely die," that the reference to death is fundamentally spiritual, for he did not die physically when he ate the fruit. Thus, death in Genesis 2:17 must be spiritual death. The second aspect deals with physical death as seen in Genesis 3:19, where, after Adam had fallen, it was said that he should eventually become dust. The third aspect, eternal death, is hinted at in Genesis 3:22 – 24, where man is driven forth from the garden of Eden, and the way back is barred to sinning man forever. Eternal death is seen in its culmination in Revelation 20:11 – 15. To sum up, when Adam sinned, he immediately died spiritually.

The remedies of death are set forth in the Word of God also. The remedy for spiritual death is eternal life, the gift of God through faith in the Lord Jesus Christ, the suffering and crucified Savior. The remedy of physical death is the bodily resurrection, which takes place at the coming of the Lord Jesus Christ for believers. For eternal death there is no remedy!

THE IMPUTATION OF SIN AND DEATH

The apostle moves from the entrance of sin in one man to its penetration to all. He writes, "and in this way death came to all men." The death referred to is probably physical in its emphasis, but it is inseparable from spiritual death. The most interesting words are "passed upon all men" (KJV). The Greek word is one that means literally "passed through." Since Paul adds "upon all men," it is clear that he thinks of the diffusion of sin as universal in its scope. "Oh, the awful power which sin had thus to turn the world into one vast cemetery and to slay the whole human race," Mr. Spurgeon said.[6]

THE FOUNDATION OF THE IMPUTATION

The final clause of the verse has been one of the major battlegrounds of the systems of theology. In what sense have "all sinned"?

First, there are many who, like Pelagius, but including such distinguished scholars as James Denney and C. K. Barrett, refer the last clause to the actual personal sins of individual people (cf. 3:23). This interpretation would be more likely if the present tense had been used, "for all are sinning." Further, the repeated claim is made in verses 15 – 19 that only one sin is the cause of the death of all. Five times Paul makes the point that the issue is of one sin. Finally, verse 14 is opposed to this view, for there it is stated that certain persons, part of the all and ones who suffer death as the penalty of sin, did not commit sins resembling Adam's, that is, individual and conscious transgressions. They must, then, have died because of Adam's sin. The Pelagian viewpoint must be discarded.

Second, there are many who have seen in the clause a reference to a realistic union between Adam and his descendants. This view is based on a common understanding of the relation of the final clause to the main clause. It is admitted that the death of all is grounded in the sin of all (v. 12), and that the death of all is grounded also in the sin of one, Adam (vv. 15 – 19). In some way and for some reason, Paul is able to say that one sinned and that all sinned — and in both statements refer to the same fact.[7] This solidarity and universality, or this union, must be a part of any explanation of Romans 5:12.

William Shedd contends that the union between Adam and his posterity is genealogical and biological and must be regarded as natural or seminal (cf. Heb. 7:9 – 10).[8] Thus, people were co-sinners with Adam in the fullest sense of the term. All the individuals descending from Adam participated in his humanity, which was a specific and numerically one entity and, thus, in his act of sin. They were in him really when he sinned. This interpretation does full justice to the past tense in "sinned," but there are insurmountable objections to it. Since at the time Adam sinned his posterity as individuals and persons did not exist, how was it possible for them to act in Adam?[9]

Furthermore, Romans 5 over and over relates our sin and guilt to the act of one man, but never once to the act of all people, which we would expect if realism were true. Further, the analogy drawn in the passage between Adam and Christ is broken, for our justification is not related to the fact that we were in Christ seminally when he died for our sins.

The last clause of verse 14 overthrows realism, for it suggests that there is a different modus in sinning for some people. Realism, however, cannot admit any, for by its very definition, every man is supposed to have been in Adam when he sinned.

Third, two final views involve the principle of imputation and the truth of representative union. One is called *mediate imputation*, and the other *immediate imputation*. Those holding the theory of mediate imputation contended that, instead of making Adam's first sin the ground of human condemnation and the corrupt nature a consequence, the corrupt nature inherited from Adam is the ground of condemnation. The guilt of the first sin becomes, then, dependent on participation in the corrupt nature. Aside from the fact that the word "sinned" cannot mean "became corrupt," as those who held this view contended, it is inconsistent with the parallelism drawn between Adam and Christ in the passage. Just as we are not justified by inherent righteousness, so we are not condemned by inherent corruption. And also, if inherent depravity is a punishment — and it is hardly possible to argue otherwise — then guilt must have preceded it. What, then, could the guilt be other than the guilt of Adam's first sin?

Fourth, we come, then, to the theory of immediate imputation. This is the biblical view. According to it, people are understood to have stood their probation in Adam, their representative head. Thus, his act was deemed their act; his sin was deemed as their sin. As the Scriptures say, they sinned in Adam (cf. 5:12, 18 – 19; 1 Cor. 15:22). This is immediate imputation. Adam was a representative head, for the promises of dominion given to him were also given to the race, as the unfolding of the Word of God indicates.

First, the threats given to Adam were threats for the race, and the consequences of his sin fully indicate that. The penal evils have affected the whole race. Second, it is implied in the fact that people are born spiritually dead, evidently under a curse (cf. Eph. 2:1 – 5). Third, it is most suitable to the illustrative analogy between Adam and Christ drawn by Paul in the section. He says all die because all have sinned (cf. v. 12). Then in verses 13 – 19 he says that all die because one sinned. He is hardly dealing with two different things; the one fact may be expressed in terms of both plurality and singularity. The sin of all is the sin of one. The solidarity must be that of federal, or covenantal, representation. Fourth, it enables us to see why only the first sin of Adam and not his subsequent sins, nor the sin of Eve, is imputed to people. Fifth, it is the only interpretation that satisfies the requirements of the relation of verses 13 – 14 to verse 12. The "for" indicates that verses 13 – 14 are designed to substantiate the statement of verse 12. If, however, verse 12 means that all people are sinners (cf. Pelagius), or that all have become corrupt (mediate imputation), or even that all actually sinned in Adam (realism), the verses do not substantiate the assertion of verse 12. If, however, verse 12 asserts that all have sinned in their representative, then everything is clear.

If we reflect on the divine scheme here, we will soon come to the conviction that it is the best possible method of saving men and women. If the testing, or probation, of humans were individual, then most of us would admit we would have fallen. We would not have had the fact of being the representative for all of our posterity as a check on us to prevent us from easily falling. The representation by Adam makes it possible for the principle to be operative in the case of Christ. He may become our representative in our salvation. The angels sinned individually, and they have no representative for salvation. We fell through no personal fault of our own; we rise through no personal merit of our own. When a father strikes oil, the children get rich. And we have hit a gusher in the last Adam!

THE NONIMPUTATION OF PRELAW SIN

[13]for before the law was given, sin was in the world. But sin is not taken into account when there is no law.

Pre – Mosaic Law Sin (Romans 5:13a)

Verse 12 introduced a comparative declaration, as the "just as" indicates. The conclusion is not stated until verses 18 – 19, where the ideas are picked up again and fully stated. Thus, verses 13 – 14 are parenthetical, explaining the statement of verse 12, namely, that all people sinned in Adam's sin by imputation. The "for" indicates that verse 13 is an explanatory statement. If Paul meant in verse 12 only that death passed on all people because of their many individual transgressions, then no explanation would be necessary, but the extraordinary statement that all die because of Adam's sin does require explanation. The statement of verse 13 is intended to show that the sin, referred to in the clause "because all sinned" in verse 12, is not sin against the Mosaic law. All violations of the Decalogue must be excluded when we look for the sin that brought death in the world.[10] It is plain that what Paul is saying is that people die, not for personal sins, but for Adam's one sin.

Its Nonimputation (Romans 5:13b)

The sin for which people died is not the breaking of the Mosaic law, for it was not yet given during this period. And yet sin is not reckoned if there is no law, but people died during this time. Now sin presupposes a law against which it is committed. If it was not the Mosaic law, it must have been some other kind of law. What other law could there have been of which they were guilty? It was the first law given Adam in the garden of Eden (cf. Gen. 2:16 – 17). Death supposes sin, and sin implies some kind of law that has been broken. It could only be the law that Adam broke. Thus, they died for the sin of the first man. The conclusion confirms the interpretation of verse 12, "because all sinned." That is spelled out in the next verse.

THE DOMINION OF DEATH

[14]*Nevertheless, death reigned from the time of Adam to the time of Moses, even over those who did not sin by breaking a command, as did Adam, who was a pattern of the one to come.*

The Fact of Its Dominion (Romans 5:14a-b)

The clause that begins with "even"[11] implies that it would not have been expected that death should reign over this class of persons, and that their case is the difficult one to explain. What is meant is that if these persons had sinned after the similitude of Adam's transgression, it would *not* have been strange that they died. But they did not sin after the similitude of his sin. To whom does the clause refer?

Three things are true of this last class. First, they were a part of the "all" of verse 12. Second, they were under a law of some kind, for sin was imputed to them. Third, they died. A sin like Adam's would have been a particular act of transgression, either of the written (Gen. 2:16–17) or unwritten law (cf. Rom. 2:14–15: law of conscience). This kind of sin, Paul says, they have not committed. Therefore, if their sin was not one like Adam's, neither against a written or unwritten law, nor a transgression of Mosaic law, it must have been Adam's first sin itself for which they were responsible. They sinned Adam's very sin in their representative, Adam. Shedd is right, "The relation between their sin and Adam's is not that of resemblance, but of identity."[12]

The clause "because all sinned" in verse 12 cannot refer to individual acts of transgression. Only the first sin of Adam can be meant. If people did not die because of Mosaic sin, nor by transgression of the law of conscience, the unwritten law, which would also be "like" Adam's transgression of a specific law, then they could only die for Adam's first sin itself. This was imputed to them. The probationary statute is the reason for their guilt.

Those referred to in the middle clause of the verse, then, are probably those who died in infancy. As Murray says, "For nothing evinces the sin of all and the death of all in the sin of Adam more than the death of little infants."[13]

Paul traced man's fall to the one sinning act of Adam, the first man. As a direct result of Adam's transgression, four things have come to pass. First, Adam's sin was imputed immediately to every member of his posterity, that is, to every member of the human race. Thus, every individual became guilty of

Adam's sin and, therefore, of condemnation and death. Second, Adam's nature became corrupted, and he passed on his corrupt nature to every member of the race. Since Adam, all people have been born in sin (cf. Eph. 2:1 – 3), inheriting a corrupt nature from the first man. Third, as a consequence of Adam's fall, all people are unable to respond savingly to the Word of God and the gospel (cf. Rom. 8:7 – 8; 1 Cor. 2:14). Finally, eternal punishment has come as the consequence of Adam's sin (cf. Gen. 2:16 – 17; 3:17 – 19). Humankind is now "under foreign domination."

As we read the chapter, it becomes evident that Adam is a type primarily by contrast, the unity of the many in the one. In Adam's case, it is the unity of the many in a representative who fell. In Christ's case, it is the unity of the many in a representative who overcame, including in his victory all who are in him.

The Illustration of the Dominion (Romans 5:14c)

The final clause of verse 14 introduces the reader to the Adam-Christ typology, as a preparation for what is to follow in the next section. The noun translated "pattern" denotes the mark made by a striking object (cf. John 20:25), an impression made by an object that is in turn used to mold or shape something else (cf. Rom. 6:17). Thus, Adam is an example, or type, of Christ. It is proper to speak of him as the first Adam and of Christ as the last Adam (cf. 1 Cor. 15:45). The typology is, nevertheless, largely contrastive in this context. The two men are heads of their posterity, but the first Adam affects his posterity for death, while the last Adam gives life to his people.

THE EPIC CONTRAST BETWEEN THE TWO REPRESENTATIVE MEN

> [15]But the gift is not like the trespass. For if the many died by the trespass of the one man, how much more did God's grace and the gift that came by the grace of the one man, Jesus Christ, overflow to the many! [16]Again, the gift of God is not like the result of the one man's sin: The judgment followed one sin and brought condemnation, but the gift followed many trespasses and brought justification. [17]For if, by the trespass of the one man, death reigned through that one man, how much more will those who receive God's abundant provision of grace and of the gift of righteousness reign in life through the one man, Jesus Christ.

With the final clause of verse 14, when Paul said that Adam was a type of Christ, it might have been expected that he would introduce a comparison of the two men. The "but" of verse 15 indicates that he will stress the contrast between the two. The first thing he says is that the offense of Adam is not like the free gift of righteousness (cf. vv. 17, 18, 20, 21). In Adam's case, the one offense has resulted in the death of many. In Christ's case, however, the one individual is responsible for the gracious gift of righteousness from God. The "much more" has a further significance. Paul indicates by its use that the work of Christ provides more than simply restoring what was lost by Adam. Not only is the sinning man restored to the condition of Adam before the fall; he is given a righteous standing in holiness before the Lord God, which is immutable.

The offense of Adam is called a "trespass" (lit., "falling beside"), which is fitting for a description of the fall of Adam. The "much more" and the "overflow" support the idea that Christ has done more than restore man to Adam's relation to God in the garden. The "many" who died and the "many" who have received grace are not coextensive; otherwise we should have the apostle teaching universalism. The many who receive grace are the people of God, the company for which Christ stood as representative.

The apostle becomes more specific in verse 16, the second of the two statements of dissimilarity between the first man and the second Man. The gift of God cannot be compared with the sin of Adam, Paul says. Adam's offenses led to judgment and condemnation. In the case of Christ, there is the free gift of righteousness by the sacrificial blood of the Redeemer. The judgment came from one deed, but God's gift is his answer to a multitude of misdeeds, the accumulated sins of the centuries since Adam.

The "for" of verse 17 introduces an explanation, which is probably primarily related to the first part of verse 16 rather than the last part.[14] There is again on Adam's side one offense, followed by the reign of death (cf. v. 14). On Christ's side, it is through him that those who receive the abundance of grace and the gift of righteousness reign in life. There is an important new fact added in this reiteration of the principal thought of the section. The apostle refers to those "who receive God's abundant provision of grace and of the gift of righteousness." In these words there is a hint of how the work becomes the possession of those for whom it was intended. From the human perspective, they are to "receive" it. It becomes theirs by the appropriation of faith. Each representative man's action is determinative for the life of the many to whom they are related.

Cranfield says at this point:

> In vv. 15 – 17 Paul has made clear the essential dissimilarity between Christ and Adam that has to be firmly grasped if the comparison between them is not to be altogether misunderstood. He has shown that, apart from the one point of the formal similarity between the relation of Christ to all men and

the relation of Adam to all men, they stand over against each other in utter dissimilarity. This having been made clear, Paul can now go on to make his comparison.[15]

THE FORMAL COMPARISON BETWEEN THE TWO MEN

[18]*Consequently, just as the result of one trespass was condemnation for all men, so also the result of one act of righteousness was justification that brings life for all men.* [19]*For just as through the disobedience of the one man the many were made sinners, so also through the obedience of the one man the many will be made righteous.*

The word "consequently" (lit., "consequently then") introduces the formal comparison between Adam and Christ. The text is related to verse 12, actually forming the conclusion to the comparison begun there. The opening clause, "just as the result of the one trespass was condemnation for all men," repeats the content of the original opening clause of the comparison in verse 12.

The expression "one act of righteousness" is probably correct, giving the rendering "the righteous act of one," the reference being to the atoning death of Christ on the cross. Cranfield disagreed: "We take it that ... Paul means not just His atoning death but the obedience of His life as a whole, His loving God with all His heart and soul and mind and strength, and His neighbour with complete sincerity, which is the righteous conduct which God's law requires."[16] This view is doubtful because the singular is surely more suitable for a reference to the cross.

What does Paul mean by saying that the free gift came "for all men" unto justification of life? Can we really say that all people are, have been, or are to be justified? That is hardly true, going against all the Scripture teaches in many places. Can it mean that the free gift has come to all people potentially or that it is offered to all? The context is as usual helpful in determining the meaning. In the immediately preceding verse, the apostle pointed out that they reign in life who "receive God's abundant provision of grace and of the gift of righteousness." The free gift comes "for all men," that is, for all people who received abundance of grace. The same type of thought is found in 1 Corinthians 15:22, and there too Paul limits the force of the "all" who are made alive by the phrase "in Christ." All die in Adam, and all in Christ will be made alive.

The expression "justification that brings life" in verse 18 refers to the process of justification that issues in life, the word "life" being a genitive of effect or result. The righteous status that follows the act of justification has life for its result. This parallels the reference to reigning in life (cf. v. 17) and to eternal life by Jesus Christ (cf. v. 21).

In verse 19, Paul introduces another analogy by way of explanation ("for") of the inward causes of the two facts of verse 18, condemnation and justification. The analogy is indicated by the words "just as ... so also." The reference to disobedience and obedience locates the transgression and the obedience with reference to the revealed will of God. Adam disobeyed it, while Christ obeyed it.

Verse 19 intends the reader to see a parallel between the two men's actions. Since that is so, as Otto Michel points out,[17] then the word "made" is to be understood forensically. Shedd, after pointing out that the verb never means "to make," says it means "to place in the class of," referring to a declarative act.[18] It is based on the causative acts of the first sin of Adam and the obedient act of Christ.

THE FUNCTION OF THE LAW

> [20] The law was added so that the trespass might increase. But where sin increased, grace increased all the more, [21] so that, just as sin reigned in death, so also grace might reign through righteousness to bring eternal life through Jesus Christ our Lord.

The Statement of It (Romans 5:20)

What is the reason for the giving of the law? In the words of Shedd, "The question naturally arises: If sin and death occurred in the way that has been described, previous to the Mosaic law, and without its use, then why its subsequent introduction?"[19]

The word translated "added" in verse 20 means to enter alongside like an actor who does not occupy the front of the stage and who appears only to play a supporting part.[20] The important subject is not the law, but sin. If sin is to be effectively dealt with in humankind, it must become manifest among people as the exceedingly vicious and wrong thing that it is. Thus, the purpose expressed here is an intermediate purpose of God, not an ultimate purpose. The manifestation of sin is for the ultimate purpose of the salvation of people. Actually, the law was given for three purposes at least, namely, that the sin of people might become fully manifest, that its inherent ungodly nature might be seen, and that it might increase in quantity, as people sought to defend themselves in their sin against the attack of the law.

"But," the apostle says, "where sin increased [in Israel], grace increased all the more." The sins of the religious, to whom revelation has come, are infinitely more heinous than the sins of the irreligious, or pagans. Paul, however, may have had in mind the abounding sin of Israel in rejection of the law in the sense of disobedience to it, and also the climax of sinfulness in the crucifixion of Jesus Christ. Grace, nevertheless, did much more abound — in fact, superabound, as the Greek intensive verb suggests — in the provision of forgiveness for sinners by that very act of disobedience, for it is by the cross that grace comes to people. As Charles Spurgeon said, "The Law is a storm that wrecks your hopes of self-salvation, but at the same time washes you up on the Rock of Ages, not only rescued, but restored and raised to the side of the Eternal God."[21] Who would not want to cry out in joy?

The Purpose of It (Romans 5:21)

The law set in motion a purpose that leads to the reign of grace through righteousness unto eternal life by Jesus Christ, our Lord. Where sin reigned and ruined, now grace is to reign and bring to life.

The phrase "through righteousness" is to be noted. God does forgive sin, but he does it righteously. To teach that he forgives sin because of tenderness of heart, like an indulgent grandfather forgives a grandson who has done something wrong, is to pervert the doctrine of divine grace. Nor does he pardon as does a governor who exercises clemency. That type of pardon would detract from the work of Jesus Christ.

God forgives people only because the Son, the divine substitute, has paid the full penalty for their sin. Everything God does in pardon and forgiveness is done righteously. Those who possess the pardon of God have a right to heaven, and no angel can bar us from entering. The grace of God is seen in the gift of the Son; the righteousness of God is seen in the work he did and in the pardon that results from it. Grace reigns not through the great-heartedness of God but through the righteousness of God. Believers are victorious in Christ!

The chapter that began on the note of security, the certainty of our salvation "through our Lord Jesus Christ" (5:1), ends on the note of eternal life by that same one, "through Jesus Christ our Lord" (5:21).

DISCUSSION QUESTIONS

1. How are you related to Adam?

2. Federal representation is clear in the Bible, but do Western civilizations utilize federal governments?

3. Is it right that something Adam did before you were born affects you? How is it fair for God to impute Adam's sin to you?

4. Do you think you would have fared better than Adam did during his probation in the garden? Would you have sinned sooner, later, or never?

5. Why is Jesus called the last Adam and not the second Adam in 1 Corinthians 15:45?

6. Is Adam's sin the last word for those who turn in repentance and faith to Jesus Christ? Explain.

7. How much greater is the last Adam's gracious work than the first Adam's sin?

CHAPTER 9

"SHALL WE CONTINUE IN SIN?"

ROMANS 6:1–14

Among Bible teachers it is generally conceded that Romans 6:1 – 8:17 is the normative passage for Christian living. When the teaching is followed, there follows relief and release from constant defeat in the believer's life. Wrath and justification, in Romans 1 – 5, yield to the discussion of sanctification. Justification brings us from the tomb; sanctification delivers us from the old "threads" of the unbelieving life.

Two questions are the key to the chapter. The first is found in verse 1. That question is answered in verses 2 – 14. The second is found in verse 15, and it is answered in verses 15 – 23. The first question arises out of the message of "free grace" that the apostle has been propounding (cf. 4:5; 5:20 – 21). We might reason in this way: "Paul, you have been setting forth a way of justification by grace, and we are not saved, you say, by anything that we do. It is all of grace. God is giving heaven, you are implying, for nothing on our part, for we simply are to believe a message. But if we get something for nothing, do we not then tend to think less of it? And, further, you have just said, 'But where sin increased, grace increased all the more.' You imply that if we sin, then grace covers our sin. Why not, then, go on sinning so that grace may go on covering our sin? God would be getting more glory by our sinning through the covering of our sin." Thus, the question of Paul in chapter 6 comes naturally, "Shall we go on sinning so that grace may increase?"

THE PRECEPT OF DELIVERANCE: KNOWLEDGE

[1]What shall we say, then? Shall we go on sinning so that grace may increase? [2]By no means! We died to sin; how can we live in it any longer? [3]Or don't you know that all of us who were baptized into Christ Jesus were baptized into his death? [4]We were therefore buried with him through baptism into death in order that, just as Christ was raised from the dead through the glory of the Father, we too may live a new life.

[5]If we have been united with him like this in his death, we will certainly also be united with him in his resurrection. [6]For we know that our old self was crucified with him so that the body of sin might be done away with, that we should no longer be slaves to sin — [7]because anyone who has died has been freed from sin.

[8]Now if we died with Christ, we believe that we will also live with him. [9]For we know that since Christ was raised from the dead, he cannot die again; death no longer has mastery over him. [10]The death he died, he died to sin once for all; but the life he lives, he lives to God.

The Inference (Romans 6:1)

The opening questions of Romans 6 are inferences drawn from the preceding section (particularly 5:20–21). If we say that where sin abounded, grace did much more abound, then shall we continue in sin, in order that grace may abound in the free forgiveness of it? One thing is immediately clear: Paul has been preaching a free salvation; otherwise, the objection raised would have no force. The question can only arise out of a free gift of righteousness apart from works. If salvation depended on works, then the objection could never have been offered.

The Greek verb translated "Shall we go on?" emphasizes that the action the apostle has in mind is a habitual action. There is no question about whether one may lapse into sin, but as Shedd says, "He cannot contentedly 'continue in sin,' without any resistance of it and victory over it."[1]

The Answer (Romans 6:2)

The apostle's answer to the questions is very forthrightly "By no means!" The expression translated by those words has been rendered by such expressions as "Good heavens, no!"[2] and "What a ghastly thought!"[3] Literally, the Greek means, "May it not come to be." Thus, Paul's first response to the inference dismisses it as unthinkable and blasphemous.

Paul next answers the questions by a statement of the believer's death to sin in the death of Christ (cf. v. 2). Since "we died to sin," Paul asks, "how can we live in it any longer?" The believer's death to sin is out of harmony with a living in it. The apostle refers to sin as a power in the light of the context (cf. vv. 1, 10,

12 – 14). The Lord Jesus died, then, not only for sin, but he died *to* sin. And we too died in him who was our representative. This is a once-for-all "definitive breach with sin, which constitutes the identity of the believer," John Murray says.[4] It is not our deadness but our death that Paul has in mind. The word "live" implies more than a lapse into sin; it speaks of the element in which we live, our moral atmosphere.[5] To die to sin is to die with respect to sin.

He means that a believer cannot, in the light of what has happened to him in his representative, go on living in sin. If a man lives in sin, he is not a believer.[6] The entire chapter argues for the doctrine that a believer cannot persist in sin as the bent of his life. Trust in the atoning work of the representative, the Lord Jesus Christ, is incompatible with self-indulgence in sin and increasing depravity because of our union with Christ (cf. vv. 3 – 14) and of the nature of the human will and of voluntary agency (cf. vv. 15 – 23). Or, to put it another way, justification is incompatible with nonsanctification!

The Explanation (Romans 6:3 – 10)

Paul details the believer's union with the last Adam, and the stress here rests on the positive side of things. We are judicially and mediatorially represented by our Lord in his dealing with sin through the work of the cross. We died with him, and we were buried with him. Further, we rose with him, and his work has severed us from the dominion of sin. Verse 3 begins with "or," which introduces us to the positive side of the matter. Paul vindicates the premise of the believer's death to sin by an appeal to the force of baptism. It involves identification with Christ in his death, the covenant sacrifice. But what is the baptism that is in the mind of the apostle? Is it a Spirit baptism or a baptism in water? Bible teacher George Guille used to say, "Now we have come to Romans 6, and let us hope that we can get through it without getting wet!"

Those who believe that Romans 6 speaks of water baptism point to the following points. First, they emphasize the "all of us who were baptized," suggesting by their emphasis that evidently some of the Romans were not baptized. But, as many grammarians have pointed out, the quantitative relative pronoun translated by "all of us who" is often equivalent merely to a simple relative pronoun. In this case, the rendering would be simply, "we who were baptized."

Second, they emphasize the word rendered "like" in verse 5. Does not this prove, they say, that the baptism that Paul has in mind is only a symbol? In that case, the meaning would have to be water baptism. From a careful reading of the text, we come to the conviction that it is much more likely that the likeness to which Paul refers is not that of the real to the unreal but that of the physical and representative (the death of Christ) to the judicial and spiritual (our death in him). Both are real deaths (cf. 5:14; 8:3; Phil. 2:7).

Nevertheless, some things point strongly to the view that the baptism here is the baptism of the Spirit (cf. 1 Cor. 12:12 – 13). In the first place, so far as the text is concerned, the death spoken of is a real death. If so, how can water baptism be in view? That rite does not produce a real death. Further, Colossians 2:12 obviously runs in the same train of doctrine, and there the reference is to the baptism of the Spirit, as the words "not ... done by the hands of men" indicate (cf. Col. 2:11).

Finally, we must remember that water is not mentioned in the text at all. It is probable, however, that the apostle's thoughts did include water baptism as the background of the ideas expressed here. Does it not express in symbolic fashion the truths accomplished in the baptism of the Spirit? As far as method is concerned, the chapter is not conclusive. Should we not, we ought to ask ourselves, use the method that best pictures our identification with Christ? Thus, when our mediator and representative Jesus Christ arose on the first day of the week, we arose in him. This is our inviolable position and relation to him.

The "therefore" of verse 4 introduces an inference as a kind of consequence of the preceding. If we are united with him in his death, then it follows that we were united with him in his burial and resurrection. And this union is for the purpose of life, as the comparative clause indicates.

The "if" (literally, "for if")[7] of verse 5 introduces a corroborative statement in explanation of the preceding. Union in death means union in resurrection and, therefore, a walk in newness of life. Death is a prerequisite to sharing in his life. The reason for this conviction is assigned in verse 6. The "old self" — all that we were as unregenerate humans in the first federal man, Adam — has been crucified together with Christ. This has taken place in order that the body as the seat, or instrument, of sin might be annulled. The aim of it all is "that we should no longer be slaves to sin." A life of service to sin is to be replaced by a life of service to righteousness (cf. v. 19).

We are not freed from sin in the sense of being sinless. We are freed from sin in the sense of being freed from the guilt of sin. We have been declared righteous with respect to sin (cf. 3:24). Our condition now is likened to Christ's in his resurrection. No longer is he under the power of death. As Paul says, "Death no longer has mastery over him" (cf. v. 9). We too are no longer under the power of sin by virtue of our identification with our covenantal head, the Lord Jesus Christ.

What is meant by the expression to die "to sin"? It occurs three times in the passage (cf. vv. 2, 10, 11). Twice it is used of believers, once of Christ. For Christ, it cannot mean that he has died to sin in the sense that he is a person who has now gotten victory over it in his life. The death he died was for the wages of the sin of others, not himself. John Stott was right, "The death that Jesus died was the wages of sin — our sin. He paid its penalty, He accepted its reward, and He did it 'once,' once and for all."[8] We have died in Christ, then, in the sense that in him we have the penalty for our sin paid. The old life has come to an end, and a new life has begun.

THE PRACTICE OF DELIVERANCE: RECKONING

[11]In the same way, count yourselves dead to sin but alive to God in Christ Jesus.

The apostle now calls on his readers to reckon that in their covenantal head, the Lord Jesus Christ, they have come to an end of the old life. The debt has been paid, and a new life has begun, a life of deliverance from the dominion of sin. They have a new standing and a new life, and believers are to grasp the fact that they are dead to the penalty and guilt of sin by faith and live in freedom from the old bondage into which their sin had brought them.

The fact that Paul's word "count" is in the present tense indicates that he refers to an attitude of faith and not to a specific act. Believers are to count on the definitive break with sin that occurred in their salvation and the new freedom they possess from the guilt and penalty of sin. That freedom and the deliverance it involves is expounded more fully in later chapters, and the apostle relates it to the continuing activity of the Holy Spirit in the believer's life in sanctification.

THE PRINCIPLE OF DELIVERANCE: YIELDING

[12]Therefore do not let sin reign in your mortal body so that you obey its evil desires. [13]Do not offer the parts of your body to sin, as instruments of wickedness, but rather offer yourselves to God, as those who have been brought from death to life; and offer the parts of your body to him as instruments of righteousness.

The keynote of the apostle's inference ("therefore") from the preceding is the command that believers not let sin reign in their mortal bodies. The saved life leads to good works, or put another way, the crucifixion of the old man leads to the yielded life. The apostle does not refer to a life of perfection; he refers simply to the reigning of sin in the believer's life (cf. 1 John 3:9). The second occurrence of the word "offer" in verse 13 is in the aorist tense, which looks at the yielding as an event. The matter is to be settled decisively, the action being illustrated by the swearing in of a soldier, one act with many consequences, or by the "I will" of a marriage, also an act with many consequences. What Paul, then, is doing here is exhorting the saints to persevere in the faith, and the very exhortation is one of the means God uses to cause them to do just that.

THE PROMISE OF DELIVERANCE: UNDER GRACE

[14]For sin shall not be your master, because you are not under law, but under grace.

The final verse of the section is a glorious promise of deliverance from the bondage and dominion of sin. It is the reason ("for") we should yield ourselves to God. He promises deliverance from the reigning power of sin. The final explanatory statement, "because you are not under law but under grace," is important. The legal principle brings servitude to sin, but grace gives the power and the desire to live a holy life, for grace is in principle God doing something for us freely. What a magnificent promise and incentive to holiness this statement is. The provision of God for a life well-pleasing to him is complete in the consummation of the union of believers with their head, who has restored his people to the lofty place of a co-session with him at the Father's right hand (cf. Col. 3:1 – 3). Reckoning on this great redemptive work and relying on the power of the Spirit of God in sanctification, believers are delivered from service to sin to a walk in newness of life, which pleases the Father and accomplishes his will in our lives.

DISCUSSION QUESTIONS

1. How does chapter 6 connect to chapter 5? How does sanctification relate to justification?

2. If a Christian does not ask the question, "Shall we go on sinning so that grace may increase," does he or she really comprehend free grace?

3. Is there any reasonable or logical explanation for a Christian who is determined to "go on sinning"?

4. Do you notice Paul's use of both the indicative (statement of fact) and imperative (commands) in Romans 6? Can the indicative/imperative paradigm be useful in all areas of Christian sanctification? If yes, how?

CHAPTER 10

ONLY TWO MASTERS

ROMANS 6:15–23

THE INTERROGATION

There is an interesting difference in the construction of the two questions of verses 1 and 15. In verse 1 the present tense is used of the verb "go on sinning," and the meaning clearly has to do with a continuing in sinful activity. In verse 15, however, the apostle uses the aorist (undefined) tense, looking at the sinning as simply an event. In fact, it is possible that the tense refers to an isolated act of sinning. The question would then be, "Paul, can we sin now and then, since we are not under the law but under grace?" Is an isolated act of sin permissible? C. E. B. Cranfield has rather neatly pointed out the sense of the verse and the section in this way:

> The burden of the verse as a whole may be expressed in some such way as this: The question of a man's being free in the sense of having no master at all simply does not arise. The only alternatives open to him are to have sin, or to have God, as his master (the man who imagines he is free, because he acknowledges no god but his own ego, is deluded; for the service of one's own ego is the very essence of the slavery of sin). The one alternative has as its end death, but the other life with God.[1]

There is no third option in the nature of the human being.

THE ARGUMENTATION

[15]What then? Shall we sin because we are not under law but under grace? By no means! [16]Don't you know that when you offer yourselves to someone to obey him as slaves, you are slaves to the one whom you obey — whether you are slaves to sin, which leads to death, or to obedience, which leads to righteousness? [17]But thanks be to God that, though you used to be slaves to sin, you wholeheartedly obeyed the form of teaching to which you were entrusted. [18]You have been set free from sin and have become slaves to righteousness.

[19]I put this in human terms because you are weak in your natural selves. Just as you used to offer the parts of your body in slavery to impurity and to ever-increasing wickedness, so now offer them in slavery to righteousness leading to holiness. [20]When you were slaves to sin, you were free from the control of righteousness. [21]What benefit did you reap at that time from the things you are now ashamed of? Those things result in death! [22]But now that you have been set free from sin and have become slaves to God, the benefit you reap leads to holiness, and the result is eternal life.

The First Answer to the Question (Romans 6:15)

Paul's first reply to the question "Shall we sin, because we are not under law but under grace," is the blunt rejection of the idea as unthinkable and blasphemous. "By no means!" is his response. Monstrous is the thought.

The Second Answer to the Question (Romans 6:16)

Saying that a man is the moral subject of his actions may summarize the second reply. William Shedd comments, "The argument, here, is derived from the nature of the human will, and of voluntary agency. Purpose and inclination in one direction are incompatible with purpose and inclination in the contrary direction.... No man can serve two masters, at one and the same moment."[2] Since the Romans are obeying from the heart the form of doctrine to which they had been delivered (cf. v. 17), the new inclination of the will to holiness makes it a self-contradictory thing to sin, because they are not under the law but under grace. The nature of the will and its inclination forbids the doing of two contradictory things at one and the same time.

The Third Answer to the Question (Romans 6:17–22)

The third reply is simply that the believer is a slave to righteousness. Reckless sinning is, therefore, always incompatible with the grace of God. The apostle commends the wholehearted obedience of the Romans. They "used to be" (imperfect tense, suggesting that the condition was their continual state) slaves to sin by nature, but now their nature has been changed.

The words "form of teaching to which you were entrusted" demands further exposition. The word "form" is the rendering of the Greek word *typos*, which referred to the mark made by the blow from an instrument (cf. John 20:25, "print"), or the impression made by a die, or even the substance of a letter (cf. Acts 23:25). Here the idea is that of a definite standard, a mold, and since it is used of teaching, it must refer to a definite body of teaching to which the Romans yielded obedience. It was not a vague set of emotional ideas; it consisted of doctrine. There can be no real vital, stable, and strong Christianity if there is no sound theology at the heart of it. The divine mold of truth is the sine qua non of vital testimony to Christ.

The metaphor behind the thought is that of a slave being transferred from one master to another. Thus, the Romans are seen as being delivered to a new master — in this case, the apostolic doctrine. Their lives would now be molded by that teaching. It was now their new master, and they were its slaves (cf. 16:25).

Verse 18 restates their obedience from the heart, just stated in verse 17, with the added mention of a necessary consequence of it, namely, enslavement to righteousness. The words "set free" do not imply a complete and absolute freedom from sin, but from the domination of sin. Shedd explains:

> Believers are free from the condemning power of sin, and from its enslaving power. They are not under the curse of the law, and their wills are not, as in the days of unregeneracy, in total and helpless bondage to the principle of evil.... As a man is physically free whose fetters have been broken, although their fragments may not have been removed, and he be much impeded by them in his movements, so a man is spiritually free, in whom sin as a nature or principle has been slain, although its remnants still hinder him in holy living.[3]

The last words of verse 18 make it clear that freedom from sin is slavery to holiness or righteousness. This slavery to righteousness is not such that a believer cannot sin, but he cannot sin in the manner of the unregenerate, that is, completely and without sorrow and shame. The believer cannot live and act as he did in the days of his impenitency. Only when he reaches heaven will the *posse peccare* ("able to sin") of imperfect sanctification yield to the *non posse peccare* ("not able to sin") of sinless perfection. Total sanctification is not immediate on earth, but it is inevitable in heaven.

In verse 19 the apostle admits that the figure he is employing (i.e., of slavery) is inadequate, perhaps even unworthy of the believer's relation to righteousness. He writes, "I put this in human terms because you are weak in your natural selves" (cf. 3:5; 1 Cor. 9:8; Gal. 3:15). It is true that the believer's relation to righteousness is not the humiliating, degrading, grievous thing (to use Cranfield's words) that slavery is.[4] It is, in reality, a perfect freedom, for we have come to love righteousness.

The remainder of verse 19 is largely explanatory of the terms "freedom" and "slavery," as found in verse 18 (cf. vv. 13, 16). In verse 20 Paul refers to the same teaching on the will that he gave in verse 18, but in a reversed form. When living in sin, a person is released from holiness, but that freedom is a false freedom. Only as a servant of righteousness is a person truly free (cf. John 8:32 – 36, "free indeed"). Verse 21 is an appeal to yield to righteousness by a reference to the consequences that follow when one follows the path of sin. The end of the life of sin is death. The apostle evidently refers to eternal death in the light of the use of the expression "eternal life" in verse 22 (cf. v. 23). He points out that freedom from sin and submission to righteousness leads to sanctification, which ends in eternal life.

THE CONCLUDING PRINCIPLE

[23]*For the wages of sin is death, but the gift of God is eternal life in Christ Jesus our Lord.*

The final verse of the section introduces further support for the teaching of the two previous verses. It also forms a fitting conclusion. Its climactic character reminds the reader of the climax in verse 21, for both emphasize the contrast of grace. Paul speaks first of the wages that sin pays. It operates on the remuneration principle, and it leads to death. The unmerited favor principle, the grace principle, leads to life. The sinner earns his judgment. In speaking of the opposite, the apostle does not say that the wages of righteousness is eternal life, because the imputed righteousness, by which alone a sinner may receive life, is a gratuity, a gift. "Righteousness, unlike sin," Shedd claims, "is not self-originated, and consequently its reward must be gracious."[5] The ground and the cause of it all is Christ, so Paul adds, "in Christ Jesus our Lord." Eternal life is only to be found in him.

DISCUSSION QUESTIONS

1. What roles does Old Testament law play in the life of a Christian? What about the Ten Commandments?

2. Since unbelievers are "slaves to sin" (v. 17), why do they believe they truly have "free will"?

3. Since believers are "slaves to righteousness" (v. 18), why do some Christians believe they truly have "free will"? In what way is the will tethered to the nature?

CHAPTER 11

MARITAL UNION
WITH CHRIST

ROMANS 7:1–12

In Romans 7 Paul is showing his readers how to be saved from the power of sin in their daily lives. In the final analysis, since only Christ can live the Christian life, we need him, and Paul's words are intended to indicate to us how we have him through union with him. This union may be seen in these aspects: first, by judicial union (6:1 – 14); second, in moral union (6:15 – 23); third, by marital union (7:1 – 6); fourth, in dynamic union by the Spirit (8:1 – 17).

The figure of marriage, which the apostle draws on here, is a significant one. The aim of the natural life of marriage is the establishment of a home and a family (cf. Gen. 1:28). Involved in marriage is a courtship and the marriage itself, and the natural result is a physical progeny. The aim in the spiritual life is the establishment of a relationship with the God of heaven. Involved in that is a courtship carried on by the Spirit (cf. 2 Cor. 11:2), a marriage (Rom. 7:4), and a spiritual progeny (7:4).

THE ILLUSTRATION OF PAUL

> [1]*Do you not know, brothers — for I am speaking to men who know the law — that the law has authority over a man only as long as he lives?*

109

The Connection with the Preceding Context (Romans 7:1)

The Greek is literally, "or are you ignorant," introducing the alternative to something in the preceding chapter. The connection is found in 6:14 – 15, where the apostle had said that the believer was not under the law. After answering an objection that might have arisen immediately in the mind of his readers — that is, "Shall we sin because we are not under the law but under grace" — Paul felt it necessary to further support the claim, "you are not under law." The terminology of chapter 7 along with 7:1 also supports the connection the apostle has with 6:14. The occurrence in the opening statement of chapter 7 uses the same Greek word root that the apostle used in 6:14, *kyrieuō* (translated "be your master" in 6:14 and "has authority" in 7:1). Thus, there now follows in the opening verses of chapter 7 elucidation of the claim that believers are not under the law.

The apostle opens the explanation by appealing to the principle that the authority of the law controls a person as long as he or she lives. In the midst of the statement is a parenthetical one, "I am speaking to men who know the law" (referring to the Old Testament law). If you accept the principle of verse 1 and the conclusion of verses 4 – 6 from its application in verses 2 and 3, you will have to accept the claim made in 6:14, "you are not under law."

The illustration follows in verses 2 and 3. The married woman is bound to her husband by the law so long as he lives. If, however, the husband should die, she is released from the law binding her to her husband. The word translated "man" in verse 1 is the generic word, which may refer to either a man or a woman. Thus, the apostle in verse 1 states the general principle that pertains to both a man and a woman. In his illustration, since he needs to use the female to make marriage to the male Christ understandable, he uses the woman.[1]

THE INTERPRETATION OF PAUL'S ILLUSTRATION

> [2]*For example, by law a married woman is bound to her husband as long as he is alive, but if her husband dies, she is released from the law of marriage.* [3]*So then, if she marries another man while her husband is still alive, she is called an adulteress. But if her husband dies, she is released from that law and is not an adulteress, even though she marries another man.*

The husband in Paul's example, in the light of the preceding context in chapter 6 and the picture of the death of the believer there, is designed to represent the old man under the law. It is what Paul speaks of in Romans 6:6, "For we know that our old self was crucified with him so that the body of sin might be done away with, that we should no longer be slaves to sin." The fifteen hundred years of bondage under the law of Moses was over (cf. Gal. 4:1–7).

The wife in Paul's illustration "represents that inmost self, or personality, which survives all changes, moral or physical, and retains its identity under all conditions of existence."[2] She is the "I" of Galatians 2:20 who survives in the "me" of the same verse.

The death is the same death referred to in the preceding chapter (cf. 6:6, 7, 8, 11).

The law is the Mosaic law (cf. 5:20; 6:14). When we look at Paul's illustration, clearly Paul is making essentially the same point he made in chapter 6. In this chapter, however, there is need to relate the representative death of our Lord to a new matter, the law, and so he does it by means of a new analogy.

THE APPLICATION OF PAUL'S ILLUSTRATION

[4]So, my brothers, you also died to the law through the body of Christ, that you might belong to another, to him who was raised from the dead, in order that we might bear fruit to God. [5]For when we were controlled by the sinful nature, the sinful passions aroused by the law were at work in our bodies, so that we bore fruit for death. [6]But now, by dying to what once bound us, we have been released from the law so that we serve in the new way of the Spirit, and not in the old way of the written code.

The Fact of Freedom (Romans 7:4, 6)

In the application,[3] Paul makes several important points. The first is the fact of the believer's freedom from the law. In chapter 6 he made the point that the Christian is free from sin's dominion (cf. 6:18, 22) and now is free from the law. The apostle writes that the Romans have been put to death to the law. He was thinking of the event of the cross as the point of death, and the passive voice may indicate that he wished his readers to recognize that the death in the past was "God's doing."[4] Death to sin (cf. 6:2–10) is necessarily death to the law. As we often sing, "Free from the law, oh, happy condition, Jesus hath bled, and there is remission! Cursed by the law, and bruised by the fall, Grace hath redeemed us once for all."[5]

The phrase "through the body of Christ" is a reference to the death of our Lord on the cross. In our representative we have died with respect to the law of Moses. The purpose of the death of Christ is expressed in the clause, "that you might belong to another," and the identity of that person to whom the believer is to be married is further explained as being the one raised from the dead, that is, the risen Christ. Finally, the marriage relationship that is established by the death of Christ has its intent, "in order that we might bear fruit to God." The fullness of the application Paul makes from the illustration indicates he intended it to suggest a number of parallels.

The Means of Freedom (Romans 7:4, 6)

The death of Christ is the basis of our justification (cf. 5:9) and is also the basis of our sanctification (cf. 6:6). Here in chapter 7 Paul makes the point that the death of Christ is also the basis of our emancipation from the law of Moses (cf. 7:4, 6).

The Results of Freedom (Romans 7:4 – 6)

Paul points his readers to the marriage that has been consummated between the Lord and his own bride. A marital union has been accomplished by the death of Christ. From the negative side of things, this means emancipation from the law of Moses, but the results from the positive side are astounding. Believers have been married to the risen Christ.

What a beautiful figure of our relationship to Christ is the figure of marriage! Marriage is one of the most blessed of all relationships. The wife surrenders herself, and in her surrender she meets in a high sense the surrender of her lover to herself. She says, "I am his," but she is able to add, "and he is mine." A mutual possession flows from the relationship. Thus, a believer can speak of his relation to the Lord, who is the groom. Moreover, marriage is the sphere of privilege, bringing the wife into the intimacies of her husband's life and he into the intimacies of hers. There is a mutual sharing of love, purposes, aspirations, and experiences. In marital union there is a unity not found elsewhere. Thus is the relation of the risen Christ to his bride.

The reference in verse 4 to "fruit to God" reminds us that true spiritual fruit can come only from union with One who is able to produce it. We are only the instrumentalities of his inner working that produces fruit. At this point, we call to mind the teaching of our Lord in John 15:1 – 12, and an exposition of that passage would at this point fittingly make the point plain that "apart from me you can do nothing," but with him nothing is impossible.

Freedom from the Mosaic law is often misinterpreted as leading to antinomianism (lawlessness). The apostle would not have understood such reasoning. In this passage, where he makes it crystal clear that believers are delivered from the law, he nevertheless makes it also patent that they are to "serve" (v. 6). This verb is in the present tense, which suggests a continuous bondage. Freedom from the law of Moses leads to another life of bondage, a bondage to the Lord

God — but a willing bondage, for it flows out of a love and gratitude wrought by thanksgiving for the grace that has brought us from spiritual death to marital union with the Son of God. The believer is not freed from the obligation to live in a righteous manner. In fact, Paul says, it is expected that they will serve "in the new way of the Spirit" (cf. 7:6). Finally, the use of the term "Spirit" in this phrase may be an allusion to the work of the Spirit, which is largely before the reader in the next chapter.

Our relationship to the Lord Jesus Christ is a wonderfully marital one. And a life in love, his love to me, as well as mine to him, is the prerequisite for a life of happy, joyous fruitfulness in his service.

IS THE LAW SIN?

The obvious objection to the thinking of the apostle now surfaces. It might be phrased in this way: "Paul, you have said that we believers died to sin in the death of Christ (6:1 – 14), and you have followed that by saying that we have also died to the law of Moses (7:1 – 6). Are you not, then, putting the two in the same category, sin and God's law? Are you not implying, if not saying, that the law is sinful?"

The question itself plunges us into the subject of sin, a most unpopular subject in today's climate of opinion. Calvin Coolidge, one of the lesser-known presidents of the United States in the twentieth century, visited a church and was asked what the preacher spoke on. He replied in his taciturn way, "Sin." "What did he say about it?" he was asked. "He was against it," was the reply.

THE PROBLEM STATED

7What shall we say, then? Is the law sin?

The problem raised by the apostle is, "What shall we say, then? Is the law sin?" That the apostle means by "the law" the Mosaic law is clear, since in a moment he will cite one of the Ten Commandments. God gave Israel the Mosaic law with its commandments and ordinances since the Abrahamic covenant promises did not lay much stress on sin (cf. Gen. 12:1 – 3). It was necessary for the education of the nation that they be taught their sinful nature, for only in this way would they be likely to respond to the ministry of the Messiah who was to come. In this sense, the giving of the law of Moses was an act of grace on the part of the Lord. If, as Paul says, we have in Christ died to sin and to the law, is there any implication in his teaching that God erred in the gift of the law of Moses?

THE PAULINE ANSWER

⁷Certainly not! Indeed I would not have known what sin was except through the law. For I would not have known what coveting really was if the law had not said, "Do not covet." ⁸But sin, seizing the opportunity afforded by the commandment, produced in me every kind of covetous desire. For apart from law, sin is dead. ⁹Once I was alive apart from law; but when the commandment came, sin sprang to life and I died. ¹⁰I found that the very commandment that was intended to bring life actually brought death. ¹¹For sin, seizing the opportunity afforded by the commandment, deceived me, and through the commandment put me to death. ¹²So then, the law is holy, and the commandment is holy, righteous and good.

The Law Revealed Sin to the Apostle (Romans 7:7b)

Of course, the apostle knew that commandment, but evidently there came a time when its teaching really struck home. The law revealed his lust.

The Law Stirred up Sin in Paul (Romans 7:8; cf. 5:20)

Evidently some conceived of the law as taking away their freedom. Thus, there arose resentment and rebellion, or sin, against the law. And sin makes use of the commandments as a means of arousing all manner of covetousness. When sin sees the law, it "runs wild," hurrying into rebellion and wickedness (cf. v. 5). Charles Spurgeon wrote:

> That must be a very terrible power which gathers strength from that which should restrain it, and rushes on the more violently in proportion as it is reined in. Sin kills men by that which was ordained to life. It makes heaven's gifts the stepping stones to hell, uses the lamps of the temple to show the way to perdition.... Sin is that strange fire which burns the more fiercely for being damped, finding fuel in the water which was intended to quench it. The Lord brings good out of evil, but sin brings evil out of good.[6]

The final statement of verse 8, "For apart from the law, sin is dead," is of note. "Even without the law," C. E. B. Cranfield points out in explanation, "sin is indeed present, but it is inactive — or at least relatively so."[7]

The Law Revealed Paul's Spiritual Death (Romans 7:9 – 11)

It is the opinion of some commentators that the "I" of this section is not that of Paul individually, but is the "'I" of general reference. They believe Paul is really referring to man's condition before the giving of the law, along with which he probably had in mind the state of man as he is pictured in Genesis 1:28 – 29.[8] I am not inclined to accept that interpretation, because Paul's "I" is to be taken in its common sense. He means simply, as Augustine and John Calvin have said, that he was alive in the sense that the sin within him was not yet active. He was living the life of an unconvicted sinner, without remorse and in the enjoyment of his unbelieving life. When the law came home to him, that which was inactive became active, and he realized that he was really dead. William Shedd points out that the reference to death in verse 9 does not imply that previously he was not dead, any more than the reviving of sin implies that previously there had been no sin. As the "coming" of the commandment brought him to the consciousness of a sin that was latent, so it brought him to the consciousness of a death that was already within him, and resting upon him.[9]

The expression "the very commandment that was intended to bring life" points to the original intent of the law (cf. Lev. 18:5). There may be a reference to Genesis 3:13 and to Eve's deception in the apostle's words of verse 11, but we must not press it too far, for Adam, it is distinctively said, was not deceived (cf. 1 Tim. 2:14). There are several senses in which sin deceives people by means of the law. In the first place, instead of pardoning people, as many supposed, it curses and condemns them (cf. Gal. 3:10). Second, instead of removing sin, it stirs up and exasperates it (cf. Rom. 3:20; 7:5).

THE PLAIN CONCLUSION

The conclusion to be drawn from the argument is given in verse 12: "So then, the law is holy, and the commandment is holy, righteous and good." That is the specific answer to the question Paul asked in verse 7, "Is the law sin?" The problem clearly with the sin of man is not the law, for it is holy, just, and good. The difficulty lies elsewhere, and the apostle dwells on that in the verse that follows.

DISCUSSION QUESTIONS

1. Why is it rare for Christians to think of their relationship to the Lord Jesus Christ as a marital one?

2. What are the obligations of a married person to their spouse? How does this apply to the Lord and his bride?

3. How would you define spiritual adultery? Is there any way that a wife can yield herself to two husbands? Can a spouse have any love for another and remain loyal?

4. The Reformers emphasized both the law and the gospel. Why are both needed? Are they related? Do they overlap? Explain.

CHAPTER 12

THE STRUGGLE
ROMANS 7:13–25

Paul had argued in the preceding context that the believer had died with respect to sin and the law of Moses. Then in answer to the expected question, "Is the law sin?" he had replied, "No, the law is holy, and the commandment is holy, righteous and good" (cf. 7:7, 12). That answer, however, raised another question: "Is, then, that which is holy and good the ultimate source of death for me?" No, Paul points out, it is not the law that is the cause of the believer's death. The law is the instrumentality of sin (cf. 7:7, 8, 11), and it is indwelling sin that is the culprit. Even though possessed of the law of Moses, the believer, by himself or herself, is impotent to deal with the enemy — inherited, inherent corruption (original sin in the narrow sense). The problem that he deals with is alluded to in the words of verse 18, "For I have the desire to do what is good, but I cannot carry it out."

THE BELIEVER: A BOND-SLAVE SIN

> [13]Did that which is good, then, become death to me? By no means! But in order that sin might be recognized as sin, it produced death in me through what was good, so that through the commandment sin might become utterly sinful.
> [14]We know that the law is spiritual; but I am unspiritual, sold as a slave to sin. [15]I do not understand what I do. For what I want to do I do not do, but what I hate I do. [16]And if I do what I do not want to do, I agree that the law is good. [17]As it is, it is no longer I myself who do it, but it is sin living in me.

Is Paul writing about the regenerate man or the unregenerate man? As we peruse the arguments pro and con, it becomes obvious that much can be said for the opinion that Paul is writing of an unregenerate man under the law. Nevertheless, I will argue for the view that Paul is writing of a saved man.[1]

SAVED MAN

In the first place, the general flow of the epistle's argument supports the view. While it is true that not every passage after the completion of the theme of condemnation refers to the believer (cf. 8:5 – 8), it is true that we have logically come through the doctrine of sin and justification into the doctrine of sanctification. The section, then, would belong to a believer's experience. Since the apostle has already demonstrated that the law cannot justify anyone, it would be unnecessary to demonstrate that he cannot live by, or keep, the law.

Second, the burden of proof rests with the opposing viewpoint in the light of two things when combined: (1) Paul's use of the first person; (2) his use of the present tense in this section. When an author speaks of "I, myself" and uses the present tense, we must begin with the assumption that he is expressing his feelings at the time of writing.[2] The apostle uses this language uniformly throughout the passage. Further, it is even more important when the contrast with verses 7 – 12 is noted. There the apostle uses the past tense almost exclusively, while in verses 13 – 25 he uses largely the present. We are led irresistibly to conclude that in the preceding section we have historical facts, while in this next section we have present experiences.[3]

Third, it is difficult to imagine an unsaved man diagnosing his case so perfectly or affirming such things of an unsaved person. Paul has a clear view of himself (vv. 18, 24) and a noble view of the law (vv. 16, 19). He hates sin (vv. 15 – 16), he delights in God's law (v. 22), and he looks for deliverance to Christ alone (v. 25). John Stott comments, "Now let me repeat that anyone who acknowledges the spirituality of God's law and his own natural carnality is a Christian of some maturity."[4] F. F. Bruce writes,

> In this section Paul continues to speak in the first person singular, but he leaves the past tense and uses the present. Not only so, but also there is an inward tension here, which was absent from verses 7 – 13. There, sin assaulted him by stealth and struck him down; here, he puts up an agonizing resistance, even if he cannot beat down the enemy. There, he described what happened to him when he lived in "this present age"; here, "the age to come" has already arrived, although the old age has not yet passed away.[5]

Is Paul drawing on his own experiences, or is he using himself as representative of one in the throes of this spiritual condition? It is not a question of an either/or but of a both/and. He is using himself as an example based on his own experiences. What we have is no abstract argument, but the personal struggle of an agonizing soul. Christians struggle as long as they are in the flesh, but there are occasions of glorious victory in the believer's life, although complete victory awaits the future (cf. 8:1 – 11).

What we have, then, in Romans 7:13 – 25 is the picture of a believer seeking to keep the law (cf. 7:22; 8:4) with the resources of the law and his new life alone (cf. 8:3). Sixteen times we find *egō* (Greek for "I") used, while the Holy Spirit is not discussed at all in 7:13 – 25. The law is mentioned in chapter 7 over twenty times but only a handful of times in chapter 8. In chapter 8 there are at least twenty references to the Holy Spirit. These facts are the key to the section.

There are three cycles in the argument of 7:13 – 25 (cf. vv. 13 – 17, 18 – 20, 21 – 25). We can see this by the recurring refrain in the last verses of the first two sections and the synonymous idea in the third. Each of the sections reveals the unhappy condition of the one who is a bond slave to indwelling sin in his members. In each cycle a pattern appears. First, there is an acknowledgment of his condition (cf. vv. 14, 18, 21). Second, each cycle continues with a description of the conflict (cf. vv. 15 – 16, 19, 22 – 23). Finally, each section ends with a summary of the believer's condition and a fixing of the cause of it all, indwelling sin (cf. vv. 17, 20, 25). The last section is, no doubt, an advance on the preceding, for in it Paul gives not only a description of the conflict but also its cause. He sets forth the matter "as a philosophy, in terms of 'laws' or principles at work in his situation."[6]

In the first cycle, the apostle shows that, apart from the Spirit's power, he is a slave to indwelling sin. While the law is spiritual, he is carnal and sold under sin. The figure of the apostle is a vivid one. E. H. Gifford comments, "A slave that has been sold is more wretched than a home-born slave; and man is said to have been sold, because he had not been a slave from the beginning (Bengel). Slavery to sin is not the rightful condition of our nature."[7] The believer is not master in his own house! C. E. B. Cranfield comments,

> The more seriously a Christian strives to live from grace and to submit to the discipline of the gospel, the more sensitive he becomes to the fact of his continuing sinfulness, the fact that even his very best acts and activities are disfigured by the egotism which is still powerful within him — and no less evil because it is often more subtly disguised than formerly.[8]

Incidentally, there is no question in Paul's mind that while the believer is unable of himself to win the battle, he is nevertheless responsible for his failure.

The apostle does not speak of two "I's" in the section. There is only one *egō*, but the one person has two sides to his being. The "I" is used comprehensively, referring to the person as actuated both by the new man, or the man within (cf. v. 22), and the evil flesh, or old nature. And the "I" is used limitedly, referring to the new principle of life, or the new man, minus the elements of the old man (cf. vv. 17, 20). This latter sense is also found in the term "the inner being" (v. 22; cf. vv. 23, 25). Thus, there is one person, but he has both a mind (a property of the new man) and flesh (here the old nature).

THE BELIEVER IMPOTENT FOR THE GOOD

> [18]*I know that nothing good lives in me, that is, in my sinful nature. For I have the desire to do what is good, but I cannot carry it out.* [19]*For what I do is not the good I want to do; no, the evil I do not want to do — this I keep on doing.* [20]*Now if I do what I do not want to do, it is no longer I who do it, but it is sin living in me that does it.*

In the second cycle (vv. 18 – 20) the apostle's emphasis passes from the positive side of things to the negative and inner side of things. We are impotent to produce righteousness. The Greek of verse 18 contains "for," which introduces the amplifying explanation and confirmation of verses 14 – 17. Paul sees himself as a divided person. The "in me" is the comprehensive person, but he limits the statement to "my sinful nature [flesh]" by the restrictive "that is." What he says is that the flesh is utterly corrupt; it can do nothing for God. There is, however, a part of him of which this cannot be said. In effect, the believer is somewhat of a divided person, and the lesson is one that every follower of the Lord Jesus must learn.

THE BELIEVER ALWAYS IN A LOSING CONFLICT

> [21]*So I find this law at work: When I want to do good, evil is right there with me.* [22]*For in my inner being I delight in God's law;* [23]*but I see another law at work in the members of my body, waging war against the law of my mind and making me a prisoner of the law of sin at work within my members.* [24]*What a wretched man I am! Who will rescue me from this body of death?* [25]*Thanks be to God — through Jesus Christ our Lord!*
> *So then, I myself in my mind am a slave to God's law, but in the sinful nature a slave to the law of sin.*

In the final cycle of the apostle's reasoning, he points out that the enemy within is stronger than his renewed self. The new life alone is not sufficient for overcoming in the struggle for victory. The "another law" that always wins the battle against the law of his mind and brings him into captivity is the "law" of indwelling sin (cf. vv. 21, 25). The believer, thus, is always in a losing conflict. The present tenses of verse 23 vividly portray the habitual struggle that always ends, it seems, in defeat. Finally, there comes the agonizing cry of verse 24, "What a wretched man I am! Who will rescue me from this body of death?" The body is the body looked at as that in which the death of indwelling sin is located. Paul is now at the end of self, the only time God will come in and deliver the believer. No longer is he looking within; it is "Who will rescue me?" It was Alfred Lord Tennyson who wrote, "Oh! that a man would arise in me / that the man I am may cease to be."[9]

That is the cry of the concerned Christian, cognizant of his or her own weakness and longing for deliverance from the thralldom of indwelling sin. In the final verse of the section, the apostle breaks forth with a cry of victory, "Thanks be to God — through Jesus Christ our Lord!" There *is* such a man! Trusting in Jesus Christ is the answer to the longing for deliverance. Paul will expand this in the next chapter (cf. 8:1 – 11). The victory is found in the continuing ministry of the Holy Spirit and in Paul's final deliverance at the resurrection. The last sentence of the chapter is a concluding statement in which he summarizes the major point of the preceding section. The believer's struggle is that between the mind and the flesh.[10] These two entities within the believer struggle for control as long as the believer is in the flesh and until the resurrection of the body.

The flesh has no ability to give victory, even though the believer now possesses a new principle of life in the new nature. God must do something for us if we are to be saved from the penalty of sin, and he must do something in us if we are to have deliverance in this life. And God must do something for us and in us at the resurrection if we are to have ultimate deliverance from sin and its consequences. That he has done, is doing, and will yet do, the Scriptures say. It all adds up to the sufficiency of Jesus Christ and his saving work for our inability, whether that of the unconverted man (cf. 8:8) or of the converted man (cf. 7:24). We do thank God "through Jesus Christ our Lord." This sufficiency is received only when our inabilities are acknowledged. When we give up, he takes up.

DISCUSSION QUESTIONS

1. Can the flesh ever grant the believer victory over sin and temptation?

2. True or false? If Christians are to have deliverance from sin in this life, God is the one who must do it for us. Explain.

3. How is Christ's sufficiency seen when our inabilities are acknowledged?

4. How does prayer relate to the inadequacy of the flesh? Do you regularly pray for the ability to please him with a holy life?

CHAPTER 13

THE DELIVERING POWER OF THE INDWELLING SPIRIT

ROMANS 8:1–17

Romans 8 is one of the great chapters of the Bible. Philipp Spener affirms this almost universal sentiment, "If Holy Scripture was a ring and the Epistle to the Romans its precious stone, chapter 8 would be the sparkling part of the jewel."[1]

All genuine Christians have an interest in how to live the Christian life. Unfortunately, it is not clear to many believers how this is to be done. One answer to the question, "How is the Christian life to be lived?" is the answer of legalism. Modern legalism erects a number of human taboos as the divine standard of life and urges the Christian to live in conformity with them in order to enjoy spiritual sanctification. The New Testament speaks out strongly against the legalistic spiritual life in its many exhortations to a life of faith. If the just are to live by faith, then life is not by the law, for they are opposed to one another (cf. Rom. 1:17; Heb. 10:38; et al.).

There are others who, in their opposition to life by the law or by legalistic principles, go to the other extreme and offer the believer a sanctification that borders on license. That such was a tendency in human nature in the apostle's day is indicated by such passages as Galatians 5:13.

Romans, and the apostle's teaching in general, provides a third alternative: life by the Spirit. It is life under the sway of the third person of the Trinity, the

Holy Spirit, and it is he who lifts the believer above the exhausting life of many Christians and the law.

It is the Holy Spirit who supplies the dynamic for the new life created in believers by the new birth. Just as faith in Christ's work is indispensable for our justification, so faith in the power of the Spirit is indispensable for our sanctification. Chapter 8 is intimately connected with chapters 6 and 7. In chapter 6 believers are identified with Christ in his representative death to sin. In chapter 7 we are identified with Christ in his representative death to the law (7:4 – 6). In chapter 8 we have the positive side of the two preceding chapters. We are introduced to the powerful one who can meet the two requirements, the third person of the Trinity. Without the help of the Holy Spirit, we are slaves to indwelling sin. Romans 8 gives us a vivid picture of who our deliverer, the Lord Jesus Christ, uses in his deliverance of us from the power of indwelling sin. It is the Spirit of God whom he uses to subdue the power of the flesh and give liberty for the fulfilling of God's will in our lives.

THE FACT OF FREEDOM

> [1]*Therefore, there is now no condemnation for those who are in Christ Jesus,*

The apostle indicates the connection of the present section with the preceding by the use of the conjunctions "therefore" and "now."[2] The words "in Christ" seem to limit the apostle's thought to that section of the epistle in which union with Christ has been developed. That would mean that the reference of the words must not go back further than 5:12. The use of the root "condemnation" in 5:16, 18, and 8:3 argue for stress on the judicial sense of the term. The fruit of sanctification is the product of justification, and there is no problem in 8:1 to the latter truth.

Romans 8:1 is connected with 7:6. We have understood 7:7 – 25 as an excursus on law and sin, answering two questions that arose out of the conclusion of 7:1 – 6, namely, that believers are no longer under the law of Moses as a code. Romans 7:7 – 25 form something of an aside in the progress of Paul's argument, the purpose being the clearing up of possible difficulties in the minds of his readers. Thus, at 8:1 he returns to the ongoing argument he has been developing on the doctrine of sanctification. In 7:1 – 6 believers were said to have died to the law, which is the strength of sin (cf. 1 Cor. 15:56). Therefore, he now says, there is no condemnation from that which the law reveals, sin, either as guilt or pollution. Romans 8:2, introduced by the explanatory "because," follows naturally.

There is no condemnation, for the law of the Spirit of life has freed us from the law of sin and death.

The word "no" is in an emphatic position in the original text, and it bears a great deal of stress in the apostle's thought. "No condemnation" is the thrilling judgment the apostle affirms concerning the position of the believer before the Lord God. We might paraphrase by saying, "There is no condemnation of any kind." The "now" is probably temporal, but one cannot give it the force of the Arminian lady, who was giving her testimony and cried out, "I thank God I'm saved; I'm saved up to the present date!"

The word "condemnation" is not to be confused with the word "judgment." It is a stronger word and refers to final judgment or eternal judgment. There is no condemnation for believers, although they still face the necessity of appearing before the judgment seat of Christ for works (cf. 2 Cor. 5:10). They are freed from condemnation, the condemnation of the law of God, because their penalty has been paid by a substitute, the Lord Jesus Christ. They are also freed from bondage to sin by the Holy Spirit, a product of the payment of the penalty by Christ.

Paul locates this status "in Christ Jesus" (cf. 6:11, 23). It is found in union with Christ. That status, the keystone of Pauline theology, is the place of safety and liberty. It is the place of safety in that we in Christ have the security of eternal life, a life that can never be taken from us and that we cannot lose by definition. Believers are secure "in Christ Jesus," because the Lord has placed us in the Lord, locked in by saving grace.

THE GROUND OF FREEDOM

> [2]*because through Christ Jesus the law of the Spirit of life set me free from the law of sin and death.* [3]*For what the law was powerless to do in that it was weakened by the sinful nature, God did by sending his own Son in the likeness of sinful man to be a sin offering. And so he condemned sin in sinful man,*

The "because" of verse 2 introduces the reader to the reason there is no condemnation to the one in Christ. The gift of the Spirit is the fruit of justification (cf. 5:5; 7:6), and he operates in the believer's life with the fixedness of a law.[3] His leading is not a matter of "sporadic impulse, but the believer's habitual experience"[4] (cf. Rom. 8:14; Gal. 5:18). The presence of the sanctifying Spirit, always at work in the life of the believer, confirms the liberation of 8:1. Thus, a twofold salvation results from union with Christ: salvation from the penalty of sin, and salvation from the power, or bondage, of sin in the daily life. The law of the Spirit of life aids and supports the "law of my mind" (cf. 7:23) on the road to liberty.

The indwelling Spirit does what we cannot do of ourselves. The key to the deliverance of the believer from indwelling sin is the indwelling Spirit of Christ. The Spirit of life constantly works, and he will accomplish his work of conforming Christians to the image of the Son (cf. 8:29 – 30).

The apostle puts the liberty in the past tense, saying that the law of the Spirit of life in Christ Jesus "set me free."[5] We are not to struggle for freedom, but to stand in the freedom we have (cf. 6:18, 22; Gal. 5:1), even though the ultimate realization of the freedom in its final sense awaits the future (cf. Rom. 8:21). William Shedd comments, "But there is freedom in the sense that sin shall not have 'dominion,' or 'lordship.'"[6] Sinless perfection is not meant, for remnants of corruption are the objects of the Spirit's ministry as long as we are in the flesh, but at the time of regeneration the liberty was begun and established.

The "for" of verse 3 introduces the second reason why there is no condemnation, and the stress is on the sacrificial work of Christ. His death for sin is the judicial basis for all of our freedom, past, present, and future. The work of the Spirit in sanctification, referred to in verse 2, is itself grounded in the work of redemption. The apostle's words reiterate a theme of Pauline teaching, that is, the inability of the law of Moses to save. "The law," Shedd says, "was powerless to perform the double function of condemning sin, and saving the sinner."[7] The impotence of the law did not lie in itself; it lay in the material with which it had to work, man. James Stifler comments, "The anchor of the law was strong in itself, but it would not hold in the mud bottom of the heart."[8]

"His own Son" is a remarkable phrase. The sending of the Son is the official work of the first person, God the Father. Jesus is called here "his own" Son. The three Greek epithets (*heatou*, *monogenēs*, and *idios*) mark out the eternal sonship of the second person, the Lord Jesus Christ, from the adoptive sonship of believers, spoken of in Romans 8:14 – 17.

The phrase "in the likeness of sinful man" is a carefully chosen one. We should note that he does not say, "in the likeness of man," as if he did not have real flesh and was only a docetic Christ, nor does he say, "in sinful man," as if he took to himself fallen nature. Jesus possessed genuine human flesh, but it was only like sinful human flesh.

"To be a sin offering" refers to the fact that Christ became the sin offering (cf. 3:24 – 25; Gal. 3:13; et al.). The word "condemned" refers to the cross, where God in Christ gave "judgment against" (the meaning of the Greek word) sin, wrecking sin's dominion over the people of God. As a result, sin no longer has rights over us. While we are not immune to sin, we have been freed from the necessity of sinning.

THE PURPOSE OF FREEDOM

> [4]*in order that the righteous requirements of the law might be fully met in us, who do not live according to the sinful nature but according to the Spirit.*

The design of the triune God in this work is given in verse 4, as the "in order that"[9] shows. It is the fulfillment of the righteous requirement of the law in believers, who walk after the Spirit. That requirement is summed up in 13:9, "Love your neighbor as yourself" (cf. Lev. 19:18), a product of the realization of the new covenant (cf. Jer. 31:33 – 34; Ezek. 36:26 – 27). F. F. Bruce echoes Paul's thinking: "Christian holiness is not a matter of painstaking conformity to the individual precepts of an external law-code; it is rather a question of the Holy Spirit's producing his fruit in the life, reproducing those graces which were seen in perfection in the life of Christ."[10] Believers are responsible to have produced in their lives "the righteous requirements of the law." While believers are not under the law as a code, the Christian's life is to be such that the law of Moses in its moral demands can find no flaw in that life.

A Christian's holy life is the product of the Holy Spirit, which is suggested by the passive voice of the verb, "might be fully met in us." The meeting of the righteous requirement of the law is done by Another in us.

THE REASONS BELIEVERS WALK AFTER THE SPIRIT

> [5]*Those who live according to the sinful nature have their minds set on what that nature desires; but those who live in accordance with the Spirit have their minds set on what the Spirit desires.* [6]*The mind of sinful man is death, but the mind controlled by the Spirit is life and peace;* [7]*the sinful mind is hostile to God. It does not submit to God's law, nor can it do so.* [8]*Those controlled by the sinful nature cannot please God.*

The Control of the Inward Inclination (Romans 8:5)

Here the apostle gives the first of the reasons why believers walk after the Spirit. The "for" of the verse (in the Greek) is connected with the last clause of the preceding verse. People walk according to the inward inclination, bent, or disposition that they have. To "live according to the sinful nature" is to exist only for the flesh, and this clause, then, refers to the unbeliever. Unbelievers mind the things of the flesh; that is, they think and will according to the desires of the flesh. Their conduct follows accordingly.

By contrast, they who are after the Spirit ("live in accordance with the Spirit") think and will according to inclinations implanted by him in the inmost being of the believer. They are inclined to holiness, just as unbelievers are inclined to unholiness. The renewed nature of the believer, upheld by the Spirit, determines the bent of the life.

The Issues of the Flesh and the Spirit (Romans 8:6 – 8)

Another reason believers walk after the Spirit is that the walk after the flesh issues in death. The inclination of the Spirit (the word here may be a reference to the human spirit in its inclination), however, is life and peace, realities associated with the life of holiness, and the effects of the justification and sanctification that coexist in the believer.

In the remaining verses of this section (vv. 7 – 8), the apostle argues the last point, giving the reason why the mind of the flesh is death. It is hostile to God, the only source of human blessedness. Shedd comments on the clause "the mind of the flesh is enmity against God" in this way: "This is one of the tersest definitions of sin."[11]

The middle of verse 7 in the Greek has the word "for," which explains why the mind of the flesh is enmity against God: "it does not submit to God's law." Unsubmission to the law is the evidence of enmity toward the One who gave the law. But the fulfilling of the law by the Spirit is the evidence that the law's demands are being met. When we say that the standard for the believer is life by the Spirit and not life according to the Mosaic law, as a code under which the believer is put, we are not implying a lower standard of life or dishonoring the holiness of the law.

The natural man, the one the apostle has in mind here, is characterized by enmity against God, by rebellion against him, and by the fact that he is dominated by the mind of the flesh. He is as unable to hear the voice of God in the Word as is a deaf man judging a music contest. He is the totally depraved man, whose whole being is touched by sin. Further, Paul says that the man cannot be subject to the law of God (v. 7c). In fact, in verse 8 he says the same thing again in a more concrete form. He is the man who "cannot please God." His sphere of life is in the flesh (cf. v. 5). The verse is a clear statement of human inability to please God.

Verse 8 is one of the clearest texts teaching that an unbelieving man cannot please God until a work of the Spirit has been performed on his inner being. It plainly teaches that regeneration must precede faith. The reason is clear. Faith pleases God (cf. Heb. 11:6), but those who are in the flesh (the unsaved individuals) cannot please God. Thus, they cannot exercise faith as long as they are in the flesh. They exercise faith only after the Holy Spirit in efficacious grace takes them out of the flesh and puts them in the Spirit by giving them new life. The first activity of the new life is to believe (cf. 1 John 5:1). The person dead in sins is given new life, which manifests itself in saving trust through the gospel.

THE BELIEVER'S LIFE AND HOPE

> *⁹You, however, are controlled not by the sinful nature but by the Spirit, if the Spirit of God lives in you. And if anyone does not have the Spirit of Christ, he does not belong to Christ. ¹⁰But if Christ is in you, your body is dead because of sin, yet your spirit is alive because of righteousness. ¹¹And if the Spirit of him who raised Jesus from the dead is living in you, he who raised Christ from the dead will also give life to your mortal bodies through his Spirit, who lives in you.*

In verses 9 – 11 we have the full and final answer to the question of 7:24, "Who will rescue me from this body of death?" The basis of the deliverance is traced to the indwelling Spirit of God, who is life and peace for the believer on account of righteousness. And the blessing that finally makes everything complete is the resurrection of the body.

The Believer's Life (Romans 8:9 – 10)

In verse 9 the apostle makes the statement that the believer is not in the flesh but in the Spirit, if indeed the Spirit of God dwells in him. The syntax of the conditional clause assumes the reality of the indwelling and expresses no doubt. Remarkably, the believer is said to be in the Spirit, but the Spirit is also said to be in him. The force of the terms is to stress the closeness of the relationship that exists between the believer and the Spirit, a kind of mutual indwelling.

The apostle also points to the absolute necessity of the possession of the Spirit for one to belong to Christ. This is the test of spiritual life (cf. Gal. 4:1 – 7). The apostle in verse 10 turns to the contrary. "But if Christ is in you" is a clause that indicates that he is in the believer by means of the Spirit. Thus, the union of the believer with Christ is a spiritual one. The reference to the body as dead on account of sin is clearly a reference to its ultimate destiny by the infliction of the penalty of sin (cf. Gen. 3:19; Rom. 5:12).

The word "spirit" in the clause "yet your spirit is alive because of righteousness" is probably a reference to the human spirit and not the Holy Spirit. The contrast with "body" makes the reference to the human spirit likely, but the human spirit as regenerate. It is given new life in regeneration (cf. John 6:50 – 51; 11:26). The righteousness is both imputed and imparted, for in the context the apostle has had in mind both justification and sanctification and their indissoluble connection.

The Believer's Resurrection (Romans 8:11)

The power of indwelling sin and physical death over the believer's body is destroyed in the bodily resurrection. The logic of the apostle is clear. The presence of the Spirit of God in our mortal bodies is the guarantee of the bodily resurrection, for he is the one who raised up Jesus Christ. When Paul says that "the Spirit of him who raised Jesus from the dead," he is referring not to the Holy Spirit but to the Father. It is not "the Spirit who raised up Jesus from the dead" but "the Spirit of the one who raised up Jesus from the dead," that is, the Father God. It is the Father who raised up the Son. The reason for that is that it is important to make plain that the sacrifice of the Son is acceptable to the Father. Therefore, the almost universal testimony of the New Testament is that the Father raised the Son (cf. Acts 2:24, 32; 3:15, 26; 4:10; 5:30; 26:8; 1 Cor. 6:14; 2 Cor. 4:14). Thus, regeneration and the indwelling of the Spirit of the God of the resurrection naturally involve the resurrection of the believer's body.

THE BELIEVER'S OBLIGATION TO THE SPIRIT

12Therefore, brothers, we have an obligation — but it is not to the sinful nature, to live according to it. 13For if you live according to the sinful nature, you will die; but if by the Spirit you put to death the misdeeds of the body, you will live, 14because those who are led by the Spirit of God are sons of God. 15For you did not receive a spirit that makes you a slave again to fear, but you received the Spirit of sonship. And by him we cry, "Abba, Father." 16The Spirit himself testifies with our spirit that we are God's children. 17Now if we are children, then we are heirs — heirs of God and co-heirs with Christ, if indeed we share in his sufferings in order that we may also share in his glory.

By Reason of Righteousness (Romans 8:12 – 13)

The resurrection is a motive for the life of holiness, and that is the inference the apostle draws from the preceding. There is now no obligation to sin; we are debtors only to righteousness, a self-evident conclusion.

The "for" in verse 13 brings Paul's reasoning forward. To live after the flesh is to die. If a person lives the corrupt life that flows from a corrupt nature, then spiritual death will ensue as the natural destiny. The true believer will persevere in righteousness as the bent of his life, while the unbeliever will persevere in unrighteousness (cf. Rom. 6:15 – 23; James 2:14 – 26).

To "put to death the misdeeds of the body" is the practical, or experiential, side of Romans 6:11. It is the reckoning put into practice in the daily life, the self-abnegation that must characterize the believer. It is the result of the law of the Spirit of life and his operation within the believer, the working of the Spirit to suppress and destroy the effects of the sin principle.

By Reason of Sonship (Romans 8:14 – 15)

The "because" of verse 14 introduces the reason true believers will put to death the misdeeds of the body. Being led by the Spirit constantly, they are the sons of God. The regeneration and the mortification too are the products of the divine Spirit's work. The "sons of God" are those who are sons by spiritual adoption (cf. v. 15), not sons by creation.

Verse 15 is the evidence for verse 14, as the initial "for" indicates. When we received the Spirit, we received a disposition of adoption, or adoptive sonship. That is the element in which, and the power by which, we cry, "Father!" Fervent petition to God as Father is the result of the possession of adoptive sonship. We have in regeneration been brought to the place where we have the right to address God by the wonderfully intimate name Father. Could there be a greater blessing? "Abba" is the Aramaic term for "father" that Jesus also used of God the Father.

By Reason of Heirship (Romans 8:16 – 17)

Verse 16 gives further explanation of the preceding statement. The believer and the Holy Spirit both testify to the sonship of the believer. This co-witness confirms that the believer is a child of God. This assurance of faith is a significant stage of saving faith.

Finally, verse 17 makes a deduction from the preceding statements. Heirship of God follows from sonship of God, and this heirship is a joint heirship with Jesus Christ, he being the elder brother (cf. v. 29). Paul is saying that we share with him in the inheritance and that all believers will have the experience of some fellow suffering with him on the way to a fellow glorification with him (cf. 1 Peter 4:12 – 16).

DISCUSSION QUESTIONS

1. True or false? Christians are not condemned because Jesus was condemned on the cross. Explain.

2. True or false? When Christians live according to the Holy Spirit, they will fulfill all of God's righteous laws. Explain.

3. True or false? The context of crying "Abba" is found while Paul is discussing suffering. Explain the significance of this.

CHAPTER 14

THE DIVINE PURPOSE: FROM GROANINGS TO GLORY

ROMANS 8:18–30

Is it really true that we, God's children, are to suffer in the world? If so, how can our future be so glorious? The apostle's aim in this section is to answer that question, and at the same time he gives great consolation to the saints in his remarks regarding hope and the intercession of the Spirit for them according to the will of God. This section is bound together by a threefold groaning (cf. vv. 22, 23, 26). It all testifies to the fact that the best is yet to be (cf. Prov. 4:18) but not yet (cf. Rev. 21:4)!

THE GROANING OF THE CREATION

¹⁸I consider that our present sufferings are not worth comparing with the glory that will be revealed in us. ¹⁹The creation waits in eager expectation for the sons of God to be revealed. ²⁰For the creation was subjected to frustration, not by its own choice, but by the will of the one who subjected it, in hope ²¹that the creation itself will be liberated from its bondage to decay and brought into the glorious freedom of the children of God.

²²We know that the whole creation has been groaning as in the pains of childbirth right up to the present time.

Incomparable Glory (Romans 8:18)

In the Greek, the apostle begins the section with a characteristic "for," designed to explain the relationship of the sufferings referred to in verse 17 and the glory that is to be revealed.[1] The sufferings are not inconsistent with sonship and heirship, because they are so insignificant in the light of the weight of the glory and of the support that we receive through them. In fact, we might say that the "for" suggests one of the reasons for the enduring of the sufferings: they are the path to the incomparable glory to come.

In saying that the "sufferings are not worth comparing with the glory that will be revealed," the apostle by his own life enhances them. If Paul, the greatest of sufferers (cf. 2 Cor. 11:16–33), called his afflictions "light" and not worth comparing with the coming glory, then what must the glory be! Lüthi is right, "Suffering is a drop, glory is an ocean."[2]

Incomparable Anticipation (Romans 8:19–22)

Verse 19, with its "for" in Greek, begins an explanation of the preceding statement. It confirms the certainty of the coming glory that the saints will experience. Even physical creation is eagerly awaiting the revelation of the sons of God in their glory. The Greek word rendered "eager expectation" is a vivid word, coming from a word that is a poetic word for the head. Combined with the verb and preposition, the resultant idea is that of stretching forward the neck or head to see something of intense interest.

The following verses go on to explain why the creation is so anxiously awaiting the revelation of the sons of God.[3] What follows is Paul's commentary on Genesis 3:17–19, and the words have particular reference to the clause "cursed is the ground because of you." The creation is subject to frustration and does not attain its goal of glorying God in the fullest possible way. There are hints of it in the present creation (cf. Ps. 19:1–6), but the glory and beauty of the redeemed creation awaits the future and the unveiling of the glory of the sons.

In verse 20 the phrase "in hope" is to be connected with the words "was subjected to frustration." As C. E. B. Cranfield says, "The creation was not subjected to frustration without any hope: the divine judgment included the promise of a better future, when at last the judgment would be lifted. Paul possibly had in mind the promise in Gen 3:15 that the woman's seed would bruise the serpent's head (cf. Rom. 16:20)."[4]

The "that" of verse 21, if it is what Paul wrote,[5] gives the reason why there is hope for the creation. It will be delivered from corruption and will partake of the liberty of the glory of the children of God.

The final explanatory statement (v. 22), containing another Greek "for," introduces a truth known generally among the believers. It is that the creation is groaning and travailing even at the present moment. It sums up what Paul has been saying in verses 20 and 21, which in turn support the statement of verse 19. The groaning is not only under the decay manifest in the creation; it is also for the coming glory. As the Lutheran commentator F. A. Phillipi said, "The entire creation ... sets up a grand symphony of sighs"[6] in longing anticipation of the glorious day when the creation is born again.

THE GROANING OF THE CHILDREN

23Not only so, but we ourselves, who have the firstfruits of the Spirit, groan inwardly as we wait eagerly for our adoption as sons, the redemption of our bodies. 24For in this hope we were saved. But hope that is seen is no hope at all. Who hopes for what he already has? 25But if we hope for what we do not yet have, we wait for it patiently.

The apostle turns to a consideration of the groaning of the children for liberation. The section is closely connected with chapter 7, where the apostle groaned, "What a wretched man I am! Who will rescue me from this body of death?" (7:24). Here he speaks specifically of groaning. In spite of the beautiful expressions of deliverance through the Spirit in the earlier part of chapter 8, we are not to think that the Christian life is without struggle and groans. Although we have the Spirit now, we earnestly await (the very word is another occurrence of the intensive one that means "to eagerly await"; cf. vv. 19, 25) the adoption with groaning anticipation.

The adoption is defined here as "the redemption of our bodies." That is the final installment in the possession of the fullness of sonship (cf. v. 15). Now we have redemption of the spirit, then of the body too in its resurrection.

The firstfruits of the Spirit is a reference to the barley harvest and the offering of the firstfruits of the barley harvest (cf. Lev. 23:9 – 14). The thought behind the ritual is that the barley offered is a sample and an earnest of more in the field. So the Spirit is a sample of the life that is to come. We will experience more of the life by the Spirit than we experience today even though he already indwells us.

THE GROANING OF THE COMFORTER

26In the same way, the Spirit helps us in our weakness. We do not know what we ought to pray for, but the Spirit himself intercedes for us with groans that words cannot express. ²⁷*And he who searches our hearts knows the mind of the Spirit, because the Spirit intercedes for the saints in accordance with God's will.*

The apostle now turns to further aid given by our sovereign and merciful God to his suffering saints. We also have the help of the Holy Spirit in dealing with the infirmity of our body.

The Spirit aids us in our wrestling with the present situation, in which we suffer and long for deliverance, and yet are burdened down by the presence of indwelling sin and its judgment and effects. The singular word "weakness" seems clearly to refer to the weakness felt in the struggle with indwelling sin (cf. 7:13 – 25), expressed in the cry for help (7:24) and in the groaning (8:23). Our longing for release finds aid in the third person of the Trinity, who belongs to the saints (cf. 8:9).

Thus, we have two intercessors from heaven, one in heaven, the Son (cf. v. 34), and another in us, the Holy Spirit. The Spirit, when we reach the limit of our little, unglorified minds, intercedes for us with loving groanings for our release and needs. The reference is not to ordinary prayer primarily, but to our longing to be released from the bondage of the corruption of this life for the glorious liberty we will enjoy in the future as the children of God. The phrase "in accordance with God's will" is the assurance that his prayers are always answered. We have someone within, a divine person who prays for us in a divine way, and the inevitable result is that the Father answers the prayers. Such is the comfort, assurance, and security of the saints. God praying to God, and we are the objects of those prayers!

THE DIVINE PURPOSE: THE FOUNTAINHEAD OF ALL SPIRITUAL BLESSING

The apostle turns to the source of all the blessings, the divine purpose, made in ages past and soon to be consummated as the end-time events reach their appointed fulfillment. In Romans 8:28 – 30, Paul encourages those who are going through suffering by pointing to the great purpose of God, a fivefold chain of salvation: foreknowledge, predestination, calling, justification, and glorification. For many, suffering is alleviated only by a cessation of their suffering. Paul instructs trial-laden saints to focus on the eternal plan of almighty God. Charles Spurgeon encapsulated Paul's sentiment:

> I do not wonder, therefore, that in his epistles he often discourses upon the doctrines of foreknowledge, and predestination, and eternal love, because these are a rich cordial for a fainting spirit. To be cheered under many things,

which otherwise would depress him, the believer may betake himself to the matchless mysteries of the grace of God, which are wines on the lees well refined. Sustained by distinguishing grace, a man learns to glory in tribulations also; and strengthened by electing love, he defies the hatred of the world and the trials of life. Suffering is the college of orthodoxy. Many a Jonah, who now rejects the doctrines of the grace of God, only needs to be put into the whale's belly and he will cry out with the soundest free-grace man, "Salvation is of the Lord."[7]

Paul knows struggling saints need doctrine. Doctrine lifts the sagging soul and directs it to focus on what God is doing and how he is going about his purposes.

THE PRINCIPLE OF THE PURPOSE OF GOD

> [28] And we know that in all things God works for the good of those who love him, who have been called according to his purpose.

The Objects of His Purpose Humanly Considered (Romans 8:28a-b)

Paul emboldens the Roman readers by describing one grand, divine, and continuing purpose that encircles and supports the saints of God, even as they suffer. He begins, "And we know," writing as if this providence is something concerning which there can be little question. For Paul, the truth about God is a known commodity.

Far from speculation, Paul speaks confidently and with assurance that God's reinforcing sovereignty is for those "who love God." The Holy Spirit inspires the writer to begin by looking at the objects of God's providence from the human standpoint. In the original text these words are thrown forward in the clause in which they are found to give them added emphasis. It is for those who love God that providence is especially concerned.

The Nature of the Purpose Explicated (Romans 8:28c)

Paul then lays out the nature of the purpose itself, "all things God works for the good." Far from fatalism or a random, blind chance affecting Christians haphazardly, Paul instructs the readers about the plan of the loving Father. The concept of a personal and gracious Father negates any notion of stoic resignation, distance, or apathy. The transcendent God of eternity is also the immanent God for every believer, in the person of Jesus Christ. Every hour and minute, God personally superintends the life of every believer, even when they are hurting and suffering.

Some of the ancient manuscripts insert the word "God," saying, "we know that *God* causes all things to work together for good." Thus the "all things" become the object rather than the subject of "work together." There are actually eight different ways to translate the two readings, so it is a rather complicated textual problem.[8] Ultimately the meaning is essentially the same, whether it reads, "God works all things together for good" or "All things work together for good in accordance with God's purpose." Either way, God is the one causing all things to work together for good. The God of eternity becomes the God of the hour for each of his saints when they become the recipients of his providential care and concern.

The Objects of His Purpose Divinely Considered (Romans 8:28d)

The apostle further describes those who are the objects of the divine providence in the last words of the verse as "who have been called according to his purpose." This clause points out that the divine cause for the enjoyment of providence is ultimately the purpose of God. The meaning of "purpose" is defined in the following two verses, and there the subject of the verbs is "God." Further, in 9:11 the noun rendered "purpose" occurs again (the only other place it is found in the letter), and it clearly refers to God's purpose there. The sense of the final clause, then, is this: behind the love of the believers is the sovereign purpose of God. Their choice of him results from his prior choice of them (cf. 1 John 4:19; cf. Gal. 4:9). The man or woman who loves God is the individual who has been brought to faith by God, and thus he or she is a person who has responded according to the sovereign purpose of God. The divine perspective must never be forgotten or eclipsed, because seeing life, especially filled with trials, from an eternal viewpoint is Paul's elixir for every believer.

THE PROGRAM OF THE PURPOSE OF GOD

> [29]*For those God foreknew he also predestined to be conformed to the likeness of his Son, that he might be the firstborn among many brothers.*

The First Step: Foreknowledge (Romans 8:29a)

The "for" of verse 29 introduces the reason that all things work together for good for the saints, the called of God. In fact, verses 29 and 30 explain just what the divine purpose is, namely, that all the called ones will be ultimately glorified by being made conformable to the image of God's Son, Jesus Christ. In verse

29 we have the pretemporal steps in the divine plan, and the first of these is foreknowledge.

Does this verse suggest that God elected on the basis of his foreknowledge of what people would do? The Hebrew word used to indicate "foreknow" is *yada*, which means to know in an intimate sense. For example, it is the word for sexual knowledge, as is illustrated in the text, "And Adam knew Eve his wife; and she conceived and bare Cain, and said, I have gotten a man from the LORD" (Gen. 4:1 KJV).[9] Further, in the Old Testament, it often means simply to choose, and it has this sense in such passages as Genesis 18:19 and Amos 3:2 (Amos writes of Israel, in the KJV, "You only have I known of all the families of the earth"). No one could contend that God did not know about all the families of the earth.

The word "foreknowledge" has to do with an intimate choosing beforehand.[10] T. W. Manson said, " 'Foreknew' means 'chose in advance' — a Hebraic use of 'know' (Jer. 1:5; Amos 3:2)."[11] Matthew Black wrote, "The divine foreknowledge, i.e. choice and election (the divine 'fore-ordination') is virtually synonymous; cf. Acts 4:28."[12] Even Rudolph Bultmann, the well-known German New Testament scholar, concurred, although not at all a genuine believer in the sovereignty of God: "In the NT *proginōskein* is referred to God. His foreknowledge, however, is an election or foreordination of His people (Romans 8:29; 11:2) or Christ (1 Peter 1:20)."[13]

Third, if we look at the text carefully, it is easy to see that it says, "For *those* God foreknew," not "*what* God foreknew." The Arminian doctrine of election, according to foreseen faith, in effect says, "He loves us, because we first loved him," while John says the reverse: "We love because he first loved us" (cf. 1 John 4:19). The text says God foreknew people. God sets his love on individual sinners. That is the marvelous news. It would not be great if God looked ahead to see what people would do, but it is wonderful that God sets his love on people ahead of time! Think "whom," not "what." God never chooses based on what people can or will do for him.

Fourth, it should be noted that there are five divine acts in this "golden chain of salvation," and they are all the sovereign works of God. That itself confirms the meaning of foreknowledge as dealing with God's action, not man's work or belief. The individual does not make the ultimate choice. God does not ratify their choice; rather, God chooses sinners sovereignly and accomplishes his purposes. In fact, Charles Haddon Spurgeon once said, "I'm so glad he chose me before he saw me, because, if he had waited until he saw me, he might not have wanted me!" The ground of the choice is only God's good pleasure and the counsel of his own will (Eph. 1:5, 9, 11; cf. Deut. 7:6 – 9; 9:4 – 8).[14]

The Second Step: Predestination (Romans 8:29b-c)

The second of the five great acts of God is predestination. Predestination looks to the goal of the electing work of God (cf. Eph. 1:5, 11), and it is at the same time the ground of the work. Just as foreknowledge stresses the past love of God that issued in intimate choice, this word stresses the aim of the work. The word *election*, which is not used here (cf. 9:11), stresses the relation of the elect to the masses out of which they are chosen. The goal of predestination is that the elect might be conformed to the image of Christ. The Father so loved the Son that he determined that the whole universe should be peopled with humans like his beloved Son.

Christlikeness is the future goal. Conformity to Jesus Christ, not the prophets or apostles, is the ultimate goal. Nothing could be more final or ultimate than a person's conformity to Christ. God is every believer's Father and Jesus is every Christian's brother. Paul says that there will be many siblings who share this relationship. Out of all those ever born of a woman, Christ is the preeminent one — the firstborn. The focus of "firstborn" language is not on the temporal, but on first in ranking and greatness. His supremacy as firstborn is a magnificent expression of the working of God for his glory.

THE PROCESS OF REALIZING THE PURPOSE

[30]*And those he predestined, he also called; those he called, he also justified; those he justified, he also glorified.*

Every link to salvation's chain exclaims divine activity. The apostle, after speaking of the eternal purpose, now highlights the steps that have to do with the temporal performance of God's overarching purpose.[15] Paul has already discussed foreknowledge and predestination, but he reiterates them in 8:30 before he moves to the purpose of God in time — namely, called, justified, and glorified.

The Third Step: Calling (Romans 8:30a-b)

The general call of God is his command to believe in the Lord Jesus Christ. It goes out indiscriminately and is regularly rejected by sinners. The effectual call signifies God's work in actually bringing unbelievers to faith. Every time the word "called" is used in the New Testament epistles, it means "effectual call." The Holy Spirit causes the unbeliever to be born again (1 Peter 1:3). The call is "effectual" because the sinner cannot resist it. In Romans 8:30, "calling" is part of the sure and certain activity of God. God's grace in the effectual call is irresistible and results in the justification of the individual called (cf. 2 Thess. 2:13–14).

The Fourth Step: Justification (Romans 8:30c-d)

As discussed earlier in Romans 3, justification means "to declare righteous." All Christians possess by imputation the righteousness that God's righteousness requires them to have. Christ's perfect life of obedience is credited to the life of the sinner, while simultaneously the sinner's sin is credited by divine reckoning to Jesus, the sin-bearing substitute (2 Cor. 5:21). God treats Jesus as if he sinned, but Jesus never actually sinned. God treats the sinner as if he or she actually obeyed with perfect obedience, even though the sinner did not actually obey. God confirms justification by raising Jesus from the dead, thus vindicating his great atoning sacrifice.

The Fifth Step: Glorification (Romans 8:30e-f)

The fifth and last link in the golden chain of salvation is the grand finale of the divine redemptive program. Paul utilizes the aorist tense of the verb "glorified," writing as if the act has already been finished, even though the glory is still future (cf. 5:2). The end result of the past tense verb is the stress on the certainty of our glorification. "Why does Paul move directly here from justification to glory, without saying anything about the Christian's present experience of sanctification under the power of the Spirit?" F. F. Bruce asks. "Partly, no doubt," he continues, "because the coming glory has been in the forefront of his mind; but even more because the difference between sanctification and glory is one of degree only, not one of kind.... Paul looks forward to the completion of the work — a completion guaranteed by its inception: 'whom he justified, them he also glorified.'"[16]

The five links are impressive evidence of the eternal security of the believer in Christ. In the repetition of the pronoun "those," Paul emphasizes that no one is lost in the process. "Those" he foreknew, he also predestined. "Those" he predestined, he called, no more and no less. "Those" he called, he justified, no more and no less in number. "Those" God justified, he glorified. Not a single one is lost in the process that began with the intimate choice of foreknowledge and is completed in the certain act of glorification.

In God's eyes, every Christian's glorification is an absolute fact. Why would Paul speak of glorification in such a confident manner? Since the suffering of this present time is not worthy to be compared with the glory that will be revealed, Christians must turn to the Lord's promises in the midst of sufferings. Superficial solutions will not suffice. Believers will need to turn to the Lord and his golden chain of salvation. When saints realize that suffering is part of God's plan, the sting of pain will fade in light of eternity and their future glorification.

The Lord will sustain every Christian in the midst of every trial. He will hold up and support the believer, while giving the assurance of his presence as they lean on the great truths in Romans 8:28 – 30.

Samuel Rutherford, the old Scottish Presbyterian who had a large part in the writing of the Westminster Confession of Faith, used to say, "Whenever I find myself in the cellar of affliction, I always look about for the wine." The golden chain of salvation in Romans 8:28 – 30 is the wine of the Christian faith. Sovereign grace comforts and encourages every true Christian.

DISCUSSION QUESTIONS

1. How does theology influence Paul's view of God's care for suffering Christians?

2. God's sovereign choice never randomly occurs in Scripture. Why?

3. How could God's sovereign purposes comfort someone who lost a child? A job? A parent? What would be an appropriate way to talk to people who suffer such losses? What would be an inappropriate way?

4. Is it possible to enjoy your salvation more by knowing you are chosen by God (Eph. 1:3 – 6)? If so, how?

5. Can you make a list of Christian pastors and missionaries who taught unconditional election (think along the lines of William Carey and Hudson Taylor)? Why is the list so long?

CHAPTER 15

GOD FOR US

ROMANS 8:31–39

God for us. Anything else added to that statement merely detracts from its force. It is the occasion for silence and worship. And, not surprisingly, the commentators are also reserved at this point, finding it difficult to muster up words to adequately expound the meaning of the simple expression.

"But Paul and all the witnesses of the Holy Scriptures see it differently," Lüthi claims, adding,

> They would not be at all surprised if God were against us. They know that God would have good reason for being against us. That God is for us is something we do not deserve. It would serve us right if God were against us. So since He is for us, can it be that there is something wrong with justice and righteousness? Surely God who loves justice has not become weak, and evaded and offended against justice? If that were so, how could He expect us men to respect His commandments.... The Eternal Keeper of eternal justice does not deviate from the law: He is not God at the expense of justice. That would be the end of moral order and the end of the world.[1]

The evidence that God is for us is found in the cross of Christ. That is the sign of love fulfilling justice. It is a magnificent display of the nature of man and of the nature of God. It is a display of the justice of God in that in order to find a way for man to be forgiven, the Son of God must be sacrificed. The same God who three times is said by Paul in Romans 1 to have given up men and women (cf. 1:24, 26, 28) is now said by Paul to have given up his only Son for us (cf. 8:32).

Why? So that he might justly forgive sinners through the Son's suffering of their penalty by his sacrifice of blood. Thus, the cross shows that God is just and righteous in his dealings, and he does not deviate from his law even when he wishes to save people out of love for them.

In spite of the sinful nature of humanity, God is for believers! Paul's words in Romans 8 are addressed to believers. It is for them that he affirms God's faithfulness. What led Paul to think of God's committal of himself to us? He has just been thinking and writing of the divine purpose, his foreknowledge of us in his intimate choice of us for salvation; his foreordination of us as destined to become conformed to the image of the Son of God; his calling of us in time by the efficacious working of the Holy Spirit; his justification of us, declaring us righteous before his heavenly court of justice; and his glorification of us. These are magnificent truths, representing God's full sovereign salvation. It is no wonder that Paul speaks of God being for us. What more assurance could we need or have than the recital of such wonderful working of the Godhead for us?

THE GENERAL QUESTION

³¹What, then, shall we say in response to this? If God is for us, who can be against us? ³²He who did not spare his own Son, but gave him up for us all — how will he not also, along with him, graciously give us all things?

The apostle is so involved in his own exposition of the wonderful work of his God that he flings out a series of questions in fuller explanation of what is meant by the thrilling truths he has been setting forth. He asks a general question followed by a series of specific ones.

The general query opens 8:31, "What, then, shall we say in response to this?" which is more pointedly expressed next: "If God is for us, who can be against us?" There is no doubt to be found in the conditional clause "if God is for us." The apostle is merely stating the condition as a basis for argument. It would not be wrong to translate the clause "Since God is for us."[2]

When the apostle adds, "who can be against us?" we are not to think that he is saying that Christians do not have adversaries. We do have them, and in the following verses he speaks of some of them (cf. vv. 35 – 39); but they will not prevail over us.

Verse 32 is offered in support of the preceding: "He who did not spare his own Son, but gave him up for us all — how will he not also, along with him, graciously give us all things?" Paul argues that, having given the Son of God over for the saints, God will give everything else that is necessary for our salvation.

The verse is clearly an echo of Genesis 22:12, 16, in which is found the same term used here ("spare/withhold").[3]

It seems that the apostle had Abraham's offering of Isaac in mind, thinking of the sacrifice of the Son as the offering of the Father for the elect (cf. v. 33, "whom God has chosen"). It is justification for considering that incident in Genesis as typical of the sacrifice of Christ, only in this instance there is no one to call out from heaven as the angel did when Abraham, with upraised hand and knife, was about to plunge it into Isaac's heart. In the antitypical case, the blows of divine wrath must fall on the Son as he cries out, "My God, my God, why have you forsaken me?" (cf. Matt. 27:46). There is no substitute for the Substitute!

The positive statement follows: "but gave him up for us all." It was the Father who delivered him up, not Judas, nor the Jews, nor Pilate ultimately. We do not owe our salvation to the greed of Judas, nor to the fear of Pilate, nor to the envy of the Jews, but to the love of the Godhead for us. "Along with him" suggests that the greatest gift is not things, nor even justification, although that is essential, but God himself (cf. 2 Cor. 9:15).

The final clause is climactic. If he has given us that which is "unspeakably great and costly"[4] in the gift of Christ, he will certainly give all that in comparison is less. In the world of divine salvation, there is a series of things required, such as election by the Father, redemption by the Son, and the application of that redemption by the Spirit. Now there are two ways to take Paul's words. One can argue that since he gave Christ for us all (taking the "all" in the sense of every soul), he must give to all the work of the Holy Spirit in the application of redemption, for surely the greatest gift is the gift of the Son in his death. Everything is less than that. But if this is Paul's meaning, then the apostle would be teaching universalism, that is, that every human being will be saved. That, however, is plainly contrary to the thought of Paul and the Scriptures.

There is only one other interpretation that can be given Paul's words. The "us all" is a reference to the elect, who are specifically referred to as such in verse 33. The text, then, becomes another of the many passages in the Word of God that proclaim the particular redemption of the Son of God. If he gave the Son as a sacrifice for sinners, for "us all," then, having given the greatest gift, he will not withhold lesser cries, such as the work of the Holy Spirit in efficacious grace bringing the elect to salvation. The "us all," then, must refer to the elect. Since Jesus died for the elect, the elect may rest confidently in the possession of all other spiritual blessings, from the application of the work of redemption by the Spirit to all the blessings involved in the fullness of every believer's salvation.[5]

What a magnificent source of assurance this text is! If God gave his best, the

Lord Jesus, he will give the least, everything else his children need. If he gave the best, then he will give the rest. What confidence we may have in him and in his covenantal faithfulness!

THE SPECIFIC QUESTIONS

[33]Who will bring any charge against those whom God has chosen? It is God who justifies. [34]Who is he that condemns? Christ Jesus, who died — more than that, who was raised to life — is at the right hand of God and is also interceding for us. [35]Who shall separate us from the love of Christ? Shall trouble or hardship or persecution or famine or nakedness or danger or sword? [36]As it is written:

"For your sake we face death all day long;
we are considered as sheep to be slaughtered."

[37]No, in all these things we are more than conquerors through him who loved us.

The Justification Question (Romans 8:33)

The first question, having to do with justification, spans Romans 1:1 – 5:11, where that subject is discussed. Paul's point is a simple one: to attack the elect is to attack God, for he has justified them. One cannot expect to attack with impunity the Judge himself (cf. Isa. 50:8 – 9).

The Sanctification Question (Romans 8:34)

The next query seems closely related to the question of divine sanctification, the subject Paul discussed in Romans 5:12 – 8:17. The boldness of the apostle in his questions, incidentally, is not to be traced to the fact that he had discounted the effects of sin. No one, outside of our Lord, has had a deeper grasp of the heinousness of sin. Nor is he bold because of any sense of accomplishment on his part. He is bold because of what Christ has done for him and for us, and he finds in Jesus Christ a fourfold protection against the ravages of sin. It is Christ who has died, and it is Christ who has risen from the dead as the evidence of the acceptance by the Father of the work he did. Moreover, it is Christ who has ascended to the right hand of God, and, finally, it is he who lives to make intercession for the saints. He offered as priest the atoning sacrifice and now makes intercession as priest for those for whom it was made, the guarantee that all for whom it was made should possess its benefits. The beneficiaries of the atonement are coextensive with those for whom it was made, and it is the great High Priest who works to that end. Thus, there is no condemnation to those who are in him (cf. John 17:24, the high priestly petition).

The Glorification Question (Romans 8:35 – 37)

The apostle now turns to matters that relate to glorification, the subject that he has just handled in 8:18 – 30. He asks, "Who shall separate us from the love of Christ?" The apostle suggests some things that might be thought to do just that, even citing an Old Testament text that likens believers to sheep led to slaughter. But even in such things as these, Paul says, we are "more than conquerors through him who loved us" (cf. v. 37). He says "in all these things," not "away from these things." There is no promise that we will not experience such things, but there is a promise from the Lord that we will not be overcome by them (cf. Matt. 16:13 – 18).

Our victory is, however, only a victory "through him," but with him it is a rousing victory.

PAUL'S GRAND PERSUASION

> [38]*For I am convinced that neither death nor life, neither angels nor demons, neither the present nor the future, nor any powers,* [39]*neither height nor depth, nor anything else in all creation, will be able to separate us from the love of God that is in Christ Jesus our Lord.*

Death cannot separate us from the love of God, as Lazarus and the thief on the cross show (cf. Luke 23:43; John 11:43). Concluding the listing of the things that might be considered as enemies, Paul writes, "nor anything else in all creation." Everything else is a created thing, but we have the Creator on our side. And even we cannot overthrow his purposes for us, for we too are creations, and no creation can separate us from the love of God in Christ Jesus our Lord (cf. 2 Tim. 2:13). We cannot separate ourselves: even our faith is a gift from him. His hand will never relax his grip on us. The love of God will stand any test. It is the love of which hymn writer George Matheson wrote, "the love that will not let us go."

The chapter that began with "no condemnation" concludes with "no separation," for eternal life is ours. Like a graft in a strong shoot, we partake of the heredity and inheritance of the divine Son, with whom we are forever united.

DISCUSSION QUESTIONS

1. What do you say in response to the fact that God is "for you"?

2. Does "nor anything else in all creation" (v. 39) include people? What should your response be when you hear, "But I can take myself out of God's hand"? Explain.

3. What role does the Holy Spirit have in keeping someone's salvation secure and safe?

CHAPTER 16

DISTINGUISHING GRACE

ROMANS 9:1–13[1]

I s Paul's gospel true?" The apostle has pictured an election according to grace in Romans 1 – 8, but astoundingly Israel is lacking among them. What about the promises made to the nation Israel through the fathers? Either Paul's gospel is true and the promises nullified, or the promises are true and Paul's gospel is false, and Jesus Christ is an imposter. "Has God failed in his program?" Is it possible that man's "no" to God in the rejection of his promises is able to overcome God's "yes" in the offering of his promises?

Paul's answer is the theodicy of Romans 9 – 11, a vindication of God according to the principles of justice. He traces the divine purpose in history, or, as William Manson put it, "the righteousness of God in history,"[2] showing that the divine intention of saving a remnant according to the election of grace has been accomplished, is being accomplished, and will be completed in the future.

To sum up Paul's treatment of Romans 9 – 11, the apostle makes three points. First, he shows in Romans 9:1 – 10:21 that Israel's failure is not to be traced to divine unfaithfulness to his promises but rather to Israel's spiritual pride and self-sufficiency. God never intended that every single Israelite should be saved. The principle of distinguishing grace has been operative in history all along. Israel sought salvation by human works instead of by divine trust and thus did not submit to the righteousness of God (cf. 10:3); by this they failed as a nation to find that which they were seeking.

Second, the apostle points out that the failure is not total, for there is a remnant of saved Israelites, proving that God is still faithful to his Word (cf.

11:1 – 10). Finally, he reaches the climax of the theodicy by affirming that the day is coming when Israel as a nation shall be saved. Their failure, then, is not final (cf. 11:11 – 27), a fact that is really a part of the overall program of the ages (cf. 11:28 – 32). Ultimately it will be seen that "from him and through him and to him are all things. To him be glory forever!" (11:36).

PAUL'S GRIEF OVER ISRAEL'S FAILURE

> [1]*I speak the truth in Christ — I am not lying, my conscience confirms it in the Holy Spirit —* [2]*I have great sorrow and unceasing anguish in my heart.* [3]*For I could wish that I myself were cursed and cut off from Christ for the sake of my brothers, those of my own race,*

The Declaration of It (Romans 9:1 – 2)

The apostle is speaking here of a deep pain from God, his conscience bearing him witness in the Holy Spirit.[3] The words are the more touching when we remember that Israel not only did not like Paul; they hated him (cf. Acts 22:22; 25:24).

The Explanation of It (Romans 9:3)

The apostle continues with a wish, both grammatically and theologically. It is a beautiful picture of a true soul-winner's heart, and it inevitably reminds us of Moses' great words in Exodus 32:3 – 35, where he pleads with God for the salvation of Israel from divine judgment when the nation sinned by making the golden calf. It also reminds us of David Brainerd, who had a great ministry to the North American Indians early in the nineteenth century. He wrote, "I dream of lost souls. I care not what sufferings I undergo, as long as I see souls saved."[4]

THE JUSTIFICATION OF PAUL'S EMOTION

> [4]*the people of Israel. Theirs is the adoption as sons; theirs the divine glory, the covenants, the receiving of the law, the temple worship and the promises.* [5]*Theirs are the patriarchs, and from them is traced the human ancestry of Christ, who is God over all, forever praised! Amen.*

The Adoption (Romans 9:4)

In seeking to show the reason for his grief and his compassionate desire that Israel be saved, the apostle laments their privileges and lost opportunities. His description of Israel's favor being lost includes eight great blessings, the first of which is adoption. He refers to the fact that God called Israel his firstborn son (cf. Ex. 4:22; Deut. 32:18). Their failure seems more terrible in the light of what God had done for them.

The Divine Glory (Romans 9:4)

The second of the great blessings is "the divine glory," an expression that refers to the pillar of cloud and the pillar of fire, by which God miraculously, moment by moment, guided the nation through the wilderness to the promised land.

The Covenants (Romans 9:4)

"The covenants" is an expression that can include both the conditional and the unconditional covenants of the Old Testament, but in light of the specific mention of the giving of the law in the next phrase, it is likely that the stress of the words lies on the unconditional ones, that is, the Abrahamic, the Davidic, and the new covenant.

The Receiving of the Law (Romans 9:4)

Paul refers to the giving of the Mosaic law, a code in which the saints of the old covenant rejoiced because of the beauty of its revelation of the righteousness and justice of a holy God, as well as because of its foreshadowing in the cultus of the coming, saving, priestly ministry of the Messiah (cf. Ex. 19:1 – 20:1; Ps. 147:19 – 20).

The Temple Worship (Romans 9:4)

"The temple worship" refers to the priesthood, the offerings, and the tabernacle and temple, in which the service was carried on (cf. Heb. 10:1 – 3). If ever a religion had a beautiful liturgy, Old Testament Israelite religion was that, and best of all, it pointed tellingly to the ministry of the Lord Jesus Christ.

The Promises (Romans 9:4)

By "the promises" Paul refers to what Reformed theologians call the covenant of grace. Paul points to the messianic promises, that is, the promises of the coming Messiah and their application to the elect of God. The messianic promises have their beginning in the *Protevangelium*[5] of Genesis 3:15 and encompass all of the promised program of the Old Testament, including the promises of the Great Prophet, the Priest after the order of Melchizedek, and the promises of the King to come.

The Patriarchs (Romans 9:5)

Not the least of the blessings of the nation are those traditions seen in the life of the fathers of the faith, men such as Abraham, Isaac, Jacob, Joseph, and Moses. In fact, we might include here all of those mentioned in the "Hall of Faith" (Heb. 11:1 – 12:2).

The Messiah (Romans 9:5)

And, finally, there is the Messiah, related to them according to the flesh, but also "God over all, forever praised!" Liberal theologians have generally contended for a punctuation of the original text that attributes deity to "God," not to the Messiah. Conservatives have generally taken the words "who is over all, God blessed forever" to refer to Christ. The decision must be settled by exegesis, for it cannot be settled with certainty by grammar or by textual concerns.[6] The context of the passage suggests a lament over the blessings of Israel, of which they have not availed themselves, rather than the offering of praise to God at this point. Israel has turned from God in spite of large spiritual advantages. How much more appropriate, then, for this to be a reference to the deity of the Messiah! To have rejected one who possesses deity makes Israel's rejection of him the more lamentable. The text, then, is one that proclaims the deity of the Son of God. Jesus is "God over all, forever praised."

This, then, was Israel's supreme privilege. Of them came the Messiah, the God-man, but they, with the Gentiles, crucified him. In the future, however, awakened by the Spirit of grace and supplication, they will perceive their sin and folly at his coming, and a nation will be converted in a day. In the meantime, with Paul we lament their lost opportunity, although we look forward to the day when Israel will say with their greatest prophet, "For to us a child is born, to us a son is given … he will be called Wonderful Counselor, Mighty God, Everlasting Father, Prince of Peace" (Isa. 9:6).

DISTINGUISHING GRACE, OR JACOB LOVED AND ESAU HATED

Although Paul has just said that nothing can separate the believer from the love of God in Christ Jesus our Lord, can it be said that Israel has been able to separate themselves from the love of God as seen in their election and unconditional covenants? Paul's answer to the question is not put in the style of an either/or type of matter, but in a both/and frame. Paul's gospel, he will show in Romans

9 – 11, is true, but the promises are also true, and ultimately "all Israel will be saved" (cf. 11:26).

DISTINGUISHING GRACE AND THE DIVINE ELECTING PURPOSE

> [6]It is not as though God's word had failed. For not all who are descended from Israel are Israel. [7]Nor because they are his descendants are they all Abraham's children. On the contrary, "It is through Isaac that your offspring will be reckoned." [8]In other words, it is not the natural children who are God's children, but it is the children of the promise who are regarded as Abraham's offspring.

The Word of God and the Purpose (Romans 9:6 – 8)

Israel's basic failure was a failure to read the Scriptures properly. If they had, they would have realized that even in old covenant days the principle of distinguishing grace was at work. The Word of God did not fail and will not fail. It was never the intent of God that every Israelite would be saved. There was a rejection of portions of the elect race in ancient times. "Israel," C. K. Barrett points out, "is not a term like Ammon, Moab, Greece, or Rome."[7] There always were two elements in Israel, the elect and the nonelect. The word translated "had failed" means (literally) "to fall out of" or "to fall from." It is as if Paul is saying, "The Word of God has not fallen off its straight course, the purpose of God. The trouble is with the passengers, who have disembarked at the port of scriptural ignorance and unbelief."

The statement "for not all who are descended from Israel are Israel" has nothing to do with Gentiles, although some have tried to make it include them. What it says, and says plainly and simply, is that there are two kinds of Israelites. Just because a person is ethnically an Israelite does not mean that he or she is an Israelite in the truest sense, for the term is a religious one. To be a true Israelite, one must be a believer, walking in the steps of father Abraham (cf. 4:12). It is to the believing seed of Abraham that the promises are given. Paul discusses a division within the nation of Israel, not Gentiles.

The Seed of Abraham and the Purpose (Romans 9:7)

In fact, Paul continues, simply because persons are physical descendants of Abraham does not mean that they are true children of the patriarch. It is strictly "through Isaac" that the seed is called, which means that those who are only ethnically the descendants of the patriarch are not the recipients of the blessings from the promises.

The Underlying Principle (Romans 9:8)

Paul concludes by saying that the children of the promises are counted as the seed. In back of the belief there lies a divine sovereign promise and calling (cf. Luke 19:9).

HISTORICAL EXAMPLES OF DISTINGUISHING GRACE

[9]For this was how the promise was stated: "At the appointed time I will return, and Sarah will have a son." [10]Not only that, but Rebekah's children had one and the same father, our father Isaac. [11]Yet, before the twins were born or had done anything good or bad — in order that God's purpose in election might stand: [12]not by works but by him who calls — she was told, "The older will serve the younger."

Ishmael and Isaac (Romans 9:9, 7)

We can easily see that the apostle did not fabricate his theology in a rationalistic way. Instead, Paul simply exegeted the Scriptures, constructing his views from what he had found by reading and interpreting, under the Spirit's guidance, the texts. If we read Genesis and ponder the story of Abraham, Isaac, and Jacob in connection with the divine covenantal promises, we will come to the same theology that Paul taught. The word "promise" in verse 9 is emphatic in the Greek text. Paul lays stress on it, for it is a word of grace. When people are blessed by divine promise, they are blessed in grace, for the unconditional promise is something freely and sovereignly given.

The illustration of Ishmael and Isaac has been alluded to in verse 7. In a citation from Genesis 18:10, it is referred to again here in verse 9. The words of the Lord God to Abraham constitute a gracious promise of the birth of Isaac to Sarah. Ishmael is not to be the promised seed, although he is Abraham's first-born. Here is the principle of the distinguishing grace of God, for the election of Isaac was not on the basis of works of any kind.

Esau and Jacob (Romans 9:10 – 12)

Here the law of limitations is contracted further. There is no problem of complex parentage now, for Rebekah was the mother of twins by one man (in the Greek text the emphasis rests on the fact that the two sons came from one man). Yet the destiny of the two was to be infinitely different, for Jacob was loved but Esau was hated. The story on which the apostle builds his teaching is found in Genesis 25:19 – 26, where the birth of these twins is recorded. God had promised Isaac that he should have a seed, but Rebekah was barren (cf. v. 21). So the patriarch entreated the Lord for his wife, which illustrates aptly that divine predestination is not contrary to earnest supplication, that the patriarch was being taught patience, and that God accomplishes the fulfillment of his promises in his own way, not in ours.

The Lord answered the prayer, and Rebekah was pregnant with twins. As they struggled within her womb, she, troubled by the meaning of it all, went to ask the Lord about it. She received this prophetic word: "Two nations are in your womb, and two peoples from within you will be separated; one people will be stronger than the other, and the older will serve the younger" (Gen. 25:23). History makes it plain that the prophecy is one that covers the history of the descendants of Jacob and Esau, but as the final clause makes clear, it also refers specifically to the destiny of the two individuals, Jacob and Esau. Contrary to ancient Eastern custom, the elder son will serve the younger.

The important words for Paul in Romans 9 are the last ones of the prophecy, "The older will serve the younger" (cf. v. 12). It is from them that Paul reasons to his conclusions. The blessing of the unborn Jacob and the preferring of him to Esau, before they had had an opportunity to do anything good or evil, teaches the doctrine of sovereign distinguishing grace in election. He points out that the children were not yet born when the choice was made. Further, they had not done any works. Thus, the election of Jacob was according to the divine purpose, and it was not based on works but on the will of the one calling, that is, God. Furthermore, the choice involved individuals, not simply nations.[8]

We may sum it up by saying that, first, the sovereignty of the divine choice is taught in the choice of Jacob (v. 11). Second, the particularity of the choice is taught in the preferring of Jacob to Esau (vv. 12 – 13). This prenatal love of God for Jacob raises, of course, the doctrine of election and the basis on which God makes his selection. There are no other alternatives, since God does not choose on the basis of moral qualities. The ultimate choice is that of God, who freely chooses. God is not simply a ratifier of man's fundamental choice.

In addition, if God looked down through the years of time and saw who would believe, he would have gained in knowledge. Thus, before that time, he would not have been omniscient. Instead, God elects those whom he has purposed to save through faith in Jesus Christ. Is the reason in man or in God? The Bible teaches that election is not grounded in a man's will (cf. Rom. 9:16), nor in human works (cf. 2 Tim. 1:9), nor in human choice (Eph. 1:4). It is grounded in the divine good pleasure of his will (cf. Eph. 1:5, 11; 2 Tim. 1:9). Faith is the effect, not the ground or basis of election (John 6:44; Rom. 8:7 – 8).

THE PROOF TEXT OF DISTINGUISHING GRACE

¹³Just as it is written: "Jacob I loved, but Esau I hated."

The Text in Its Context (cf. Malachi 1:2)

Paul's final citation of the section is from Malachi 1:2. At that point, God is defending his love for Israel by reminding them of the definite distinction he has made throughout history between Israel and Edom, the nation that came from Esau. History, for the time of the prenatal love of Jacob and the rejection of Esau, reveals God's love for the nation. The text includes within it not only the individual heads of the two peoples, Israel and Edom, but their descendants. God's love is individual, national, and distinguishing.

The Text in Its Application (Romans 9:13)

The apostle uses the passage here to show that the electing purpose of God may be clearly seen in Israel's history. They should not have been surprised by their rejection when they as a nation lapsed into unbelief, an unbelief that reached its climax in the crucifixion of their Messiah, the Lord Jesus Christ. Some have sought to avoid an individual election by God to salvation by suggesting that Paul has in mind only the election of nations in Romans 9 – 11. But, if it is unjust to elect a man to salvation on the ground of free grace alone, then how much more unjust is it to elect an entire nation of individuals on that ground?

But what is meant by "Esau I hated"? There is no personal animosity in the term "hated." What is meant is the decisive rejection of another claim on God's mercy and grace. A comparison of Luke 14:26 with Matthew 10:37 indicates that the term "hate" can be another term for "love less." That is also the force of the context in Genesis 29:30 – 33. Barrett comments, "The Hebrew idiom means 'I preferred Jacob to Esau.' "⁹ The words, then, indicate the election of distinguishing grace.

DISCUSSION QUESTIONS

1. Should election be preached? Should we exclude anything from our pulpits and Bible studies that God has included in his Word?

2. What does election teach us about divine mercy and grace?

3. How does election promote humility?

4. If God were to look down the corridors of time, would he see anything in us worthy of choosing? Explain.

5. Is John Calvin responsible for originating the doctrine of election? Explain.

6. Is the term "sovereign grace" redundant? Is the term "free gift" redundant?

CHAPTER 17

VESSELS OF WRATH AND VESSELS OF MERCY

ROMANS 9:14–33

I t is not easy for people to understand and appreciate the fact that God operates in sovereign and distinguishing grace in his dealings with us. Complicating the matter is that the minds of people have been affected by the sin of Adam, and they are unable to perfectly understand the Word of God. Knowing that the previous verses brought forth questions and objections, Paul now turns to a discussion of them. The statement raises the question, "Is God righteous in his sovereign choice of some and rejection of others?" That is the question he seeks to answer, and he looks at it both from the godward and the manward side.

"IS THERE UNRIGHTEOUSNESS WITH GOD?"

> [14]What then shall we say? Is God unjust? Not at all! [15]For he says to Moses,
> "I will have mercy on whom I have mercy,
> and I will have compassion on whom I have compassion."
>
> [16]It does not, therefore, depend on man's desire or effort, but on God's mercy. [17]For the Scripture says to Pharaoh: "I raised you up for this very purpose, that I might display my power in you and that my name might be proclaimed in all the earth." [18]Therefore God has mercy on whom he wants to have mercy, and he hardens whom he wants to harden.

The Word to Moses (Romans 9:14 – 16)

God is not responsible for humanity's predicament. Human beings, because of the disobedience in the garden of Eden, are responsible for their condition in sin, disobedience, and coming judgment. Further, it is important to remember that God does exercise mercy with absolute freedom. Therefore, it is not unjust for him to do so, for God is not unjust. In fact, whatever he does is right. God himself is the standard of right and wrong. Election and reprobation are both divine prerogatives.

Since his audience recognized the authority of Scripture, Paul turned to the Word of God for evidence of the truth of his message. He cites the words that God spoke to Moses in Exodus 33:19, "I will have mercy on whom I will have mercy, and I will have compassion on whom I will have compassion" (cf. v. 15). Even though Israel had failed abysmally before Yahweh, he nevertheless acted in mercy toward them, and he acts in mercy sovereignly.

Thus, the apostle concludes, "It does not, therefore, depend on man's desire or effort, but on God's mercy" (cf. v. 16). If ever a text indicated the unscriptural nature of "free will," this one does. "It is not of him that wills," the apostle says in the original Greek. The doctrine of free will — that it is in the power of a man to turn to God by himself — is contrary to the grace of God. Salvation becomes, then, the work of God and the work of man, and the purity of the grace of God is compromised. Salvation is only of the Lord.

Man is unable to come to God of and by himself. Jesus put it as strongly as anyone in Scripture: "No one can come to me unless the Father who sent me draws him, and I will raise him up at the last day" (John 6:44). We are unable to make a decision of the will for God and salvation until God has first worked in our wills to make us willing. Salvation is first of his willing (cf. James 1:18), and only then, of our response of faith.

The Word to Pharaoh (Romans 9:17 – 18)

Pharaoh was Moses' natural opponent as the Exodus account shows, and it is natural for Paul to cite a text that pertained to him. God was not in the debt of Moses, much less was he in debt to Pharaoh. As he said to Pharaoh, "I have raised you up for this very purpose, that I might show you my power and that my name might be proclaimed in all the earth" (Ex. 9:16). "Therefore," Paul adds, "God has mercy on whom he wants to have mercy, and he hardens whom he wants to harden." The words are difficult, but they indicate that God sovereignly reprobates as well as elects. Yet God was long-suffering with the Egyptian monarch, for he could have cut him off at his first refusal to let Israel leave their captivity in

Egypt. Instead, he was patient with Pharaoh and dealt with him by the miracles of Moses for a lengthy period of time.

"THEN WHY DOES GOD STILL BLAME US?"

[19]One of you will say to me: "Then why does God still blame us? For who resists his will?" [20]But who are you, O man, to talk back to God? "Shall what is formed say to him who formed it, 'Why did you make me like this?'" [21]Does not the potter have the right to make out of the same lump of clay some pottery for noble purposes and some for common use?

[22]What if God, choosing to show his wrath and make his power known, bore with great patience the objects of his wrath — prepared for destruction? [23]What if he did this to make the riches of his glory known to the objects of his mercy, whom he prepared in advance for glory — [24]even us, whom he also called, not only from the Jews but also from the Gentiles? [25]As he says in Hosea:

> *"I will call them 'my people' who are not my people;*
> *and I will call her 'my loved one' who is not my loved one,"*

[26]and,

> *"It will happen that in the very place where it was said to them,*
> *'You are not my people,'*
> *they will be called 'sons of the living God.'"*

[27]Isaiah cries out concerning Israel:

> *"Though the number of the Israelites be like the sand by the sea,*
> *only the remnant will be saved.*
> *[28]For the Lord will carry out*
> *His sentence on earth with speed and finality."*

[29]It is just as Isaiah said previously:

> *"Unless the Lord Almighty*
> *had left us descendants,*
> *we would have become like Sodom,*
> *we would have been like Gomorrah."*

We look now at the matter from the manward side. The apostle brings forward the common objection to his teaching in verse 19, "One of you will say to me: 'Then why does God still blame us? For who resists his will?'" It is a loaded question, for it implies that God is responsible for man's lost condition. It is the human being who is responsible for his position of sin and inability to respond to the commands of God.

Paul's reply is, "But who are you, O man, to talk back to God? Shall what is formed say to him who formed it, 'Why did you make me like this?' " (v. 20). The attitude of the objector is repelled rather than refuted in detail, for the question reveals an attitude of antipathy and rebellion against God. The creature must not challenge the Creator. "Does not the potter have the right to make out of the same lump of clay some pottery for noble purposes and some for common use?" (v. 21). We are the clay, and he is the divine potter, and his authority over us is sovereign and complete. He may do with us as he wills. We are "vessels" in his hands.

Actually, Paul says, the Lord has been long-suffering in his dealings with people. He did not have to deliver Abraham from bowing down before the moon god Nannar. Nor was he compelled to deliver other Old Testament saints from bowing down to sticks and stones. He was not required to save the thief on the cross but could have left him in the same state as his friend who passed into eternity blaspheming the God who could save him forever. He was not required to save and transform the murderous Pharisee Paul. But he did in his goodness exercise long-suffering patience with them and delivered them in his marvelous grace (cf. 2 Tim. 1:9).

In verses 22 and 23 we have a strong indication of why God determined that evil should exist in his universe. The greatest good that people can have is the knowledge of God, and the revelation of God would be incomplete if we did not know him in his justice and in his mercy. But we can never know him in these attributes if sin does not exist in the universe. Thus, God has evidently determined that sin should exist in his world in order that the angels and humans can know him in his justice by his judgment of sin, and that people alone should know him in his mercy by virtue of the saving ministry of the Lamb of God. There are vessels of wrath, who are exhibitions of his justice and wrathful power (cf. v. 22), and there are vessels of mercy, who are exhibitions of his rich glory in mercy (cf. v. 23). Some have been prepared for destruction, while others have been prepared for glory by the marvelous grace of the Holy Spirit, who has wooed and won them by effectual grace, giving them life and faith (cf. Rom. 8:7 – 8; 1 John 5:1) when they were dead in trespasses and sins. The unwilling, by his saving mercy, have been made willing to the praise of his grace (cf. 3:11).

Further, Paul says, the riches of the glory of his grace have been manifested not only to the Jews but also to the Gentiles (cf. v. 24).[1] Paul follows with a series of Old Testament quotations in support of the fact that God has called Gentiles to faith and left Israel with a remnant in the earth. Divine calling unites the continuing work of God thoughout time. If Israel had read and obeyed the Scriptures, they would have understood what might happen if they should reject the revelation of God climaxed in the appearance of their Messiah, the Lord Jesus Christ (cf. vv. 25 – 29).

"WHAT SHALL WE SAY, THEN?"

> [30]*What then shall we say? That the Gentiles, who did not pursue righteousness, have obtained it, a righteousness that is by faith;* [31]*but Israel, who pursued a law of righteousness, has not attained it.* [32]*Why not? Because they pursued it not by faith but as if it were by works. They stumbled over the "stumbling stone."* [33]*As it is written:*
>
> > *"See, I lay in Zion a stone that causes men to stumble*
> > *and a rock that makes them fall,*
> > *and the one who trusts in him will never be put to shame."*

The Facts (Romans 9:30 – 31)

We must never, in our stress on the divine sovereignty, overlook the important truth of human responsibility. We are saved by divine grace, but we are lost by reason of our sin. The apostle makes the important statement that the Gentiles have found what they were not seeking, God's righteousness (cf. v. 30). In this way, he stresses that God initiated the work of salvation before they began to seek him. Salvation always begins with God. He seeks us before we seek him, and he has sought and saved vast numbers of Gentiles. Israel, by contrast, has not found the righteousness of God for the simple reason that in self-righteousness they had sought it by works (cf. v. 31). In seeking to bring God into their debt by seeking justification by what they did, Israel failed to take the place of sinners hoping for mercy.

The Cause (Romans 9:32 – 33)

The cause of Israel's failure is set forth plainly. In the first place, they sought the righteousness of God not by faith but by the works of the law. If we are to be saved, there must be a substitute, able to take our penalty on himself and give us life. Israel's only hope is suggested in the last clause, "the one who trusts in him will never be put to shame" (v. 33).

DISCUSSION QUESTIONS

1. Paul regularly utilizes Scriptures to reinforce difficult concepts. What is the benefit of quoting the Bible in theological controversies?

2. In light of our sin, should any human ever question what God does? Why or why not?

3. What is the significance of Paul's reference to people as "clay" and not robots, automatons, or puppets?

4. Paul simply accepts divine sovereignty and human responsibility. Why don't some modern evangelicals follow Paul's example?

CHAPTER 18

CHRIST, THE LAW, AND ISRAEL'S INEXCUSABLE UNBELIEF

ROMANS 10:1–21

The vital question with which the apostle Paul deals is no doubt, "How shall a person be saved, and how does my salvation relate to the Gentiles and the Jews and, in fact, the whole world?" Paul has stressed the divine side of our salvation in Romans 9, laying great emphasis on the sovereignty of God in saving and hardening. But divine sovereignty should always be balanced by human responsibility (not human free will). We are required by God to respond to the message of grace.

PAUL'S EAGERNESS FOR ISRAEL'S SALVATION

¹Brothers, my heart's desire and prayer to God for the Israelites is that they may be saved. ²For I can testify about them that they are zealous for God, but their zeal is not based on knowledge.

The Declaration of It (Romans 10:1)

The chapter opens with a beautiful expression of the apostle's concern for his own flesh and blood.

The Explanation of It (Romans 10:2)

In 9:1 – 5 the apostle had spoken of his great heaviness of heart over Israel's lost condition; yet, in spite of all Israel's privileges, only a remnant of Israel was saved. The great mass of the nation had turned from the Lord in unbelief and, with the Gentiles, had crucified their Messiah. The apostle's consideration of their condition in chapter 9 is from the objective side of things, that is, from the side of their privileges and their failure to measure up to them.

In chapter 10 Paul looks at things more definitely from the subjective side. He speaks of his great desire that they be saved because they have a zeal for God, even though it is not according to genuine spiritual knowledge. How many of us have heard people say, "It does not really matter what someone believes as long as they sincerely believe it. If we do the best we can, God surely will accept us." Sincerity, however, is no substitute for truth. The people who sincerely believe in the solvency of an insolvent bank and put their money into its hands for safekeeping are soon disillusioned. In spiritual things, sincerity in the acceptance of false doctrine will not get us saved. The Lord Jesus Christ alone saves.

THE ERROR OF THE JEW

> [3]*Since they did not know the righteousness that comes from God and sought to establish their own, they did not submit to God's righteousness.*

Their Regard for Legal Righteousness (Romans 10:3a - b)

The apostle now explains what the error of the Jew was, but he does it negatively. He tells the Romans how not to be saved in his review of the failure of Israel. Their mistake lay in seeking to establish their own righteousness by good works before God and in failing to receive, as a free gift, the righteousness of God. They did not realize that they were sinners and could not earn a righteous standing before God. In this they were ignorant of God's righteousness. The Jews, like a wrecked automobile by the sign of a steep curve in the road ahead, were a warning to all that salvation is impossible for religious, zealous people who think they do not need a Redeemer but can stand by their own good works. The Jews are the living illustration that people may come to grief over Jesus Christ if they fail to see why he had to come (cf. Gal. 2:21).

Walter Lüthi has some good words here: "It is as if, having received the gift of 'Moses and the prophets,' they have refused to allow God to give them the Redeemer in Christ. At the point where God intends the very best for them, they turn down his offer. They will not 'submit to God's righteousness.' "[1] The Jews loved their legal righteousness and set about establishing it out of pride and arrogance.

Their Rejection of God's Righteousness (Romans 10:3c)

"God's righteousness," to which the nation Israel by and large did not submit, was the imputed righteousness that flows out of the penal substitutionary sacrifice of the Lord Jesus Christ.

THE END OF THE LAW

[4]*Christ is the end of the law so that there may be righteousness for everyone who believes.*

The expression "Christ is the end of the law" is a notoriously difficult one because the term "end" may be given several different senses. First, some have taken the word "end" in the sense of the goal. That is, Christ is the goal of the law. The law was intended to point forward to Christ by acting in its office of convicter of sin (cf. Rom. 3:20). In that sense, it was the slave guardian that led people to Christ (cf. Gal. 3:24).

Second, it has been taken to mean "end" in the sense of antitype. In this context, it would mean that all the types of the Old Testament pointed to Christ. He is the one to whom the Levitical cultus pointed, being the burnt offering, the peace offering, the meal offering, the sin offering, the trespass offering, the Passover, and so on (cf. Heb. 10:1). The Old Testament is full of illustrations that point to the coming Redeemer.

Third, most of the commentators have taken the word "end" in the sense of termination, finish, or windup. The old order, the legal age, is done away with in Christ, even as a hypothetical means of salvation (no one could be saved by the law, for all people are sinners, Christ excluded; cf. Gal. 3:10 – 12). The new order of the Spirit is here. This is likely the force of the text. Righteousness is available only in Jesus Christ and his sacrifice.

THE RIGHTEOUSNESS OF THE LAW

[5]*Moses describes in this way the righteousness that is by the law: "The man who does these things will live by them."*

The apostle begins by commenting on the righteousness of the Mosaic law. There is a righteousness set forth in the law, but it is a righteousness of human works (cf. Phil. 3:9). Ideally, or hypothetically, it might be possible for a man to attain to righteousness by the law. Of course, that is impossible by reason of the fall of Adam. Only Jesus Christ has ever among humans kept the Mosaic law. But hypothetically, the law sets out a legal righteousness. If a person, from the moment he or she draws their first breath to the moment they draw their last, should live in perfect obedience to the two tables of the law, they might claim heaven by works. Thus, the legal way to life is by 100 percent holiness in deed and word throughout one's lifetime, a standard too high for sinful humanity. As the verse has it,

> Run, John, and work, the law commands,
> Yet finds me neither feet nor hands,
> But sweeter news the gospel brings,
> It bids me fly and lends me wings![2]

The law was given to bring people to the knowledge of their sin — and that work it performs admirably — when we seriously consider what it is saying. As a result, not one of us is able to stand and testify that we have kept God's law during our lifetime perfectly.

THE RIGHTEOUSNESS OF FAITH

[6]But the righteousness that is by faith says: "Do not say in your heart, 'Who will ascend into heaven?'" (that is, to bring Christ down) [7]"or 'Who will descend into the deep?'" (that is, to bring Christ up from the dead). [8]But what does it say? "The word is near you; it is in your mouth and in your heart," that is, the word of faith we are proclaiming: [9]That if you confess with your mouth, "Jesus is Lord," and believe in your heart that God raised him from the dead, you will be saved. [10]For it is with your heart that you believe and are justified, and it is with your mouth that you confess and are saved.

Its Old Testament Expression (Romans 10:6 – 8)

In the next few sentences, the apostle, leaning rhetorically on Deuteronomy 30:10 – 14, points out that the Scriptures teach a righteousness by means of faith. In the context of Deuteronomy, Moses is setting forth details of the Palestinian covenant, a covenant that regulated Israel's enjoyment of the land that had been promised to her by the Abrahamic covenant. In essence Moses said that if Israel kept the Lord's commandments (note the plural) and if they turned to the Lord with all their heart (note the singular nature of this command), they would enjoy the possession of the land. If they were disobedient, they would be scattered to the four corners of the earth. Moses says, in his own rhetorical way, that grace is nearby in the Old Testament and that it is not the product of great physical endeavors. Grace comes through a simple inclining of the heart toward the Lord, the act of faith.

The apostle, in Romans 10, trading on that rhetorical expression of the simple nature of faith and that it is not a matter of works by which we obtain God's blessings, writes, "Do not say in your heart, 'Who will ascend into heaven?' (that is, to bring Christ down)" (v. 6). What he suggests is that we do not have to precipitate the incarnation. The divine act has already occurred. He has come, and not as a reward for human works, but in sheer grace. The next sentence, "or 'Who will descend into the deep?' (that is, to bring Christ up from the dead)" (v. 7), points to another impossibility. He, the Messiah Christ, has already risen (cf. Matt. 28:6).

Thus, the apostle says, salvation is not by human merit (cf. v. 6) or by any human supplement of the work of God (cf. v. 7). It is not something attained but something obtained through faith. What is needed is not a new start in the attempt to provide ourselves with a robe of righteousness but a new heart by regeneration. The latter is an immediate possibility, for "the word 'is near you; it is in your mouth and in your heart,' that is, the word of faith we are proclaiming" (v. 8). God seeks faith alone, and he provides it too (cf. Eph. 2:8–9).

Its New Testament Expression (Romans 10:9–10)

The apostle now explains the nature of faith in its New Testament expression, namely, the confession of Jesus as Lord and his resurrection, a confession that arises out of one's heart. Paul is not speaking of two unrelated matters when he speaks of confession and belief. As C. K. Barrett affirms, "The confession is believed and the faith confessed."[3] One is the outward side and the effect of the other. Faith is the inward side of the matter and the cause of the confession.

In confessing "Jesus is Lord," a person confesses the divine nature and attributes in him. This acknowledgment can be made only by the Holy Spirit (cf. 1 Cor. 12:3), which indicates, in an incidental way, that faith is the gift of God.

The second article of the faith, that "God raised [Jesus] from the dead," is an important corrective for those who use the term "Lord" too broadly (cf. 1 Cor. 8:5). There is only "one Lord, Jesus Christ, through whom all things came and through whom we live" (1 Cor. 8:6). All other "lords" are not lords at all. The Christian faith is not one among many, as Peter puts it so plainly in Acts 4:12. Salvation is only through Christ, "for there is no other name under heaven given to men by which we must be saved." Christianity is an exclusive truth.

The fact that Jesus is Lord and has been raised from the dead is an affirmation that he stands both within history and outside history, and not as a teacher, but as the conqueror of death. As he said in his encounter with Martha, "I am the resurrection and the life. He who believes in me will live, even though he dies; and whoever lives and believes in me will never die. Do you believe this?" (John 11:25 – 26).

Paul concludes with that statement that righteousness and salvation come from believing and confessing (cf. v. 10).

FREENESS, UNIVERSALITY

[11]As the Scripture says, "Anyone who trusts in him will never be put to shame." [12]For there is no difference between Jew and Gentile — the same Lord is Lord of all and richly blesses all who call on him, [13]for, "Everyone who calls on the name of the Lord will be saved."

The Universality of the Gospel (Romans 10:11 – 12)

From the Old Testament (Isa. 28:16), the apostle shows that the way of salvation is by faith. The universality of the gospel in its invitation is affirmed ("anyone"). There is no difference between the Jew and the Gentile. All are poor, but God is rich to both, and Jew and Gentile are to be saved in the same way. The expression "the same Lord is Lord of all" confirms that the similar expression in 9:5 is to be referred to Christ (cf. Phil. 2:5 – 11).

The Sufficiency of the Gospel (Romans 10:11, 13)

The gospel delivers from the shame of sin, guilt, and condemnation. As a corollary, we have the freedom of perfect access to the Lord by virtue of his atoning work.

The Accessibility of the Gospel (Romans 10:8, 11, 13)

The gospel is accessible to all who call on the Lord. When Paul mentions that we may be saved by calling on the Lord, he means a true calling on him for personal salvation from sin, guilt, and condemnation.

ISRAEL'S INEXCUSABLE UNBELIEF

"But, Paul," someone might say, "what is this faith that you keep talking about? How can I obtain it?" The questions are, it seems, almost eternally relevant, illustrative of the truth of the applicability of Scripture to our everyday concerns and needs.

Paul has just explained that salvation has been prepared for the elect of God, and in that fact is to be found the clue to the failure of the nation Israel to be predominant among the elect as in old covenant times. Israel had forgotten that they must respond in faith to the invitation to receive the forgiveness of sins and eternal life through the gospel.

ISRAEL AND BELIEVING

> [14]*How, then, can they call on the one they have not believed in? And how can they believe in the one of whom they have not heard? And how can they hear without someone preaching to them?* [15]*And how can they preach unless they are sent? As it is written, "How beautiful are the feet of those who bring good news!"*
>
> [16]*But not all the Israelites accepted the good news. For Isaiah says, "Lord, who has believed our message?"* [17]*Consequently, faith comes from hearing the message, and the message is heard through the word of Christ.*

Five Links in the Chain of Evangelization (Romans 10:14–15)

Israel's necessity of calling on the Lord for salvation turns the apostle's mind to the steps by which the evangelistic program of God is carried out. We begin with Paul's methodology with verse 15. The first step in the chain of evangelization is the necessity of the sending of the messenger. The apostle, citing Isaiah 52:7, comments on the beauty of the work of evangelizing, and every saved soul can empathize with that sentiment. But, first, God must send the preacher.

The second link in the chain is found in the words "someone preaching" or "preach." The evangelist must not only be sent; he must preach. "Preach" comes from a Greek word that means simply to proclaim. Those who are God's messengers are to set forth God's truth. In gospel preaching there can be no innovating with the truth, although there may be varied ways of offering the message. The third link is hearing. God's messenger is heard through the message, but the main stress is on the necessity of hearing. The fourth link is belief. It is not enough to hear; hearers must believe.

Finally, we must call on him (cf. vv. 14–15). This is *the* invocation. Its content is found in verses 9 and 10, "That if you confess with your mouth, 'Jesus is Lord,' and believe in your heart that God raised him from the dead, you will be saved. For it is with your heart that you believe and are justified, and it is with your mouth that you confess and are saved."

The divine program of saving the people of God begins with God and ends with him.

Israel's Failure in the Fourth Link (Romans 10:16)

Paul places the failure of Israel squarely on their unbelief. Verse 16 expresses their unbelief, and it is linked to Scripture. The text from Isaiah is the lament of the nation of Israel when they will have discovered at the second advent of Jesus Christ that they have crucified their Messiah. The verb forms of Isaiah 53:1 – 9 make the verses that open that chapter a confession on their part of how they treated him at his first coming. They confess and mourn over their unbelief and rejection of him.

Additionally, the citing of Isaiah 53:1 in support of the claim they did not believe is appropriate, of course, but in the use of the text here it also becomes clear that to Paul that obedience is faith. Notice what he says: "But not all the Israelites accepted the good news. For Isaiah says, "Lord, who has believed our message?" The second statement is designed to confirm the first, and thus obedience is linked with faith. I had a visit from an old friend the past week, and he told me that he heard a preacher say, "The doctrines of grace make sinners sad, saints glad, and pretenders mad." Israel was mad, but they, in the future, will be glad.

The Summary of the Links (Romans 10:17)

Faith, Paul says, comes from the message heard through the word about Christ. Faith does not come by hereditary descent, nor does it come through the sacraments (cf. Titus 3:5). As Charles Spurgeon said, "Faith cannot be washed into us by immersion, nor sprinkled on us in christening; it is not to be poured into us from a chalice, nor generated in us by a consecrated piece of bread. There is no magic about it; it comes by hearing the word of God, and by that way only."[4] It does not come by feeling, as verse 9 of this chapter indicates; nor does it come by dreams, by the eloquence or sincerity of the preacher, or by attendance at the services.

ISRAEL AND HEARING

> [18]But I ask: Did they not hear? Of course they did:
>
> "Their voice has gone out into all the earth,
>   their words to the ends of the world."

We cannot say that Israel has not had the opportunity to hear the gospel. The preaching of the gospel, Paul says, is "as worldwide as the light of the heavenly bodies."[5] He uses the words of Psalm 19:4 in a rhetorical, or figurative, way. We may refer to his later words (15:19, 23) for his conviction that Israel has been the recipient of a wide-ranging testimony to Jesus Christ as the Messiah (cf. Col. 1:23). We are all held accountable and responsible.

ISRAEL AND KNOWING

> [19] *Again I ask: Did Israel not understand? First, Moses says,*
>
> > *"I will make you envious by those who are not a nation;*
> > *I will make you angry by a nation that has no understanding."*
>
> [20] *And Isaiah boldly says,*
> > *"I was found by those who did not seek me;*
> > *I revealed myself to those who did not ask for me."*
>
> [21] *But concerning Israel he says,*
> > *"All day long I have held out my hands*
> > *to a disobedient and obstinate people."*

Refutation from the Law (Romans 10:19)

In the final verses of chapter 10, the apostle deals with the remaining excuses to the effect that ethnic Israel did not know what was going to happen if they rejected the message from the Lord. "Did Israel not understand?" is the sense of his words, which literally are, "But I say, is it that Israel has not known?" A question exists over the proper object of the verb "know." Is the sense "Is it that Israel has not known the gospel?" Or "Is it that Israel has not known that there would come a time of rejection because of their unbelief?" Or "Is it that Israel has not known that the gospel was universal in nature, comprehending Gentiles too?"

Paul's citation of Deuteronomy 32:21 leads to viewing that the second alternative is correct, although that would involve a universal gospel preaching. The apostle understands the Deuteronomy passage to predict that, since Israel will worship "no-gods," the idols, God will provoke them to jealousy by a "no-people," that is, the Gentiles, who were not the chosen people, as Abraham's descendants were (cf. 11:11, 14). Thus, if they had read Moses correctly, they would have understood their fate if they rejected the Word of God in Christ.

Refutation from the Prophets (Romans 10:20–21)

Isaiah is bolder than Moses, Paul says, for he frankly predicts that those who did not seek Yahweh, as Israel did not, will find Yahweh. The text is from Isaiah 65:1 and refers to the Gentiles rather than the Jews. It is a prophecy of the future reception of Gentiles, and Israel should have known its force (cf. Isa. 42:6–7).

Isaiah 65:2 is then cited as referring to ethnic Israel. It gives the reason for the reception of the Gentiles, referred to in the immediately preceding verse in Isaiah and in Romans. It is a remarkable text, and in a sense it sums up the idea of the whole chapter, "All day long I have held out my hands to a disobedient and obstinate people." The picture is of the unwearied love of Yahweh for his people. There is a great emphasis on the words "all day long." Paul gives a beautiful and touching figure of the incessant pleading love of Yahweh for Israel.

DISCUSSION QUESTIONS

1. Are Christians responsible for the salvation of other people? Elaborate.

2. What is the Christian's responsibility in evangelism?

3. Why is it inexcusable for a Christian preacher of the gospel, knowing that salvation is only through Jesus Christ, to fail to preach that truth? What are the consequences?

4. Must Christians "be led" to evangelize when they are told that they must (cf. Matt. 28:18 – 20)? Explain.

5. How are prayer and evangelism linked?

CHAPTER 19

IS ISRAEL'S REJECTION TOTAL?

ROMANS 11:1–24

Romans 1 – 8 has set forth an elect group justified by faith in the Lord Jesus Christ, who offered the redeeming sacrifice on Calvary's cross. A Jewish reader, familiar with the Old Testament, would have noticed what might have seemed an unusual thing: Israel seems to be missing from the elect group. Except for a brief mention of the problem of Israel in 3:1 – 8, the nation appears to have been entirely neglected by the apostle. Were they not the elect nation, recipients of the covenants of the Old Testament? How can any teaching have divine approval that does not reckon with them? Romans 11 deals with the future of Israel thematically.

Now, in 11:1 – 10, the apostle makes the point that, in spite of the nation's obvious failure, their failure is not total or final. A time is coming when all Israel will be saved (cf. vv. 11 – 27). The glorious promises of the Old Testament will have their brilliant fulfillment.

THE PAULINE QUESTION AND ANSWER

¹I ask then: Did God reject his people? By no means! I am an Israelite myself, a descendant of Abraham, from the tribe of Benjamin. ²God did not reject his people, whom he foreknew. Don't you know what the Scripture says in the passage about Elijah — how he appealed to God against Israel: ³"Lord, they have killed your prophets and torn down your altars; I am the only one left, and they are

173

trying to kill me"? [4]*And what was God's answer to him? "I have reserved for myself seven thousand who have not bowed the knee to Baal."* [5]*So too, at the present time there is a remnant chosen by grace.* [6]*And if by grace, then it is no longer by works; if it were, grace would no longer be grace.*

Direct Denial (Romans 11:1a)

Paul's question in verse 1 follows naturally in the light of the last words of the preceding chapter, where he speaks strongly of Israel's unfaithfulness: "But concerning Israel [God] says, 'All day long I have held out my hands to a disobedient and obstinate people'" (10:21). Considering their present condition, what more natural question is there than "Did God reject his people?" Hints to the apostle's forthcoming answer can be found in the way he phrases the question. First, he uses a negative particle that is used when the interrogator expects a negative answer. The question could be paraphrased, "God has not cast away his people, has he?" Further, the very use of the expression "his people" lets the perceptive reader know what kind of reply the apostle expects. When God takes a people to himself, it is forever.

There may have been changes in the divine economy (sacrifices, the priesthood, and the temple were now obsolete), but there were no negations in the promises. As is customary, the opening Pauline rebuttal is a direct denial. "By no means!" is his reply to his own question (cf. 3:3; 9:6). If God were to forsake his people, then he would become a liar, a covenant breaker.

The Case of Paul (Romans 11:1b – 2a)

The apostle further explains why God has not cast away his people. Paul, a saved Israelite, proves God's trustworthiness. But, as Walter Lüthi suggests, someone might say of the citing of the salvation of the one man, Paul, "One swallow does not make a summer."[1] So Paul states positively what he is affirming in verse 2. The use of the term "to foreknow" gives further evidence that in Paul's usage the term means "to choose in love." If the word meant simply "to know beforehand," in the sense of knowing beforehand that they would eventually believe, there would be no problem of "Did God reject his people?" It is plain that if there is a problem in connection with Israel's relation to the promises of God, it must concern their election. The problem is simply, if God has foreordained Israel's salvation, what is their status now in the light of their rejection of the Messiah? Does not that cancel their election? Arthur Way renders the last clause, "whom He marked out for His own so long ago" (cf. 8:29).[2] God, then, is not fickle, but he has had a plan within a plan. He intends to bring Israel to their promises, but the way includes the present time of Gentile blessing also (cf. vv. 11 – 15).

The Parallel with Elijah (Romans 11:2b – 6)

The apostle now introduces as an illustration of the present time the situation in the time of Elijah, the great prophet of Israel in the days of their backsliding. At that time apostasy was general, but it was not universal (1 Kings 19:10 – 18). Elijah thought that he alone had remained faithful to the Lord, but God had to remind him most vividly that he had reserved for himself 7,000 men who had not bowed the knee to the image of Baal. What a magnificent declaration of divine sovereignty! The question in verse 4, "And what was God's answer to him?" refers to the revelation from God to Elijah in "a still, small voice" (1 Kings 19:12 KJV; literally, "the voice of crushed silence"). The words reflect Paul's attitude to the Old Testament utterances: they came from God.

In verse 5 Paul indicates the contrary to the preceding — that is, general apostasy is consistent with the existence of a remnant and the presence of the remnant proves God does not cast away his people. The words "so too" draw the comparison between Elijah's days and Paul's. The "at the present time" introduces the inference implied in the preceding discussion of Elijah's day. The "remnant" refers to the Jewish converts in Paul's day, namely, Jewish believers in the church, which is by now becoming largely Gentile in character. The word refers to that which the apostle calls "the Israel of God" in Galatians 6:16.

The remnant is one that is the product of the election of grace. The term "chosen" here confirms the sense we have given to "foreknew" in verse 2 (cf. 8:29 – 30). The reference to "grace" launches the apostle to explain the negative force of the preceding phrase: "and if by grace, then it is no longer by works; if it were, grace would no longer be grace." God's grace is free, the product of the sovereign love of our mighty triune God. Augustine once said, "*Gratia, nisi gratis sit, non est gratia,*" which may be translated "Grace, unless it should be free, is not grace." It is not to be procured by works. God is not finished with Israel, because he has been saving Jewish people throughout history.

THE LOGICAL CONCLUSION

> [7] *What then? What Israel sought so earnestly it did not obtain, but the elect did. The others were hardened,* [8] *as it is written:*
>
> "*God gave them a spirit of stupor,*
>   *eyes so that they could not see*
>   *and ears so that they could not hear,*
> *to this very day.*"

⁹*And David says:*

> *"May their table become a snare and a trap,*
> *a stumbling block and a retribution for them.*
> ¹⁰*May their eyes be darkened so they cannot see,*
> *and their backs be bent forever."*

The Boon of Election (Romans 11:7; cf. 9:30 – 32)

The logical conclusion of his line of reasoning follows in verses 7 – 10. Viewed from the human side, the nation has failed to attain righteousness (v. 7a-c), but the elect have attained it (v. 7d). Thus, God has not cast away his people. Viewed from the divine side, however, something else must be said, and Paul says it bluntly: "The others were hardened." The word "hardened" is strong; it refers to the forming of a callus. Although used metaphorically here, the force is that of a deep hardening (cf. 2 Cor. 3:14). In the next verse, Paul says that God is the agent who performs the hardening. As usual, he points to election as the basis of acceptance and sin as the basis of judgment (not nonelection). There is no arbitrariness, or evidence that God prevents a seeking soul from knowing him. Nor is there injustice, for no one deserves anything good. The truth expressed by Paul may be traced to our Lord himself (cf. Mark 4:12; John 12:40).

The Blindness of the Rest (Romans 11:8 – 10)

The apostle, in customary fashion, clinches his argument and conclusion by the citation of Scripture, in this case, portions from the Law (Deut. 29:4), the Prophets (Isa. 29:10), and the Writings (Ps. 69:22 – 23). The people of Israel in Paul's day are hardened and blind like Israel in the wilderness, dazed and obtuse like the Israel of Isaiah's day. Further, David's persecutors are the forerunners of our Lord's Israel, guilty of deicide and falling under judicial hardening and blindness, which is their recompense.

THE PARABLE OF THE OLIVE TREE

Paul introduces an interlude into the argument devoted to the question of the purpose of Israel's rejection (cf. vv. 11 – 15) and a warning addressed to the favored Gentiles (cf. vv. 16 – 24).

It is important to bear in mind at this point the debate over the ethnic future of Israel. Generally speaking, amillennialists oppose the doctrine of an ethnic future for Israel, while premillennialists almost universally affirm it. A random sampling of views might be helpful here: First, John Calvin, who has often been claimed by the amillennialists (he certainly was not a premillennialist), affirmed that there was to be a restoration of the Jews (cf. 11:1). He did, however, interpret "Israel" in verse 26 as inclusive of both Jews and Gentiles (cf. Gal. 6:16), although the Jews, as God's firstborn family, will "obtain the first place."[3]

Second, John Murray, a postmillennialist, commenting on verse 12, affirmed, "Hence nothing less than a restoration of Israel as a people to faith, privilege, and blessing can satisfy the terms of this passage."[4] Since the stumbling is theirs, so is the fullness.[5] What kind of future does the nation of Israel have, if any?

THE QUESTION

> [11]*Again I ask: Did they stumble so as to fall beyond recovery? Not at all! Rather, because of their transgression, salvation has come to the Gentiles to make Israel envious.* [12]*But if their transgression means riches for the world, and their loss means riches for the Gentiles, how much greater riches will their fullness bring!*

The apostle has shown that Israel's rejection is not complete; it is only partial. He will now show that it is not final; it is only temporary. The question of the finality of their fall is a natural one in the light of the redemptive history of the Scriptures, and Paul introduces the question of finality as an inference from the preceding discussion. The "again I ask," clearly related to verse 1, opens the discussion of the matter. He turns his attention to the majority who have stumbled after handling the case of the minority who did not. He has modified the question of verse 1; now he answers it.

The section is in the form of a question (v. 11), an answer (vv. 12–15), and then an admonition (vv. 16–24). The apostle is dealing primarily with national purposes, not individual purposes. He is dealing with Israel and the Gentiles, or Israel the nation and the nations first and foremost.

First, since the word "stumble" is in a Greek tense that refers to indefinite action, looked at as an event, we might take it to refer to an utter and permanent fall. Thus, the question, which expects a negative answer, would be a denial of such a permanent fall. While the individuals who rejected Christ fell permanently, the nation's fall is only temporary.

Second, it may be, then, that Paul is reflecting on the more ultimate and gracious design of God in the stumbling of the mass of Israel in our Lord's and Paul's day. The stress of the question should be put on the purpose clause, that is, on the "so as to fall beyond recovery." Their stumbling and falling serve the purpose of Gentile salvation, and by that, the provocation of Israel to jealousy (cf. Deut. 32:21). The fall of Israel had as a designed result the salvation of the Gentiles, and that in turn was to lead to the return and restoration of Israel to divine favor.

THE ANSWER

> [13]*I am talking to you Gentiles. Inasmuch as I am the apostle to the Gentiles, I make much of my ministry* [14]*in the hope that I may somehow arouse my own people to envy and save some of them.* [15]*For if their rejection is the reconciliation of the world, what will their acceptance be but life from the dead?*

The apostle's answer is threefold. First, such a thought as a final fall for God's people is unthinkable and blasphemous (cf. 3:1 – 8). How can God be unfaithful to his unconditional promises? If that were possible, how could believers today trust his unconditional promises to us in the gospel of Jesus Christ?

Second, the false step of the Jews has led to Gentile salvation, which God has intended in his gracious purpose to provoke Israel to jealousy (cf. vv. 11 – 12). "Their recovery and not their fall was His aim," E. H. Gifford points out.[6] The apostle's text is Deuteronomy 32:21, a passage he has already referred to in chapter 10 (cf. v. 19), and in which he made the point that Israel should have known from it that a time would come when Gentiles would experience God's salvation while Israel was passed by because of their intransigence. One of the principal purposes of Gentile salvation in the present age is the provocation of the chosen people to jealousy so that they too might return to the Lord God of their fathers.

Finally, the apostle argues from the logic of the situation that the blessing of the Gentiles today by Jewish stumbling in the past, in the light of their predicted recovery and restoration in the future, demands tremendous world blessing, something like life from the dead in the future for Gentiles as well (cf. vv. 13 – 15). It was the failure of the mission of the Jews that led to the mission to the Gentiles (cf. Deut. 32:21; Acts 13:45 – 48; 18:6; 28:28), and the failure of the mission of the Gentiles will issue in the future mission to Israel and then the salvation of the world (cf. Acts 15:13 – 18). It will be seen, then, that, "the salvation of the Gentiles is subordinate to another design."[7]

The threefold reference to the third person plural pronoun in verse 12 ("their") emphasizes that the apostle is looking at the nation as a whole. The generation of Jesus and Paul could not be in view. The truth of Israel as the Lord's instrument for world blessing is certainly taught here (cf. Gen. 9:24 – 27; Ps. 67:1 – 2). The word "some" in verse 14 indicates that the apostle does not expect that all of Israel will be saved now. That will come later (cf. vv. 25 – 26). With the "for" of verse 15 Paul introduces the conclusion from verses 13 and 14, as he did in verse 12 from verse 11. The argument is again *a fortiori*. The limited reconciliation followed Israel's rejection; worldwide reconciliation will follow their receiving. Paul refers to "an unprecedented quickening for the world in the expansion and success of the gospel," Murray suggests.[8]

THE ADMONITION

> [16]*If the part of the dough offered as firstfruits is holy, then the whole batch is holy; if the root is holy, so are the branches.*
>
> [17]*If some of the branches have been broken off, and you, though a wild olive shoot, have been grafted in among the others and now share in the nourishing sap from the olive root,* [18]*do not boast over those branches. If you do, consider this: You do not support the root, but the root supports you.* [19]*You will say then, "Branches were broken off so that I could be grafted in."* [20]*Granted. But they were broken off because of unbelief, and you stand by faith. Do not be arrogant, but be afraid.* [21]*For if God did not spare the natural branches, he will not spare you either.*
>
> [22]*Consider therefore the kindness and sternness of God: sternness to those who fell, but kindness to you, provided that you continue in his kindness. Otherwise, you also will be cut off.* [23]*And if they do not persist in unbelief, they will be grafted in, for God is able to graft them in again.* [24]*After all, if you were cut out of an olive tree that is wild by nature, and contrary to nature were grafted into a cultivated olive tree, how much more readily will these, the natural branches, be grafted into their own olive tree!*

The Declaration (Romans 11:16)

The Greek particle introducing verse 16 is the word *de*, which is transitional here and means "now." It brings the reader the illustration of the olive tree, which serves as a warning to the Gentiles (cf. vv. 20 – 21, 24). It also includes some strong reasons for expecting the receiving of the Jews (v. 14). The two figures of verse 16 are similar, the firstfruits and the root. What do they represent? The following context points to Israel the nation being the branches (cf. vv. 17, 19, et al.). Thus, the lump also probably refers to the nation. The "dough," derived from Numbers 15:17 – 21, shows that the Israelites were to offer to God a cake from the dough of the first-ground flour, as it came from the threshing floor. The presentation of the cake hallowed the whole baking (cf. Lev. 23:10 – 11; 1 Cor. 15:23). The basic thought of both figures is that consecration of the firstfruits, or root, is communicated to the lump, or the branches.

But what are the firstfruits and the root? While some have attempted to refer them to Christ and others to the remnant, it seems best to refer them to Abraham and the patriarchs (cf. v. 28; 9:5; Jer. 11:16; Hos. 14:6). The point of the verse, then, is that the initial consecration to God of the patriarchs by the choice of Abraham (cf. Deut. 7:8 – 9; Luke 1:55) in making them natural branches is the basis of his expectation of restoration. The Abrahamic covenant, lying in the background of the apostle's words and thoughts, being unconditional in nature (cf. Gen. 15:7 – 21), is the ground of the assurance of Israel's future blessing.

The Illustration (Romans 11:17 – 24)

After the declaration of verse 16, the apostle expounds an illustration of the matter in verses 17 – 24. He uses the second of the figures from verse 16 "because it admits of a distinction between one branch and another, and so can be applied, collectively or individually, to believers and unbelievers."[9] In the figure there is a warning for the Gentiles (vv. 17 – 22) and a fresh argument for Jewish restoration (vv. 23 – 24; cf. vv. 11 – 15). The figure is a parable from horticulture, but it is governed by grace, as Paul notes (cf. v. 24).[10] It is the practice of grafting a cultivated bud onto a wild stock, as Paul knows.

The warning to the Gentile believers begins in verse 17 with an "and" in Greek.[11] The "some" may be compared with that which is taught in verses 1 – 10. The process described is unnatural, and that is the point he wishes to stress. The phrases "among the others" and "and now share" indicate plainly that the Gentile believers share with Israel the Abrahamic covenant promises, although they remain Gentiles (cf. Gal. 3:16, 29; Heb. 2:16). They too are heirs of the fat root of the olive tree. This statement of the apostle argues strongly against too sharp a distinction between the blessings enjoyed by Israel and Gentile believers in the church.

In the following verse (v. 18), Paul reminds the Gentiles that branches are not self-sustaining. The text is a blow to anti-Semitism (cf. 3:2). In a kind of diatribe-like reply, the Gentile comes back with, "Branches were broken off so that I [emphatic] could be grafted in." Paul's reply is that they stand by faith, and they have no reason for self-glorying, for it is God's gift. Further, Israel failed because of unbelief, not because of inferiority or because Yahweh grew tired and peeved at them (cf. 12:16).

Verse 21 gives the reason why they, the Gentiles, should not presume on their spiritual election. There is more likelihood of blessing for the original covenant people than for the heathen Gentiles. William Shedd comments, "The children of God are warned against apostasy, as one of the means of preventing apostasy. The holy and filial fear of falling is one of the means of not falling. He who has no such fear, because he presumes upon his election, will fall."[12]

On the conditional "provided that you continue" of verse 22, Murray makes the point that there is "no security in the bond of the gospel apart from perseverance. There is no such thing as continuance in the favor of God in spite of apostasy; God's saving embrace and endurance are correlative."[13]

Verses 23 – 24 constitute a massive *a fortiori* argument for the restoration of national Israel. Their rejection is not final. The only thing preventing their restoration is unbelief (on the human plane; on the divine plane it is his purpose in this age). The "for" of verse 23 in "for God is able to graft them in again" introduces the reason he can do it. He not only can restore Israel if they believe, but he can remove their unbelief itself. The "again" refers to the national reintroduction to blessing (cf. Matt. 21:43; Acts 3:19 – 21; 2 Cor. 3:16).

Verse 24 continues the reasoning. The "for" in Greek (*gar*) serves to introduce the grounds for national restoration. It is "an easier process"[14] than the salvation of the Gentiles. The last three words are emphatically climactic, recalling 3:1 – 2 (cf. Matt. 24:30 – 31). As Murray says, "The patriarchal root is never uprooted to give place to another planting."[15] It is their olive tree, and it is always theirs. The Gentiles share in their covenantal blessing.

In summary, the figure of the olive tree, representative of the Abrahamic covenant and the blessings that flow from it, was designed primarily to be a warning to the Gentiles not to presume on the Lord's mercy, simply because in the present age they are the signal objects of the divine grace. The olive tree illustration taught the fall of Israel, the blessing of the Gentiles, and the probability of the reception of Israel again into the plan and purpose of God in grace.

Paul's words are being vindicated today. There is no question but that modern Judaism is bankrupt. Divine grace has been abandoned for legalism. Jews today need divine efficacious grace and the return of the Messiah, the Lord Jesus Christ (cf. Zech. 12:10). May the Lord hasten the day!

DISCUSSION QUESTIONS

1. Is the story of the nation of Israel indicative of God's faithfulness to his promises? If so, how?

2. Some believe God's Word is inspired simply because of the nation of Israel.[16] Why would they believe this?

3. Is the church today doing a good job of provoking the Jews to jealousy today? In what ways could the church do a better job?

4. Are Jewish unbelievers helped today when Jesus is preached as a weak, sentimental, faceless, amiable carpenter instead of the God-man who has offered a penal, substitutionary sacrifice for wicked sinners, among whom are all people? Explain your answer.

CHAPTER 20

THE SALVATION OF ISRAEL AND GOD'S AGENDA FOR THE NATIONS

ROMANS 11:25–36

THE HARDENING OF ISRAEL

²⁵I do not want you to be ignorant of this mystery, brothers, so that you may not be conceited: Israel has experienced a hardening in part until the full number of the Gentiles has come in.

The Admonition (Romans 11:25a-b)

The Greek begins verse 25 with a causal "for," introducing the ultimate ground for the hope of Israel's regrafting into the olive tree. It is the scriptural basis of the matter, and Paul does not want his readers to proudly overlook the fact. Israel's restoration is expected, for their hardening is only partial, and their future has been prophesied. Israel's hardening is subject to two limitations, which sum up the chapter. First, it is "in part," used here extensively, not intensively. All people, including Israel, are equally depraved, but the depravity of Israel has been overcome by the saving work of God extended to some of them. Paul is referring, of course, to the remnant that has been saved through the election of grace and their consequent faith (cf. vv. 5, 17). Second, it is temporary; the temporal clause introduced by "until" suggests a limit to the duration of the hardening. The apostle calls these things a "mystery," that is, a divine secret, something that may be known only by divine revelation.

Paul is concerned that his readers not be ignorant of Israel's present and future status. That is why he says, "I do not want you to be ignorant of this mystery, brothers, so that you may not be conceited." The reason that Paul wanted his readers to know the things he was talking about was that the Gentiles, if they did not realize where they stood in the plan of God, might be filled with pride and arrogance over their election and salvation (cf. vv. 17 – 21). They must not become "conceited"; instead, their proper attitude should be fear (cf. v. 20).

The Description of the Hardening (Romans 11:25c)

The apostle goes on to describe the "hardening." The word is derived from a Greek word meaning "a callus." It denotes, therefore, in a metaphorical sense dullness or insensibility. The words "in part" go with "experienced." That is, the dullness has been judicially inflicted on a part of Israel, not on all. The insensibility is the judgment for the rejection of the Messiah, the Lord Jesus Christ. The nation, centering their attention on the prophecies of the glory of the Messiah and the victory he would accomplish for the nation, failed to give proper attention to the prophecies that detailed his sufferings, the ground of the atonement, and the forgiveness of sins.

Passages such as Isaiah 53 were a mystery to them because of their failure to recognize their own sinful state and need of redemption. Like the little boy waiting in a London hospital for a visit from King George V and failing to recognize him when he came because he did not wear his crown as king of England, Israel too failed to recognize their King when he came. Jesus did not have his crown on; he came in his suit of suffering. His crown was not made of gold but of thorns!

The Culmination of the Hardening (Romans 11:25d)

The apostle makes several important points in the last clause of the verse. In the first place, the "until" suggests an end to the hardness of heart (cf. 1 Cor. 11:26; 15:25); this is stated explicitly in the next verse. Second, the expression "the full number of the Gentiles" usually means the whole body.[1] The term is to be distinguished from the term "the times of the Gentiles" (cf. Luke 21:24), which refers to the lengthy period of Gentile domination of the city of Jerusalem, beginning with Nebuchadnezzar's capture of the city and concluding with the second coming of Jesus Christ. The "fullness" of the Gentiles is a soteriological term, referring to the time of Gentile salvation during the present age.

The words "has come in" can be thought of as "shall have come in," that is, into that community of the people of God signified by the good olive tree, into which some of them have already been grafted. Or, perhaps more clearly, it refers to the present Gentile community of the faithful (cf. Acts 15:14; also cf. Rom. 15:16, 18 with 11:11 – 12). The coming in, however, refers to the entrance into the possession of the blessing of the covenantal program of the Old Testament unconditional covenants.

THE SALVATION OF ISRAEL

[26]*And so all Israel will be saved, as it is written:*

> *"The deliverer will come from Zion;*
> *he will turn godlessness away from Jacob.*

The Manner of It (Romans 11:26a)

Before us now is the important statement, "And so all Israel will be saved." But what is meant by "and so"? Some have taken the words in the sense of "and in this manner" and have referred them to the manner indicated in the preceding context (cf. vv. 1 – 24). What this results in, for these people who are amillennialists for the most part, is that Israel is to be saved by Gentile provocation to jealousy, but the salvation is not one that concludes with a large outpouring of salvation on ethnic Israel at the end of the age. Instead, it is a process that continues throughout the age between the two comings of Christ in a slow trickle. Thus, there is to be expected no large-scale turning of the descendants of the fathers at the end of the present age. Basic to this view is that the words cannot be taken temporally and should be rendered "*and* then," the salvation being then referred to the future.[2]

The most common view is to take the words in the comparative sense, accepting the rendering "and so" but referring them to the entrance of the Gentiles into the family of God. Sanday and Headlam,[3] as well as Frédéric Godet,[4] take them this way. When the full number of the Gentiles has come in, Israel will come to salvation in this manner, that is, by having been provoked to jealousy by Gentile salvation. While this is the method of Israel's salvation (via Gentile provocation to jealousy), the time is clearly future from the context. The figure of the olive tree (cf. vv. 23 – 24) and the preceding verse (v. 25) suggest this. Finally, the Scripture cited from Isaiah 59:20 – 21 (Ps. 14:7) and 27:9 (Jer. 31:33 – 34) refers to the coming of messianic salvation at the time of the second advent of Jesus Christ, the Messiah of Israel.

John Calvin, a premier interpreter of the Bible, took "Israel" here to mean the church, composed of both Jews and Gentiles.

Many understand this of the Jewish people, as though Paul had said, that religion would again be restored among them as before: but I extend the word Israel to all the people of God, according to this meaning — "When the Gentiles shall come in, the Jews also shall return from their defection to the obedience of faith; and thus shall be completed the salvation of the whole Israel of God, which must be gathered from both; and yet in such a way that the Jews shall obtain the first place, being as it were the first-born in God's family."[5]

The usage of the term "Israel" in the Scriptures is opposed to this, and the usage in this section of Romans is also opposed. The word occurs about eleven times in chapters 9 – 11, and in the other ten (all those outside this instance) it refers to ethnic Israel. Further, one only has to read verses 25 – 26 with Calvin's meaning to see the weakness of it.

The Number of Them (Romans 11:26a)

Paul writes, "all Israel." What is meant? A study of such passages as 1 Kings 12:1; 2 Chronicles 12:1 – 5, and Daniel 9:11 will show that he meant Israel as a national whole, not every individual Israelite. The nation as a whole — that is, its leaders and the majority of the people — will turn to the Lord in the latter days. This meaning is confirmed by the fact that in rabbinic literature "all Israel" has this force.[6] The apostle adds the adjective "all" in verse 26 to stress the fact that he is speaking not just of a remnant, but of Israel as a nation ("his people," cf. 11:1). Paul does not mean all Israelites without exception, but Israel as a whole, not necessarily each individual Israelite. It is unlikely, both theologically and exegetically, that Paul would use the word "Israel" differently than he has in the last three chapters. Every use of "Israel" in Romans 9 – 11 refers to ethnic, or national, Israel. Never does the term include Gentiles.[7] The New Testament uses the term exactly the way Paul does in this section.

The Meaning (Romans 11:26a)

Thus, to sum up, Paul means that after the present period of Gentile ingathering into the covenantal blessings offered the fathers, there will come a time when Israel will be restored by God to her place under the blessing of the Lord.

THE SCRIPTURAL ATTESTATION

> [27] And this is my covenant with them
>   when I take away their sins."

It was not Paul's patriotism that led him to prophesy Jewish restoration; it was Scripture. Thus, in the final verses of the section (vv. 26b – 27), in a free blending of Old Testament passages, he supports his view by the Word of God. The passages are grounded in the truth of the three unconditional covenants of Israel (the Abrahamic, the Davidic, and the new). In verse 26b, the words about the coming of the Deliverer refer to the Davidic covenant, and in verse 27a the words are built on the words to Abraham in Genesis 17:4, although found in Isaiah 59:21. Thus, the Abrahamic covenant is in view. And in the final words in verse 27b, either Isaiah 27:9 or Jeremiah 31:33 – 34 is referred to, but the reference to the forgiveness of sins makes it clear that the new covenant is before the author. Thus, all the unconditional covenants find their fruition in the second advent and the events that follow. Divine logic (cf. vv. 11 – 24) and prophecy (vv. 25 – 27) look on to the restoration of Israel.

GOD'S AGENDA FOR THE NATIONS

The apostle now obliges his readers with a survey of the broad sweep of God's dealings with the nations (vv. 28 – 32), which is then followed by an overflowing doxology for the wisdom and knowledge of the God of heaven (vv. 33 – 36). The key words of the theodicy of Romans 9 – 11 are the words "mystery" and "mercy." Now mercy comes to the fore, being mentioned four times (vv. 30, 31, 32). Human history is the story of the mercy of God going out to the nations.

ANTITHESIS ONE: ENEMIES, YET ELECT

> [28] *As far as the gospel is concerned, they are enemies on your account; but as far as election is concerned, they are loved on account of the patriarchs,* [29] *for God's gifts and his call are irrevocable.*

According to the Gospel (Romans 11:28a)

Verses 28 – 32 "recapitulate"[8] what was said in verses 11 – 27, but with a broader sweep. Israel has been temporarily cast away but awaits a restoration. As C. K. Barrett points out, "the paragraph is brought to an end with two balanced sentences, each constructed on the same pattern.... The rhetorical pattern suggests that Paul is writing with care as well as feeling."[9]

In this first antithesis, the principal point the apostle makes is that Israel has an inevitable future, for God does not change (cf. Mal. 3:6). The word "enemies" might be misunderstood. The apostle is not speaking of Israel's enmity here, although he could have done that, for that has been their response to the coming of God's Messiah. The adjective here is passive in force; that is, God is treating

Israel as an enemy as the gospel goes forth in this age. They abide under a judicial hardening (11:25). Israel's treatment as enemies is "on your account," that is, for the sake of Gentile salvation in the present age.

According to the Election: Beloved (Romans 11:28b)

Looked at from the standpoint of the election of the nation, seen in the calling of Abraham, Isaac, and Jacob, with their descendants, Israel is beloved by God. The word "election," of course, refers to the covenant promises, particularly the source of the covenantal program, the Abrahamic ones. Israel is beloved, not for their sake, but for the ancestors' sakes. The promises are secured to Israel, not on the ground of their merit, but on the ground of God's fidelity to his word.

The Rationale (Romans 11:29)

The apostle's "for" introduces an explanation of the inevitability of the ethnic future of the nation Israel. The gifts and calling of God are not regretted. The immutability of the divine promises is the ground of Israel's status. The "gifts" are the effects of the calling of God, which is the electing call given to their ancestors and confirmed in the salvation of the members of the believing remnant. The gifts include those that are mentioned in 9:4 – 5 (cf. 3:3; Isa. 66:22). The election is binding on that last generation, but again, not of every individual, only of the nation as a whole.

ANTITHESIS TWO: DISOBEDIENCE AND MERCY

[30]*Just as you who were at one time disobedient to God have now received mercy as a result of their disobedience,* [31]*so they too have now become disobedient in order that they too may now receive mercy as a result of God's mercy to you.* [32]*For God has bound all men over to disobedience so that he may have mercy on them all.*

The Gentile Mercy (Romans 11:30)

The final of the balanced sentences follows. It too is a kind of reiteration of verses 11 – 27. The "for," which opens verse 30 in the original, explains the preceding and expands the argument. The end of the road for both Jew and Gentile in the divine agenda for the nations is the mercy of God, but for each of them, the nations and the nation, it leads to mercy through the experience of disobedience.[10]

That the apostle has the Gentiles primarily in mind is clear. He refers to their former disobedience in Old Testament times and their present reception of mercy by reason of the disobedience of the Jews. The plan of God is being worked out in the respective actions. As Barrett says, "In each case, behind disobedience and mercy, God wills and enacts the one as he wills and enacts the other."[11]

The Jewish Mercy (Romans 11:31)

The case of the Jews is handled in verse 31. The final "now" in the last clause is something of a problem, since some of the manuscripts do not have it, while others do. If the "now" is what Paul wrote, the apostle is referring either to the idea of verse 23, namely, that Israel's only hindrance to return to the Lord is her unbelief, or to the present messianic age, during which time, especially at its concluding hours, the nation will be saved.

Notice the process the apostle has in mind. First, there is Gentile disobedience, the apostle apparently referring to the opening chapters of Genesis and God's activity with them (cf. Gen. 1:1 – 11:26; Acts 17:30; Rom. 1:24, 26, 28). Second, there is Israel's election and then their subsequent disobedience, spanning the period of time from the call of Abraham to the cross (cf. Gen. 11:27 – Acts 1:26). Third, there is the period of Gentile election and Jewish disobedience, beginning with the day of Pentecost and concluding with the apostasy of the church (cf. Acts 2:1 – Rev. 3:22). During this time, Israel abides in rejection, being under judicial punishment as a nation (individuals, of course, are being saved as a remnant). Charles L. Feinberg reportedly remarked that his old Hebrew teacher used to say that "the Hebrews, like their language, have a past and a future but no present." The nation today still abides in unbelief. Fourth, the apostle has taught that Israel, made jealous by Gentile salvation, will be delivered and worldwide salvation may be expected (cf. Rom. 11:11 – 15, 23 – 24, 25 – 27).

The Rationale (Romans 11:32)

Verse 32 confirms and explains the preceding statement in verses 30 – 31, as the "for" suggests. The agenda of the nations has as its goal the display of the mercy of God to all the nations. The word "bound" is vivid, being used in a military context for the giving of people over to the sword (Ps. 77:62 LXX), metaphorically for the catching of fish (Luke 5:6), and also of people being shut up in prison. Arthur Way renders, "God shut the door on them all when they passed into the prison cell of disobedience, only with the intention of having mercy on all."[12]

But, as Shedd points out, conviction is prior to conversion.[13] So the goal, or aim, of God is mercy to all the nations. Universalism is not in view in the twofold use of the word "all." Paul refers to all without distinction, not all without exception. Further, the "all" here refers to the classes of nations, Gentile and Jewish, not primarily to the individuals involved. It was not that he intended to save all, and man's will defeated his purpose (cf. Rom. 8:29 – 30; 9:16, 18, 21). He intended to have mercy on all the nations, and he has succeeded. Those saved will have the testimony of Salvation Army officer John Allen, "I deserve to be damned; I deserve to be in hell; but God interfered!"[14]

THE DOXOLOGY

> [33] Oh, the depth of the riches of the wisdom and knowledge of God!
>   How unsearchable his judgments,
>   and his paths beyond tracing out!
> [34] "Who has known the mind of the Lord?
>   Or who has been his counselor?"
> [35] "Who has ever given to God,
>   that God should repay him?"
> [36] For from him and through him and to him are all things.
>   To him be the glory forever! Amen.

In Praise of Wisdom (Romans 11:33)

Paul now seems to be caught up in the spirit of Charles Wesley's song "Love Divine," with its "lost in wonder, love and praise." Why is Paul so overcome in his exultation? M. B. Riddle said, "We have learned Paul's meaning only when we can join in this ascription of praise."[15] He speaks first of the inscrutable "wisdom and knowledge of God." "Wisdom" is a reference to God's purpose for the nations, while "knowledge" refers to the means that he has employed in attaining the end. The wisdom and the knowledge of God are beyond humans. The Greek word translated "beyond tracing out" is an adjective coming from a verb that means "to track out." Shedd comments, "The divine decisions being self-moved, and wholly internal, are not traceable by the finite intellect."[16] The profundity and the meritlessness of his plans for us are beyond us, indeed.

The Challenge from the Scriptures (Romans 11:34 – 35)

Paul's "hymn"[17] is cast in Old Testament language. He cites Isaiah 40:13 in support of his preceding points, the first clause alluding to knowledge and the second to wisdom. Verse 35 continues with Job 41:11, and by the text the apostle indicates that God's goodness to us is not in repayment for human services. If it were true that God looked down through the years and saw who would believe and then chose those people on the basis of their decision in free will, then humankind would have given to God something for which we could claim recompense. In that case, the divine wisdom would not be a free wisdom and inexplicable to humans, as the apostle says in verse 33. The divine action would have been conditioned by human action, and it would then have been within the reach and cognizance of human calculation. In that case too we could not rightly say, "Salvation is of the Lord," for it would be of both man and God. But, thank God! His salvation has arisen from his determination in sovereign grace to bless his elect with eternal love (cf. Eph. 1:4 – 6).

The Rationale (Romans 11:36)

The independent sovereignty of God is a sufficient negative answer to the preceding questions from the Word of God. It is a resounding "no," for no one first gave, because all is from him. He is the source ("from"), the means ("through"), and the goal ("to") of all the divine acts of creation, providence, and redemption (cf. Dan. 2:21; 4:35).

As we might expect, the apostle concludes on the note of the ineffable glory of God in verse 36. *Sola fide* and *sola gratia*, as expounded so fully in chapters 1 – 8, lead on to the broader *soli Deo gloria!* Or, "by faith alone" and "by grace alone" lead to "to God alone be glory." His working among the nations, the Gentiles and Israel, all tends to his eternal glory. It is a monument to his faithfulness, his trustworthiness as seen in the keeping of the promises of his Word. Israel will have their future too. The promises to individual believers are just as reliable as God's promises to Israel.

Since Paul has thoroughly demonstrated that his gospel is true and the promises of Israel are still valid, the salvation of every Christian is secure.

DISCUSSION QUESTIONS

1. How is God's greatness shown through using the sin of Israel for the good of the Gentiles?

2. What is the difference between an unconditional and conditional covenant?

3. If Israel's restoration depended on their faithfulness, what would be the outcome?

4. What about the land promises given to Israel? Would the apostles, having the Old Testament, consider those Scriptures to be binding? On what basis should promises to Abraham be split into "to be fulfilled" and "to be unfulfilled" categories?

5. Can you pray this prayer: "Your kingdom come?"

6. Why should Paul's closing doxology be the doxology of every Christian?

CHAPTER 21

THE MERCIES OF GOD AND LIVING SACRIFICES

ROMANS 12:1–8

The preceding chapters in the epistle, in which the great doctrines of soteriology and eschatology have been expounded, are all practical chapters. What can be more practical than right thoughts about God? In fact, all life that pleases God can issue only from right theology and right thoughts about our triune God. Roy Harrisville insightfully begins his comments on Romans 12 by saying, "Now to what is vulgarly and erroneously called the 'practical' portion of the Romans letter."[1]

It is true, however, that with Romans 12 we come to the chapters that have an ethical stress. The theme of the righteousness of God is still in view (cf. 1:16–17), but here the righteousness of God develops in all the spheres of human activity.

THE GREAT REQUEST

[1]*Therefore, I urge you, brothers, in view of God's mercy, to offer your bodies as living sacrifices, holy and pleasing to God—this is your spiritual act of worship.*

The Motivation for Dedication (Romans 12:1a)

The "therefore" that opens the chapter is the fourth important "therefore" in the letter (cf. 2:1; 5:1; 8:1). The apostle is introducing inferential truth from the preceding chapters. He will press the entire Old Testament rite of sacrifice into symbolic service to New Testament Christianity.

"God's mercy" is the motivation for dedicating our bodies to the service of the Lord. The mercies of God are compelling and majestic. They envelop truths from election through effectual grace on to the fullness of justification, sanctification, and glorification. They are the free and unconditional product of eternal love and are conditioned by nothing but divine grace. Motivation comes from mercies.

Thus, the first step in knowing God's will and in dedicating ourselves to the Lord is the knowledge of a Savior, the Lord Jesus Christ. Walter Lüthi encapsulates Paul's strategy for motivating Christians: "Throughout eleven long chapters of his Letter to the Romans, Paul has tirelessly preached what God has done for believers, and not until the twelfth chapter do we hear the words: 'I appeal to you.' But even now that he has changed over to giving the Christians in Rome directions for their behaviour, he still addresses them as 'Brethren,' reminds them of 'the mercies of God.'"[2] It is in this spirit that the hymn writer Isaac Watts wrote, "Love so amazing, so divine, demands my soul, my life, my all!"[3]

The Content of the Request (Romans 12:1b)

The second step in the discovery of God's will is the presentation of our bodies. The language is sacrificial, although the word "offer" is not used in the Greek Old Testament of any offering. It is used primarily of the service of the priests in the Old Testament, and the reason for its choice may lie in the fact that this offering of our bodies is not a bloody offering. The tense of the verb is one that refers to the act of dedication as a definite act, like the "I do" of marriage or of induction into military service. It is an "I do" with continuing responsibilities. It is not "yield," because that connotes a passive idea; nor is it "surrender," which also has the idea of reluctance associated with it.

Many years ago I heard a preacher give a message on this text. He spoke of the glad giving of the verb, illustrating it in this way: "Let us suppose that on our next wedding anniversary I should buy some jewelry for my wife. If, in giving it to her, I should say, 'I'm yielding this to you,' or 'I'm surrendering this to you,' she might not think that I was very happy about giving the gift. The apostle speaks of the free and happy presentation of his body to the Lord for his use for time and for eternity."

God amazingly desires to use us for the glorification of the Son of God and for the gathering in of all his elect. And how rational it is to give him the key to all the doors within the house of our bodies! It is unreasonable to give the key of the soul to God and that of the body to the devil.

The Description of the Sacrifice (Romans 12:1c)

Paul, by the words "living sacrifices," implicitly draws our minds to the slain sacrifices of the Old Testament ritual that involuntarily went to their deaths. He would have us voluntarily give ourselves to him. Is it not a marvel of grace that those described in 3:9 – 20 should be a gift pleasing to him? The apostle adds that this is "your spiritual act of worship." The internal worship of the mind and heart is that to which he refers, contrasting that with the outward rites of the Levitical cultus of the Old Testament (cf. John 4:23 – 24).

THE PROCESS OF REALIZATION

> [2]*Do not conform any longer to the pattern of this world, but be transformed by the renewing of your mind. Then you will be able to test and approve what God's will is — his good, pleasing and perfect will.*

The Outward Side (Romans 12:2a)

The third step in finding the will of God is a continuing process. The words "Do not conform" represent a Greek verb dealing with the outward side of things. Christians should not model themselves after the fleeting, superficial fashions of the age. Only the truth of God is true and eternal; humanism is doomed to extinction.

The Inward Side (Romans 12:2b)

The fourth step in the discovery of God's will lies in the transformation of the inner life of the believer. Nonconformity to the outward fashion of the age is not enough. The apostle would have us be conformed to Jesus Christ, what he says is sure to eventually happen. He would, however, like for this to begin now (cf. 8:29). The word translated "be transformed" is built on the same root as the one in Philippians 2:6, which refers to an inner change that is more than superficial. If we ask, "How can we be constantly in the process of being transformed?" the answer, found in the text, is by the renewing of our mind. And if still another question is asked, "What is the renewing of our minds, and how is it accomplished?" the answer is before us. The renewing of our minds is the manner of transformation, and since the mind of Christ is found in the Word of God, it seems plain that the renewing of the mind is to be found in the contemplation of the Scriptures.

The Great Result (12:2c)

The apostle concludes the section by writing, "Then you will be able to test and approve what God's will is — his good, pleasing and perfect will." In the taking of the steps mentioned previously, one discerns, or "tests and approves," God's will. The Greek word rendered "test and approve" means to "learn by experience," according to Richard Weymouth.[4] We often wish that God would drop down from heaven a map for us. This he does with his preceptive will, found in the Bible, but his particular will for us can be found only by trial, by the experience of life.

Just as the weaver's pattern is only seen as he progresses in his work, so we discover the will of God for us as life continues. The accomplishment of his purposes for us will be found in the submissive response to God's will found in his Word. Prayer and action in the light of what we have already had revealed to us leads on to the proving of his good and acceptable and perfect will for us.

Advice for Using Spiritual Gifts

Spiritual gifts are spiritual abilities given by the Holy Spirit for service to God, not for worship. There are differences in the gifts, some of them being utterance gifts, such as teaching, and others being nonutterance, such as ruling. Some were given for a time, such as the gift of apostleship, and others have been given throughout the centuries, such as the gift of pastor-teacher. Thus, there are some that may be classified as temporary and others that may be classified as permanent.

THE EXHORTATION TO HUMILITY

[3]For by the grace given me I say to every one of you: Do not think of yourself more highly than you ought, but rather think of yourself with sober judgment, in accordance with the measure of faith God has given you.

The apostle, having just said that the offering of the body of the believer to God as a spiritual sacrifice leads to the realization of God's will in the believer's life, now turns to the first step in the realization of his will. What follows, in the exhortation to humility, is part of the Christian offering. Paul begins by saying that he speaks "by the grace given me," referring to the gift of apostleship (cf. 1:5; 15:15 – 16). He, therefore, speaks with authority.

The content of his exhortation is that the reader should "not think of yourself more highly than you ought, but rather think of yourself with sober judgment, in accordance with the measure of faith God has given you." It is to be noted, first of all, that the exhortation is one of universal application, for it is directed to "every one of you." Then, the sense of the appeal is that one is to entertain sober views of oneself, a grace singled out by the Lord for imitation by his disciples (Matt. 11:29; 18:2–4).

The apostle's words have a peculiar pungency, for there is a wordplay in his appeal. It is difficult to bring out the exact force of his use of words in English, but it has been rendered by Henry Alford in this way: "not to be high-minded above that which he ought to be minded, but to be so minded as to be sober-minded."[5] Commenting on the virtue Paul asks for here, William Shedd says, "The apostle makes humility to be the foundation of Christian ethics and morality."[6] The expression "the measure of faith" probably refers to the standard of faith, the faith by which we believe, a virtue given by God (cf. Phil. 1:29).

THE EXHORTATION TO UNITY

[4]Just as each of us has one body with many members, and these members do not all have the same function,

The apostle begins verse 4 with a connective, "for," in the Greek. Since Christians are a body and need one another, we cannot afford to neglect the grace of humility. Only a self-existent being, isolated from others by virtue of his own inherent powers, is able to neglect humility. Thus, the only person excused from the practice of the virtue is God, the only self-existent being in the universe. The apostle stresses that all the members of the body do not have the same function. Gifts are given to each, but the gifts differ.

The metaphor the apostle uses is "one body." It is likely that the apostle is using the word as a simile, and that he is not speaking specifically of the body of Christ, the church (cf. 1 Cor. 6:15; 12:27).[7] The stress on unity here is important, and an important truth undergirds Paul's words. We are one, and Ephesians 4:1–6 sets forth the spiritual unity that we enjoy; it is a unity in Christ even though it is not fully realized in our daily lives.

THE EXHORTATIONS CONCERNING DIVERSITIES

[5]so in Christ we who are many form one body, and each member belongs to all the others. [6]We have different gifts, according to the grace given us. If a man's gift is prophesying, let him use it in proportion to his faith. [7]If it is serving, let him serve; if it is teaching, let him teach; [8]if it is encouraging, let him encourage; if it

is contributing to the needs of others, let him give generously; if it is leadership, let him govern diligently; if it is showing mercy, let him do it cheerfully.

Paul reminds readers at the beginning of this section that God gives gifts (v. 6) that differ "according to the grace given us" (cf. 1 Cor. 12:11). He stresses here that they are given in grace, and in 1 Corinthians he emphasizes that they are given sovereignly. The Holy Spirit exercises a "royal freedom"[8] in their disposition. Thus, the gifts are diverse but universal among the members of the body. In light of 1 Corinthians 12:31, they are not of equal importance, although all are equally necessary.

Paul begins with the gift of prophecy, one of the more important gifts in the early church. It is not the gift of emphatic utterance, as it is popularly thought to be. Its distinguishing feature is that it is an utterance that is the result of particular divine revelation (cf. Ex. 7:1; Acts 11:27–28; 21:10–11). It was revelation, not illumination or teaching. Since the canon of Scripture has closed, the spiritual gift of prophecy no longer needs to be sovereignly given by the Holy Spirit.

Prophecy had two aspects. First, the prophet foretold the future. Second, he expressed the mind of God in the present time[9] (cf. 1 Cor. 14:3). Modern-day "prophets" do not foretell the future in any specific way and are given generally to meaningless platitudes, which, like the Delphic Oracle, may be fulfilled in many different ways. The biblical prophet was to prophesy "in proportion to his faith," an expression that refers to the rule of faith. That is, the prophecy is to agree with the faith. Shedd comments, "The injunction is the key to systematic theology. No alleged Christian tenet can be correct which conflicts with other Christian tenets. All Christian truth must be consistent with Christianity."[10]

The word for "serving" (v. 7) is one that literally is derived from words meaning "through dust," suggesting the activity that ought to characterize a person with this gift.[11]

While the prophet, as noted above, gave forth revelation, the teacher is illumined as he studies the revealed Word, and the things that he learns he communicates to the body of believers.

The gift of exhortation is similar to the gift of teaching, although there is a different emphasis and method in the exercise of the gift. The one who exhorts has his eyes on a concrete situation.

The gift of giving, the apostle says, is to be exercised with liberality. Giving is not to be exercised from ulterior motives or in ostentation. Cranfield comments, "We can hardly improve on Althaus's comment: 'Giving requires the simplicity, which without ulterior motives or secondary purposes is wholly directed toward the other person's need and has no other consideration than that of relieving the need.'"[12]

A leader is to rule and "govern diligently" and thus might usually be associated with the elder or bishop, but mercy might be just as surely associated with the deacon. His duties usually encompass ministry to the needy, the poor, the weak, and the sick.

DISCUSSION QUESTIONS

1. True or false? Serving other Christians is directly related to justification by faith alone. Explain.

2. Can diverse giftedness positively contribute to the unity of the body of Christ? How?

3. There was a time in World War II when the führer was in total command of all western Europe. Winston Churchill called the British Parliament together to give them the gloomy news concerning the fall of France and Hitler's defeat of the allies. He said to them, "The whole free world is dependent on England now." Then, after pausing a bit for the full effect of the words to take hold, he added, "Gentlemen, I find this rather inspiring."[13] How can the service of the Lord God be exciting to every Christian?

CHAPTER 22

LOVE AND SERVICE

ROMANS 12:9–21

The love that Paul wishes to see in the Romans is one that works in holiness and right living. Thomas Watson, a Puritan, spoke to that point, "Faith deals with invisibles, but God hates that love which is invisible."[1] Puritan John Trapp said most pointedly, "Affection without action is like Rachel, beautiful but barren."

The rest of chapter 12 contains a number of injunctions to "deep, unaffected and practical love."[2] The commands are reminiscent of those in the Sermon on the Mount, and in this they form a link between the law of Moses as interpreted by the Lord and the "law of Christ" as interpreted by the apostle (cf. Gal. 6:2). Commentator Alan Johnson has entitled this section "The Law of Love Applied."[3] Of course, the kind of love that Paul sets forth is a far cry from the sentimental softness that the modern world calls love. In the biblical world love is in complete harmony with the divine righteousness and holiness, thoroughly consonant with the punishment of sinners. Love to be true love must be love "in the truth" (cf. Phil. 1:9; 3 John 1). Love to our world is gushy and mushy or, as radio preacher J. Vernon McGee is fond of saying, playing on the Greek word for love, "I'm tired of sloppy agape!" Biblical love has an astringent ruggedness about it, mixed with the tenderness of the deepest commitment of the will to the object of divine grace. It is holy love, free, distinguishing, and gracious.

THE FIRST TRIPLET: A LOVE THAT CAN HATE

> *[9]Love must be sincere. Hate what is evil; cling to what is good. [10]Be devoted to one another in brotherly love. Honor one another above yourselves.*

The believer's response to the mercies of God, Paul says in 12:1–2, is the offering of our bodies as living sacrifices to God. Paul now expresses more specific exhortations, directed to accomplishing such sacrifice. These are not random commands, but they are closely related to one another.

The first of the exhortations reads, "Love must be sincere." The apostle is speaking of a genuine love, not like that of people described in Scripture whose words are "smooth as butter," but whose true feelings are "drawn swords" (cf. Ps. 55:21). Reflection on the extent of the divine grace manifested to us ("in view of God's mercy") in our lost condition ought to be sufficient to bring us to unfeigned love of the brethren (cf. 1 Peter 1:22). It is clear that if God has loved others and saved them as he has loved and saved us, we can and must love them too.

Paul then urges his readers to hate evil and cling to the good. Is this an irrelevant interruption? No. This is just as essential to the noblest love without hypocrisy as sincerity. Notice that the second precept, the clinging (or cleaving) to the good, is the ground of the first, for if we are to hate evil, we must love the good.

The apostle exhorts his readers to a familial love. Paul here speaks of a more restricted love for the family of God. The sentiment is similar to that expressed in Galatians 6:10, "Therefore, as we have opportunity, let us do good to all people, especially to those who belong to the family of believers." The Greek word rendered "be devoted" refers to family affection, like the love of a mother for a child, or of a father for a son, or simply the love that members of one family have for other members of the family, no matter how wayward they may be. Christians are to have kind affection for one another.

THE SECOND TRIPLET: WHOLEHEARTED SERVICE

> *[11]Never be lacking in zeal, but keep your spiritual fervor, serving the Lord.*

Christian Diligence (Romans 12:11a)

The second triplet has to do with Christian diligence, fervency, and service. The apostle writes, "Never be lacking in zeal." The Greek word means "diligence," and it has its application not only to a person's business but to all that he or she does.

It is true that many businesspeople are on fire for their business but are at the same time all ice for the business of the Lord. We spend long hours in business to get ahead, concentrate for most of our waking days on how to make our business bigger, go to sleep with plans for our work buzzing in our minds, but in the meantime reserve a few hours on Sunday for the most important work of all, the work of the Lord. We occupy ourselves with the temporalities and neglect the eternalities. May God enable us to be diligent in our work, diligent in our play, and especially diligent in the spiritual things of the Lord.

Christian Fervency (Romans 12:11b)

The apostle continues, "but keep your spiritual fervor" (the word "spirit" may be a reference to the Holy Spirit, in which case it should be capitalized, but the meaning is essentially the same, for all true fervency comes ultimately from him). The word rendered "fervent" comes from a root that means "boiling." Paul refers to a fire below that makes the soul's depths boil with fervent earnestness. Paul does not have in mind the indolent kind of emotion that emotes but does not lead to work for him. Biblical fervency is yoked to work for the Lord. How can one be "cool" in the light of the mercies of God? Those who understand God's gracious salvation must be fervent in spirit. And if we are not, we must go over again those "mercies," so wonderfully expounded in Romans 1 – 11.

Christian Service (Romans 12:11c)

Paul concludes this verse with "serving the Lord" — to think that we are serving, working for the Lord himself. What a privilege! And why should we be diligent? Consider the greatness of the work, the greatness of the enemy of the souls of people, the brevity of the time in which we are able to work (the night soon comes when no one can work), and the extreme gravity of the issues involved, life and death. The personal reason for our diligent service is Paul's word in Galatians 2:20, "the Son of God, who loved me and gave himself for me."

THE THIRD TRIPLET: THE INNER SECRETS

[12] Be joyful in hope, patient in affliction, faithful in prayer.

This final verse of the section is the only verse that refers to the inner secrets of the Christian life. First, the apostle asks for Christians to rejoice in the light of our hope. Joy is not a matter of temperament or of circumstances. Joy comes from faith in the promises of God, which remind us that we have an omnipotent Father, a divine continuing providence that guards our way (cf. Rom. 8:28), the abiding presence of the Lord Jesus Christ (cf. Matt. 28:19), and a heavenly home (John 14:1 – 3).

If joyful, then we can endure too (cf. Rom. 5:2 – 4). And we will have tribulation in this world because we are related to him whom the world hates. In fact, the world's hatred of Christians is simply the continuation of its quarrel with Jesus Christ (cf. John 15:18 – 19; 16:33; Acts 14:22). The Lord, however, has promised us peace and good cheer in the midst of the tribulations we face in the world.

Finally, Paul concludes with "faithful in prayer," reminding us that we endure as we pray (cf. Acts 1:14; 2:42; 6:4; Eph. 6:18; Col. 4:2). It is a fitting way to conclude the three great triplets of Christian exhortation. We cannot help but be impressed with the contrast presented between the practices of modern Christians who so vociferously claim the experience of being born again and these precepts of Paul.

THE FOURTH TRIPLET: THE LAW OF CONCERN

> [13]*Share with God's people who are in need. Practice hospitality.*
> [14]*Bless those who persecute you; bless and do not curse.* [15]*Rejoice with those who rejoice; mourn with those who mourn.*

At verse 13 Paul moves from the innermost region of communion with God to the wide field of duties in relation to people or, as Alexander Maclaren puts it, from the secrecies to the publicities.[4] Paul continues the presentation of his exhortations in the form of a series of triplets of virtues.

Concern in Needs (Romans 12:13)

We might call this triplet "the law of love," speaking of love in the biblical sense. Zeal toward believers, expressed outwardly, is before the reader. In our day of Social Security, Medicare, Medicaid, unemployment insurance, and other forms of governmental welfare, we might be inclined to forget that welfare toward the saints is often needed.

Hospitality was a needed thing in ancient days when no hotels were available. The small inns that were available were often dirty and were places of immorality. Christians needed hospitality when they traveled away from home. The apostle urges the practice of the virtue, for the word rendered "practice" is a word that means to pursue. Believers are to aggressively pursue the virtue, seeking out opportunities to be hospitable today as well.

Concern in Goodwill (Romans 12:14)

In verse 14 Paul writes, "Bless those who persecute you; bless and do not curse." This command expresses a responsibility that Christians have toward society in general.

Concern in Sympathetic Adjustment (Romans 12:15)

The apostle continues, "Rejoice with those who rejoice; mourn with those who mourn." Adjustment to others' moods and tragedies is the point. It seems to require more grace to rejoice with the rejoicing than to weep with the weeping. As Chrysostom said, it is easier to weep with those who weep than to rejoice with those that rejoice, because nature itself prompts the former, but envy stands in the way of the latter.[5]

THE FIFTH TRIPLET: THE LAW OF SELFLESSNESS

[16]Live in harmony with one another. Do not be proud, but be willing to associate with people of low position. Do not be conceited.

In True Harmony (Romans 12:16a)

All three of these clauses deal with mental attitudes, explanatory of the preceding commands. When the apostle writes, "Live in harmony with one another," he does not mean that we should see "eye-to-eye" on every point. The text refers to the cultivation of the deeper unity that has been given to all genuine believers in the possession of a common basic body of belief. All believers are partakers of the life of Christ and thus share in a common relation to him. The things that unite us should be before us always, even in the moments at which we must differ over the details of faith and practice.

In Lowliness (Romans 12:16b)

The apostle is probably thinking of things, not people, when he says, "Be willing to associate with people of low position," for the word translated as "people of low position" may be neuter in form. In the light of the preceding, "do not be proud," it seems a bit more likely that he is thinking of things here. If so, then he is exhorting the believers not to disdain the lower places, the lower stations, and the lower interests of life. He is encouraging us to remember that excessive ambition often festers into neglect of the more important things of life, the things of the Lord. In seeking the lowlier things of life, he may discover, as John Bunyan's shepherd boy did in the classic *Pilgrim's Progress,* that the flower of heart's ease grows in just such lowly valleys.

In Mind (Romans 12:16c)

Finally, in this triplet Paul adds, "Be not be conceited," speaking of intellectual conceit. A vain young man reportedly said to D. L. Moody, "You know, Mr.

Moody, I am a self-made man." Mr. Moody replied with the well-known quote, "Young man, you have relieved the Almighty of a great responsibility."

THE SIXTH TRIPLET: THE LAW OF NONHOSTILITY

[17]Do not repay anyone evil for evil. Be careful to do what is right in the eyes of everybody. [18]If it is possible, as far as it depends on you, live at peace with everyone.

In Response to Wrongs (Romans 12:17a)

"Do not repay evil for evil," the apostle continues. These words, and the words of the remainder of the chapter, for the most part, have to do with duty in the face of the world's hostility. The world will hate us because it hated our Lord, and the apostle asks us not to respond in kind.

In Noble Life (Romans 12:17b)

Paul adds, "Be careful to do what is right in the eyes of everybody." It is clear from this imperative that the apostle believed that the world had essentially correct notions of morality.

In Peace (Romans 12:18)

And now comes the well-known injunction, "If it is possible, as far as it depends on you, live at peace with everyone." Peace depends both on objective and subjective things. Objectively the Christian can never be at peace with the world, for it continues its quarrel with Jesus Christ by persecuting his followers. In fact, it is our Lord who said, "Do not suppose that I have come to bring peace to the earth. I did not come to bring peace, but a sword" (Matt. 10:34). However, from the subjective standpoint, that is, from our side, the apostle asks that we give no occasion for conflict ourselves. When the quarrel is struck up, let it be from the other side.

THE SEVENTH TRIPLET: THE LAW OF NONRETALIATION

[19]Do not take revenge, my friends, but leave room for God's wrath, for it is written: "It is mine to avenge; I will repay," says the Lord. [20]On the contrary:

"If your enemy is hungry, feed him;
*   if he is thirsty, give him something to drink.*
In doing this, you will heap burning coals on his head."

[21]Do not be overcome by evil, but overcome evil with good.

In Vengeance (Romans 12:19; cf. Deuteronomy 32:35)

In these final verses, Paul continues his stress on our duty in the face of the hostility of the world. It involves a denial of the natural instincts that come from the old self within. What he says is explanatory of how we are to maintain peace in the world (cf. v. 18).

Paul reminds the believer to "leave room for God's wrath." It is he who will render vengeance. Objections to divine retribution are both unethical and immoral. In fact, Paul suggests that it is the Christian's duty to desire that divine justice be administered by the sovereign Lord.

The text has something to say to modern attitudes toward punishment of criminals. Punishment is for requital and does not aim at the improvement or rehabilitation of the criminal. Thus, punishment is in its own nature endless, and the Supreme Being is the only one who can inflict it. Ultimately, sin is an offense against an infinite Being, and the wrong is always wrong, just as wrong ten years from the time of its doing as it was on the day it was done. Time does not reduce guilt. Such guilt can be paid for only by a method satisfactory to the Father. That method is the cross of Jesus Christ.

In Beneficence (Romans 12:20; cf. Proverbs 25:21, 22)

The injunction to feed and give drink to an enemy, because in so doing we will "heap burning coals on his head" is a metaphor for causing keen anguish in those who oppose the saints.

In Conquering Evil with Good (Romans 12:21)

Paul's concluding admonition is related to the preceding, and the apostle seems to be saying that if we do what he has just said, that is, treat an enemy well, we may gain a friend. A godly way to get rid of an enemy is to make him a friend. In this way evil will be overcome by good.

CONCLUSION

As we look over the chapter, it becomes clear that the apostle's emphasis is on the necessity of being something first, and then of doing something. Right conduct can flow only from right being and thinking. Thus, the first step in the fulfillment of 12:3 – 21 can be accomplished only by the "Christian offering" that Paul refers to in verse 1, and the transformation of the believer by the renewing of the believer's mind through the Word of God (set forth in v. 2).

DISCUSSION QUESTIONS

1. How does biblical love motivate us to action?

2. How is it possible to biblically love other people even if there are no emotional feelings toward the person or persons? Explain.

3. What are some ways in which Christians can stoke the coals of love for their Christian church family?

4. Name some specific ways believers can overcome evil with good?

CHAPTER 23

THE CHRISTIAN CITIZEN AND THE DAY

ROMANS 13:1–14

The careful and attentive reader of the epistle to the Romans notices something of a tension between the opening and closing words of the apostle in chapter 13. In the beginning, he writes, "Everyone must submit himself to the governing authorities" (v. 1), while near the end, he exclaims, "The night [in the context a reference to the present age] is nearly over; the day is almost here" (v. 12).

There is a problem here, if we remember Paul's words in 12:2, "Do not conform any longer to the pattern of this world." If we are not to be conformed to this age, should we, then, pay our federal, state, city, and county taxes? Should we vote? Did not Paul write that we were citizens of another land? What does he mean by "our citizenship is in heaven. And we eagerly await a Savior from there, the Lord Jesus Christ" (Phil. 3:20)? And did not the writer of Hebrews say much the same thing, "But you have come to Mount Zion, to the heavenly Jerusalem, the city of the living God" (Heb. 12:22)?

It may be helpful to remember that a believer lives in many spheres. In the first place, there is the personal sphere of life encompassed by the Lord and the believer only. In this sphere he is to live according to the preceptive will of God, expressed in the Word of God.

Second, the believer lives in a family, and in this sphere is responsible for obedience to the Scriptures that address family life. The husband is the head of the wife and is to render to her the love that Christ had and has for the church, while the wife is to be in submission to her husband. Children are to obey their parents in the Lord.

In the third place, the believer lives in the church, in the sense that he is a member of the body of those who have come by grace to faith in Christ. In this sphere of life the believer is responsible to be in submission to the elders of the church, who have the rule over us (cf. Heb. 13:7, 17).

Finally, we live in the sphere of the state. In the state we have certain responsibilities too, and it is of these that Paul now writes.

PUBLIC OBLIGATIONS TO THE STATE

¹Everyone must submit himself to the governing authorities, for there is no authority except that which God has established. The authorities that exist have been established by God. ²Consequently, he who rebels against the authority is rebelling against what God has instituted, and those who do so will bring judgment on themselves. ³For rulers hold no terror for those who do right, but for those who do wrong. Do you want to be free from fear of the one in authority? Then do what is right and he will commend you. ⁴For he is God's servant to do you good. But if you do wrong, be afraid, for he does not bear the sword for nothing. He is God's servant, an agent of wrath to bring punishment on the wrongdoer. ⁵Therefore, it is necessary to submit to the authorities, not only because of possible punishment but also because of conscience.

⁶This is also why you pay taxes, for the authorities are God's servants, who give their full time to governing. ⁷Give everyone what you owe him: If you owe taxes, pay taxes; if revenue, then revenue; if respect, then respect; if honor, then honor.

The Command (Romans 13:1)

The believer's obligations to society are now before the reader. Romans 12:3 – 21 set out our obligations that devolve on us because we are in the body of Christ, while chapter 13 sets out our responsibilities because we are in the human race.

The word rendered "submit" is the apostle's familiar word for submission. In fact, the New Testament uses it to speak of many different kinds of subjection (cf. 1 Cor. 16:16; Eph. 5:21 – 22, 24; Titus 3:1; James 4:7; 1 Peter 2:18; 5:5). Believers must submit to the government as we would to the Lord.

The Causes (Romans 13:2 – 6)

Paul gives several reasons for submission to the authorities; the first is because God has ordained the higher powers (cf. vv. 1 – 2). It is, therefore, expedient to be in submission to them until the "day" comes (cf. v. 12).

Second, the apostle points out that the powers approve that which is good and punish that which is evil (cf. vv. 3 – 6). The sentiment is the same as that given by Peter (cf. 1 Peter 2:14). In these verses, we move from authority through law and justice to the sword. The mention of the sword implies that ultimate authority, the authority over physical life, has been delegated to the higher powers. Capital punishment finds divine justification from this passage.

The Conclusion (Romans 13:7)

The apostle concludes: "Give everyone what you owe him: If you owe taxes, pay taxes; if revenue, then revenue [he has in mind certain secondary levies here, similar to our customs duties]; if respect, then respect; if honor, then honor." When the ship of state is in danger of sinking, the believers are not to forsake it like rats leaving a sinking ship. They are to stay at their posts in obedience to the will of God. Our political leaders are to have our submission as long as they do not ask us to sin.

Our Lord's words to the chief priests and the scribes, and to others, point to the principle for which the apostle is arguing. When they asked, "Is it right for us to pay taxes to Caesar or not?" Jesus replied, using a visual aid of a denarius, "Then give to Caesar what is Caesar's, and to God what is God's" (Luke 20:19 – 26). In the difference of the conjunctions "or" (v. 22) and "and" (v. 25), we have the essence of our Lord's words and viewpoint. It is not a matter of "either/or," but of "both/and," when we are speaking of submission to the human authorities and to the divine authority. We are to give obedience to both.

Someone may ask, "Are we to render obedience if the government of the land is despotic and violates the will of God, as expressed in the Scriptures?" In the matters in which there is a clear violation of the principles of the Word, we are to resist. The apostles followed this path, as Acts indicates (cf. Acts 4:17 – 21; 5:29, 40 – 42). When told that they were not to preach the gospel, the apostles continued doing just that, following the higher principle, "We must obey God rather than men." We can do nothing better than to follow the lead of the apostles (cf. Dan. 3:16 – 18).

PRIVATE OBLIGATIONS WITHIN THE STATE

⁸Let no debt remain outstanding, except the continuing debt to love one another, for he who loves his fellowman has fulfilled the law. ⁹The commandments, "Do not commit adultery," "Do not murder," "Do not steal," "Do not covet," and whatever other commandment there may be, are summed up in this one rule: "Love your neighbor as yourself." ¹⁰Love does no harm to its neighbor. Therefore love is the fulfillment of the law.

The Negative Side (Romans 13:8)

The negative side of things is taken up first, with Paul writing, "Let no debt remain outstanding, except the continuing debt to love one another, for he who loves his fellowman has fulfilled the law." John Murray comments on "let no debt remain outstanding":

> The force of the imperative is that we are to have no unpaid debts; that we are not to be in debt to any. In accord with the analogy of Scripture this cannot be taken to mean that we may never incur financial obligations, that we may not borrow from others in case of need (cf. Exodus 22:25; Psalm 37:26; Matthew 5:42; Luke 6:35). But it does condemn the looseness with which we contract debts and particularly the indifference so often displayed in the discharging of them.[1]

The Positive Side (Romans 13:8–10)

The apostle here argues that love is the fulfillment of the law of Moses, and that he who loves fulfills the ultimate obligation to people. All the particular statutes of the Decalogue, insofar as they relate to obligations to fellow humans, are summed up in the command, "You shall love your neighbor as yourself." The commands of the second table are referred to, for they pertain to the relations of people with people. In verse 10 he writes in the negative form, "Love does no harm to its neighbor," but the positive is implied: "Love doeth good," as William Shedd suggests.[2] In this way love fulfills the law.

PERSONAL ESCHATOLOGICAL INCENTIVE TO ITS FULFILLMENT

> [11] *And do this, understanding the present time. The hour has come for you to wake up from your slumber, because our salvation is nearer now than when we first believed.* [12] *The night is nearly over; the day is almost here. So let us put aside the deeds of darkness and put on the armor of light.* [13] *Let us behave decently, as in the daytime, not in orgies and drunkenness, not in sexual immorality and debauchery, not in dissension and jealousy.* [14] *Rather, clothe yourselves with the Lord Jesus Christ, and do not think about how to gratify the desires of the sinful nature.*

The Coming of the Lord (Romans 13:11)

In verse 11 the apostle introduces an incentive to the fulfillment of the obligations laid by God on believers by referring to the fact that the time for the close of the age is drawing nigh. The apostle refers to the present time as the "night" (v. 12) and, therefore, it is high time that we awake from sleep. Our ultimate salvation is nearer than when we believed. The exhortation is for drowsy believers who are allowing opportunities to slip by them.

The sleep out of which they are to awake is the sleep of selfishness, the doctrinal sleep of those who refuse to see the importance of the theology of the Scriptures, and the spiritual somnambulists who are so numerous in our evangelical churches. They are outwardly walking and alive, often teaching, praying, and reading in the assemblies of the saints, but inwardly they are asleep. Paul says it is high time they awake. The exhortation is grounded in the fact that the believers are nearer the conclusion of their race and fight of faith than they were when they became Christians. It is likely that Paul refers to Christ's second advent. "Salvation" is used here of the future salvation from the presence of sin, that is, when believers pass into the presence of the Lord at his advent (cf. 5:9).

The Conduct Expected (Romans 13:12 – 13)

Three exhortations follow in the light of the fact that the day is at hand. First, we are to cast off the works of darkness, the works that characterized the old life (cf. Eph. 4:17 – 19, 22 – 24). Second, we are to put on the armor of light, a reference to the holy life proper for believers. That the apostle speaks of "armor" may suggest that he has the Roman soldier in mind, who after his day's work laid aside his armor to carouse through the night and then donned it again in the morning to return to his work. Paul had seen many of them in his time, often having firsthand contact with them, for they were assigned to guard him. Third, Paul calls on us to walk decently in holiness, not in immorality.

The Conclusion (Romans 13:14)

The apostle's words were addressed to those who were already believers, for Christ must be in us before he can be on us. "Clothe yourselves" is an aorist tense verb that refers to a definite, positive act. The name used of our Lord here suggests the various aspects of his person and work. He is the Lord, and all the faculties belong to him. He is Jesus, the saver and sanctifier and preserver from sin. He is Christ, the Messiah, the Prophet who teaches, the Priest who has offered the offering by which we enter the veil of divine communion, and the King under whose sway is everything. The clothes of the works of darkness are to be put off, and the clothes of the Lord himself are to be put on. These are the clothes that really do make the man (cf. Col. 3:12 – 17). The negative action concludes the chapter. The tense of the verb here is instructive. It is a present imperative, and it refers to continual action of not stirring up the remainder of the flesh that abides in all believers (cf. 7:1 – 8:39).

DISCUSSION QUESTIONS

1. Is paying taxes an act of worship? Why or why not?

2. Is bad government better than anarchy? If so, how? If not, why not?

3. Why are so many Christians vehemently against the death penalty?

4. Instead of saying, "our salvation is nearer now than when we first believed," could it be said of the unbeliever, "It is high time that you should awake out of sleep, for now is your damnation nearer than when you first heard the gospel and rejected it?" Explain your answer.

5. How does anticipating the soon return of Jesus help us to submit to governmental authorities?

CHAPTER 24

THE CHRISTIAN'S FAVORITE INDOOR SPORT

ROMANS 14:1–23

"Paul enjoyed his Christian liberty to the full," F. F. Bruce has written, adding, "Never was a Christian more thoroughly emancipated from un-Christian inhibitions and taboos. So completely emancipated was he from spiritual bondage that he was not even in bondage to his emancipation."[1] Martin Luther said, "A Christian man is a most free lord of all, subject to none."[2] These expressions of freedom are harmonious with Paul's thought in Romans 14.

The apostle's concerns here have to do with food (vv. 2, 17) and festivals (vv. 5–6), which were problems for the culture of his time. It is clear that these issues are not immoral in themselves. For this reason, the section is said to be about "debatable things," or "the morally indifferent things." Our concerns today, somewhat parallel to these, are such things as the relation of a believer to tobacco, alcohol, movies, TV, dancing, and such things. Christians have differing opinions concerning these things, often differing over them in different parts of the world. It is in these differing opinions that the spiritual pride of believers is often manifested. In fact, Ray Stedman is right when he says that the desire to change one another in these debatable things is "the favorite indoor sport of Christians."[3] We want our fellow Christians to subscribe to our own list of taboos, and we often take a bit of pleasure in having them submit to us in our inhibitions. The important question, however, is this: What does the Bible say about such things?

Romans 14 is bound together with the preceding chapter, for the apostle is still speaking of the application of the righteousness of God to our daily lives. So, the subject is the application of the divine righteousness, which we now possess by imputation through faith alone, to debatable things.

FOOD AND THE RECEPTION OF THE WEAK

> [1] *Accept him whose faith is weak, without passing judgment on disputable matters.* [2] *One man's faith allows him to eat everything, but another man, whose faith is weak, eats only vegetables.* [3] *The man who eats everything must not look down on him who does not, and the man who does not eat everything must not condemn the man who does, for God has accepted him.* [4] *Who are you to judge someone else's servant? To his own master he stands or falls. And he will stand, for the Lord is able to make him stand.*

The Command for Reception (Romans 14:1)

The specific debatable things involved the eating of "meat" (v. 21), the drinking of wine (v. 21), and the observance of certain festival "days" (vv. 5–6).

The apostle speaks of brethren as "weak" (v. 2) and as "strong" (15:1). The weak are those who have scruples regarding foods, drink, and the observance of certain days. The strong are those who believe they have freedom to eat and drink what they wish and to observe certain days or not. Paul seems to be addressing both Gentile and Jewish scruples. On the one hand, the Jews had scruples concerning certain meats. They could not eat pork according to the Mosaic law and, in fact, could not even eat beef or lamb if they were not prepared according to the law. Thus, it is easy to see that some of the weaker brethren may well have been those with scruples regarding such food, derived from their acquaintance with the law. On the other hand, the Jews did not have any scruples over drinking wine. Therefore, this scruple regarding alcohol was probably one that originated from Gentile excesses stemming from their past lifestyle (cf. v. 21). Both William Shedd and C. K. Barrett are right, then, in seeing the strong as disparaging both Gentile and Jewish believers, or believers affected by both Gentile and Jewish scruples.[4]

The section begins with the Pauline command, "Accept him whose faith is weak, without passing judgment on disputable matters." The expression "disputable matters" is literally "not to disputes of doubts." The point is simply that the believers are to be received into the fellowship of the believing body, but not simply for theological argument or debate. Bruce captures the purpose of Christian acceptance: "without attempting to settle doubtful points."[5]

The expression "faith is weak" refers to a failure to grasp the nature of justifying faith that Paul expounded in Romans 3:21 – 5:21, resulting in fears that lead to ascetic opinions. When justification by faith alone is understood, Christians realize that nothing we do or don't do will affect our righteous position in Christ.

The Problem (Romans 14:2)

Paul outlines the essence of the problem in verse 2. The scruples referred to here concern meats and vegetables. Since the Jews in old covenant days were not able to eat pork, this may have been in Paul's mind. The person who is weak in the faith and has such scruples is usually a person who has not yet discovered the meaning of Christian freedom, finding it difficult to liberate themselves from a belief in the efficacy of works, if not for salvation, at least for sanctification.

The Counsel of Paul (Romans 14:3 – 4)

The counsel of the apostle consists first of a two-sided rule, followed by reasons. The rule is that the strong are not to despise the weak, and the weak are not to judge the strong in the morally indifferent things. The criticism takes two forms. The strong tend to despise the weak for their lack of understanding of Christian freedom in the new covenant. The weak on their part tend to judge the strong for their laxness in spiritual living, thinking that their freedom is not freedom, but rebellion against the standards of the divine teaching.

Christianity is grounded on our faith in the atoning Christ, not in our commitment to human scruples. Someone has defined a legalist as a person who lives in mortal terror that someone, somewhere, is enjoying himself.[6] That is not really the thing that motivates a legalist, but the legalist is one who thinks that he makes points with God, either for salvation or sanctification, by the things he does in his own strength.

The reasons for the advice of the apostle are given in these verses too. First, God has received the weaker or stronger brother (v. 3). Second, there is only one Master, the Lord Christ, and he alone is to do the judging (v. 4; also 1 Cor. 4:3 – 5).

FASTS, FESTIVALS, AND THE RECEPTION OF THE WEAK

[5]*One man considers one day more sacred than another; another man considers every day alike. Each one should be fully convinced in his own mind.* [6]*He who regards one day as special, does so to the Lord. He who eats meat, eats to the*

Lord, for he gives thanks to God; and he who abstains, does so to the Lord and gives thanks to God. ⁷For none of us lives to himself alone and none of us dies to himself alone. ⁸If we live, we live to the Lord; and if we die, we die to the Lord. So, whether we live or die, we belong to the Lord.

⁹For this very reason, Christ died and returned to life so that he might be the Lord of both the dead and the living.

The Problem (Romans 14:5a - b)

The second point of difference concerns "days." Evidently the reference is to certain feasts or festivals that were still being practiced by some of the believers, probably those who were of Jewish background. We are reminded of Paul's words to the Galatians, who, however, were Gentiles, "You are observing special days and months and seasons and years" (Gal. 4:10; cf. Col. 2:16). Perhaps some were still observing Jewish Sabbath days.

The Command of Paul (Romans 14:5c)

Paul's imperative now is, "Each one should be fully convinced in his own mind." This is the general principle for matters not essential to salvation. Each believer is to study the Scriptures, seek the mind of the Spirit in illumination, and then follow that which seems to be the teaching of the Word.

The Reason Underlying the Command (Romans 14:6 – 9)

This section is best understood as being true of all believers who become "fully convinced in [their] own mind[s]." Christians need to be convinced of the course of action after seeking the mind of God in the Word and through the Spirit.

Both the weak brother and the strong brother, when fully persuaded in their own minds, serve the Lord (v. 9 makes it plain that the "Lord" here is Christ). We all, whether weak or strong, as we earnestly and submissively seek to follow the teaching that we discern in the Word, live in a slave – Lord relation. Since God accepts all of us, we should accept into full communion those who may differ with us in debatable matters.

Verse 9 stresses that the Lord Jesus by his death and resurrection has acquired title to believers. The death is his penal, propitiatory, substitutionary death. He obtained his lordship by death and resurrection; in fact, that was the purpose ("so that") of his ministry. His lordship is over both dead and living believers (cf. Matt. 22:32). "If Christ is Lord of his people, not only when living but also when dead, it follows that they are under obligation to serve him both in death and in life."[7]

THE APPLICATION OF THE TRUTH

[10]*You, then, why do you judge your brother? Or why do you look down on your brother? For we will all stand before God's judgment seat.* [11]*It is written:*

> "'As surely as I live,' says the Lord,
> 'every knee will bow before me;
>   every tongue will confess to God.'"

[12]*So then, each of us will give an account of himself to God.*

The Interrogation (Romans 14:10a-b)

The apostle speaks plainly here of the sin that most of us believers are liable more frequently to commit, namely, criticism. Paul's point is a simple one: Christ alone has the right to judge and, when we do, we are "meddling with God's government."[8] The two questions speak to the two types of people. The first question is for the weak, prone to judge the strong; the second is for the strong, who are liable to despise the weak.

The Substantiation (Romans 14:10c-11)

The apostle reminds all the Romans that they will stand before the judgment seat of God. Christ's judgment is supported by a citation from Isaiah 45:23. Judgment belongs to Jesus the Lord.[9] At his judgment seat our attitude to our brothers will be dealt with, as well as our personal conduct (cf. 2 Cor. 5:10) and our service (cf. 1 Cor. 3:11 – 15). Christians will never be judged for their sins because of Christ's full atoning work at Calvary, but their deeds will be examined and judged.

The Conclusion (Romans 14:12)

Paul concludes with, "So then, each of us will give an account of himself to God." The words are an emphatic repetition of the thought of verses 4, 10, and 11. All of us owe an account to God (the words are emphatic in the original text, intended to remind the Romans that God judges). Therefore, no one should judge another in this regard.

AN EXHORTATION AGAINST INJURING WEAK CONSCIENCES

The Christian life is one full of freedom, but that freedom should not be the occasion of offense to a brother whose conscience is weak. Freedom is to be limited by Christian love. That is the clue to the section we now study.

13Therefore let us stop passing judgment on one another. Instead, make up your mind not to put any stumbling block or obstacle in your brother's way.

A Decision Not to Come to (Romans 14:13a)

The Jews could not eat pork, nor could they eat other meats unless they were properly prepared. No blood could be consumed. When Jews became Christians, naturally they had to face the question of freedom regarding these old laws and customs. The Jerusalem Council had to deal with the matter, and in its conclusions it called on believers to deal gently with the Jewish scruples. Paul in one sense is only following their views. In the letter to the Gentile believers of Antioch, Syria, and Cilicia they proclaimed, "You are to abstain from food sacrificed to idols, from blood, from the meat of strangled animals and from sexual immorality. You will do well to avoid these things" (Acts 15:29; cf. v. 20).

It would have been difficult for the Christians to buy meat in the butcher shops of the ancient world that had not been dedicated to some deity. Therefore, the questions arose concerning eating such food, and some Gentile believers had scruples about it. Paul's words are designed to give counsel to them. The apostle, first of all, in some words that probably pertain to both groups, says, "Therefore let us stop passing judgment on one another."

A Decision to Come to (Romans 14:13b-c)

But Paul goes on to say, "Instead, make up your mind not to put any stumbling block or obstacle in your brother's way." The Greek word translated "make up your mind"[10] is used in two ways in this verse. In its first occurrence, it means to criticize or pass judgment, while in its second occurrence, it means to make a determination, to decide. The word rendered "obstacle" was used of the bait stick of a trap. It was, thus, a death stick, something that proved fatal for an animal that took the bait. Paul, therefore, looks at the matter as a serious one. To cause a professing believer to stumble has solemn consequences (cf. vv. 15, 20–21).

SOME ARGUMENTS FOR LOVING CONSIDERATION

14As one who is in the Lord Jesus, I am fully convinced that no food is unclean in itself. But if anyone regards something as unclean, then for him it is unclean. 15If your brother is distressed because of what you eat, you are no longer acting in love. Do not by your eating destroy your brother for whom Christ died. 16Do not allow what you consider good to be spoken of as evil. 17For the kingdom of God is not a matter of eating and drinking, but of righteousness, peace and joy in the

Holy Spirit, [18]because anyone who serves Christ in this way is pleasing to God and approved by men.

[19]Let us therefore make every effort to do what leads to peace and to mutual edification. [20]Do not destroy the work of God for the sake of food.

The Statement of Christian Freedom (Romans 14:14)

The principle of freedom is stated by Paul in the opening words of verse 14, "I am fully convinced that no food is unclean in itself." The Christian is free from the scruples touching food and days. This truth is confirmed both in his other statements and in the statements of the Lord Jesus Christ (cf. Mark 7:14 – 19; Titus 1:15).

Far from theoretical, the limitation of Christian freedom is practical. The apostle continues his comments in verse 14 by saying, with the weak brother clearly in mind, "But if anyone regards something as unclean, then for him it is unclean." Thus, a man's conscience concerning right and wrong before God is important. To violate our conscience, our convictions concerning that which is right or wrong before God, is to act in rebellion against that which we regard as God's will. It is a sinful act for the weaker brother to violate his or her convictions.

The Principle of Love (Romans 14:15)

Love is the principle that binds the application of freedom. Paul writes, "If your brother is distressed because of what you eat, you are no longer acting in love. Do not by your eating destroy your brother for whom Christ died." In the original text, the verse begins with a "for," relating the words of verse 15 to the last clause of verse 14. Paul says, in effect, that there is good reason for mentioning the words about the weak brother's convictions, for our freedom may at times grieve such brethren. The grief is the grief of the weak brother, who sees one of the strong doing something that he thinks is contrary to the will of God.

Perhaps Paul's most interesting statement is the last one: "Do not by your eating destroy your brother for whom Christ died." The problem of the security of the believer is raised, the divine side of the perseverance of the saints. In fact, some consider the statement a clear proof of the fact that it is possible for a brother to lose his salvation. That, of course, would be contrary to many plain statements of the Word of God (cf. John 10:28 – 30). So what is the purpose of the admonition? This admonition of the Word to the saints is designed to aid in preserving them in the faith. The threats and warnings of the Word are means to accomplishing the unconditional promises of God, aiding in the preservation from apostasy.

The admonitions also serve as serious warnings to the professing company of persons, those who claim to be Christ's but are not. They announce to them that continuance in a certain form of activity will lead to ruin. If a brother performs in such a way as to grieve a professing saint, it is possible that such action may lead to the ruin of that person. John Murray comments, "It is a warning, however, to the strong believer that what he must consider is the nature and tendency of sin and not take refuge behind the security of the believer and the final perseverance of the saints."[11]

The point of Paul's thought is simply this: we should not think more of our food than Christ has thought of the life of the brother. Christ's ultimate sacrifice requires love toward the weak.[12]

The Influence of the Heathen (Romans 14:16-18)

In verse 16 the apostle speaks of the effect of disputes and contentions among Christians on the unbelieving world. He says, "Do not allow what you consider good to be spoken of as evil." The meaning of the expression "the good" is debatable, some referring it to the believer's Christian liberty, others to the Christian church, and still others to the Christian faith, or, most likely, the gospel.

The apostle refers in verse 17 to the motive for avoiding the reproaches of the world: "For the kingdom of God is not a matter of eating and drinking, but of righteousness, peace and joy in the Holy Spirit." The expression "the kingdom of God" refers to the realm in which God's will prevails. Over that realm the messianic King, the Lord Jesus Christ, reigns, having established it by virtue of the sacrifice that confirmed the Abrahamic, Davidic, and new covenant promises. That kingdom has been established and will become visible in our society at the second advent of Jesus Christ.

The kingdom of God consists of more than outward rites and material things. The "righteousness" is that which believers have through the merits of a crucified Savior, made available to them through faith. The "peace" is also that made by the cross between God and his rebellious people (cf. 5:1-11). The "joy" is the joy of the possession of the righteousness and peace. In this way, the one serving Christ is acceptable to God and approved of people. Shedd comments, "God takes pleasure in one who serves Christ in the evangelical manner described. The legalist is not well-pleasing to God, because 'whatsoever is not of faith is sin' (verse 23)."[13]

Concluding Words of Exhortation (Romans 14:19-20a)

The apostle concludes with an exhortation to seek to find a way of solving the problems of differing views over debatable things. The strong are to forbear and lead the weak to a more scriptural and satisfying view of Christian liberty, while the weak are to keep the strong from licentiousness by reminding him that his liberty is to be practiced before God with a good conscience.

FINAL WORDS TO THE STRONG

All food is clean, but it is wrong for a man to eat anything that causes someone else to stumble. ²¹*It is better not to eat meat or drink wine or to do anything else that will cause your brother to fall.*

²²*So whatever you believe about these things keep between yourself and God. Blessed is the man who does not condemn himself by what he approves.* ²³*But the man who has doubts is condemned if he eats, because his eating is not from faith; and everything that does not come from faith is sin.*

Sin Arising from Examples (Romans 14:20b – 21)

The figure of the edifice is retained as the apostle reminds his readers not to tear down the work of God (the Christian) for food. All things indeed are pure (he again affirms that the strong are basically right), but the strong sins if he eats in such a way as to be offensive to the weak. Commentators differ over the interpretation of the words "causes someone else to stumble" (v. 20b). Some think the offense refers to the sin of the weak in eating something that is contrary to their real convictions as a result of the liberty of the strong and the example they provide. Others think that the reference is to the sin of the strong in injuring the weaker brother by his actions in freedom. The latter view seems more in accord with the chapter, which has spoken of the offense given by the strong in the exercise of his freedom before the weaker brethren.

Verse 21 seems to confirm this, for it refers to the sin of the strong. Paul's point, then, is this: the stronger brother is right, but his freedom should be exercised in the context of Christian love. It should not be used to provoke weaker brethren who do not yet understand the extent of Christian liberty.

The line of reasoning of the apostle does raise some questions. Are the strong always to refuse to indulge their liberty? Stedman wisely remarks:

I think it is a healthy thing for a Christian who has liberty in some of these areas to indulge it on occasion. The cause of Christ is never advanced by having every strong Christian in a congregation completely forego his right to enjoy some of these things. What happens then is that the question is settled on the basis of the most narrow and most prejudiced person in the congregation. Soon, the gospel itself becomes identified with that view. That is why the outside world often considers Christians to be narrow-minded people who have no concern except to prevent the enjoyment of the good gifts God has given us.[14]

Sin Arising from Doubt (Romans 14:22–23)

Paul tells the strong, who have appropriated the practical ramifications of justification by faith alone, not to parade their faith. They should rather remember that it is to be exercised "between yourself and God." The last phrase inhibits any tendency toward licentiousness that might arise.

The final words of verse 22, "Blessed is the man who does not condemn himself by what he approves," apply to both the strong and the weak. In effect, it means that the person with a good conscience in these matters is a blessed man. The paragraph concludes with some words directed to the weak, admonishing him that he must not eat or do anything concerning which he has scruples. Doubt concerning the act is enough to mean that the believer should not do it. We must act from faith, because "everything that does not come from faith is sin." The last words touch on the nature of human sin; its essence is unbelief of the Word of God, which leads to rebellion and issues in acts of immorality. Paul's words mean, then, that it is wrong to do anything we think is wrong, although it is not always right to do what we think is right.

CONCLUSION

The weak should never act from doubt but from conviction. Incidentally, this passage also includes an implicit admonition to study Christian liberty in order that the weak may advance to strength. The strong should be free, but free in love, remembering that believers are free to say no just as much as to say yes. The strong can give up their liberty for a good cause, namely, the desire to avoid offending weaker brothers and sisters.

DISCUSSION QUESTIONS

1. If Christians struggle with their liberty, how can justification by faith alone free them to think biblically?

2. How much time should be spent on straightening out the views of other Christians in gray areas? How can time be better spent?

3. Who is the ultimate judge in areas of Christian liberty?

CHAPTER 25

THE SERVANT OF THE NATIONS

ROMANS 15:1–33

Paul continues teaching on morally indifferent or debatable things. Strong believers should avoid confirming legalists in their weakness by continually yielding on the things that offend the legalists. It is the responsibility of weak believers to grow to strength, and that can hardly be done if the strong always yield without explanation. Then the life of the body of believers becomes determined by the narrowest and the most prejudiced of its members. That would not be so bad, were it not also an inevitable result that the unbelieving world is led to conclude that the gospel itself depends on obedience to the scruples and inhibitions of the weak. The gospel issue, then, is no longer the issue of Christ and his saving cross alone, but the cross plus obedience to the scruples. Salvation appears to unbelievers to be the product of faith and works, not of faith alone, dishonoring Christ's work and confusing the good news.

The conclusion of the section on debatable things features the example of Christ. Who was freer from taboos and inhibitions? Who was more considerate of others? Who was bolder in insisting that people face up to the true teaching of the Word (cf. Luke 14:1 – 6)? The example of Christ is Paul's clinching point and must be remembered: Jesus did not seek to please himself, and he received both Jews and Gentiles to the glory of God. The crucial illustration in verses 7 – 12 amplifies Christ's ministry to the Jews and Gentiles, elucidating the outworking of the divine purpose toward the two groups, the nation and the nations. Paul wishes to make the point that he welcomed both of them, but in the course of making his point, he also has some important things to say concerning the order and significance of his reception of the Jews and the Gentiles. Jesus ministered to the Jews first, and then to the Gentiles, and Paul claims that the Old Testament foresaw both aspects of his service. He cites four passages from the Old Testament that specifically speak of Gentile blessing (cf. vv. 9–12). The apostle's ministry is directed to the same end as his Lord's.[1]

THE PERSONAL SERVICE OF CHRIST

[1]We who are strong ought to bear with the failings of the weak and not to please ourselves. [2]Each of us should please his neighbor for his good, to build him up. [3]For even Christ did not please himself but, as it is written: "The insults of those who insult you have fallen on me." [4]For everything that was written in the past was written to teach us, so that through endurance and the encouragement of the Scriptures we might have hope.

The Exhortation to Endurance (Romans 15:1–2)

The two sections of the paragraph are similar in structure, in that both descriptions of our Lord's example (vv. 1–4, 7–12) are followed by prayers, or expressions of aspiration (vv. 5–6; 13).

The apostle begins by addressing a word to the strong, classifying himself among them: "We who are strong ought to bear with the failings of the weak and not to please ourselves. Each of us should please his neighbor for his good, to build him up." The strong, those free from the inhibitions and scruples of the weak regarding food and special days, are asked to tolerate the infirmities of the weak. The word "bear" may, as in English, have the sense of "to carry," but it is clear that it means "to endure" here. The strong are not simply not to despise the weak (cf. 14:2), but to positively endure their infirmities, that is, to tolerate them in love.

The Justification of the Exhortation (Romans 15:3)

In justification of the exhortation, Paul appeals to the Word: "For even Christ did not please himself but, as it is written: 'The insults of those who insult you have fallen on me.'" The expression "for even Christ did not please himself" is a summary of the person and work of Christ in the days of his flesh.[2] The text cited is Psalm 69:9, a psalm in which David writes typically of Christ.[3] David writes of his persecution by Saul, and these persecutions are taken as typical of those of our Lord by the New Testament authors. They cite the psalm at numerous places (cf. John 15:25; 2:17; here; Matt. 27:27 – 30; 27:34; John 19:29; et al.). The reproaches that fell on David were really directed ultimately at God for his choice of David and his identification with him in his royal work. The words go on beyond David to David's greater Son, the Lord Jesus, whose enemies' reproaches were really directed at Jesus' God. Thus, the fact that they fell on Christ, and he did not resist them, indicates that he did not attempt to please himself. He sought only to do the will of God. The norm of his life was not self-gratification but God-gratification (cf. John 13:15; 1 John 2:6).

The Propriety of the Citation (Romans 15:4)

The appropriateness of the Old Testament citation is supported by a reference to the general purpose, and the more specific moral purposes, of the Scriptures. The old covenant was designed to instruct us, to the end that we might through endurance and encouragement cling to our hope of an enduring future. The practical value of the Word of God cannot be more strongly emphasized. All Scripture (both Old Testament and New Testament) gives us the power to endure affliction and temptation, and too often our contemporary believers have neglected their benefits. In difficulty we flee to our counselors, some amateur and others professional, but they can never do the work of the Word of God. It is possible through the Scriptures to have the Lord Jesus Christ as our constant companion and permanent, moment-by-moment counselor. Let us not run to people, but to him. Read the Old Testament to learn the lesson of delayed gratification.

THE PRAYER FOR UNANIMITY

>[5]*May the God who gives endurance and encouragement give you a spirit of unity among yourselves as you follow Christ Jesus,* [6]*so that with one heart and mouth you may glorify the God and Father of our Lord Jesus Christ.*

The Content of It (Romans 15:5)

The prayer-wish, or expression of aspiration, is to be connected with the statement of verse 3, namely, that Christ did not please himself. In accord with this, Paul expresses the wish that God would give the Romans the power to be like-minded toward one another. The expression in the Greek text, rendered by the NIV as "give you a spirit of unity," means literally "to mind, or think, the same thing" (to be like-minded). The unanimity that Paul wishes here is not unanimity of doctrine, but oneness in disposition and action rather than pleasing themselves.

The Intent of It (Romans 15:6)

The purpose of the prayer is that the weak and the strong may glorify with one mind and mouth the God and Father of our Lord Jesus Christ.[4]

THE NATIONAL SERVICE OF CHRIST

> [7]*Accept one another, then, just as Christ accepted you, in order to bring praise to God.* [8]*For I tell you that Christ has become a servant of the Jews on behalf of God's truth, to confirm the promises made to the patriarchs* [9]*so that the Gentiles may glorify God for his mercy, as it is written:*
>
> *"Therefore I will praise you among the Gentiles;*
> *I will sing hymns to your name."*
>
> [10]*Again, it says,*
> *"Rejoice, O Gentiles, with his people."*
> [11]*And again,*
> *"Praise the Lord, all you Gentiles,*
> *and sing praises to him, all you peoples."*
>
> [12]*And again, Isaiah says,*
> *"The Root of Jesse will spring up,*
> *one who will arise to rule over the nations;*
> *the Gentiles will hope in him."*

The Request and the Example (Romans 15:7)

"Then" (lit., "wherefore") makes the connection in the Greek text. In order that this praise and glory be rendered to God, receive one another, just as Christ received you to the glory of God. He came not to receive, but to give service, which he performed by receiving both Jews and Gentiles. It is the reception of Gentiles that illustrates most clearly the care and love of Christ, since there was no direct covenant made with them.

The Manner of His Service (Romans 15:8–9a)

Paul introduces further explanation of the service of our Lord as substantiation of the command to receive one another. The example of our Lord comprehended the reception of both Jews and Gentiles into fellowship with the Godhead.[5] He first calls attention to the fact that Christ has become a minister of the Jews (lit., "circumcision"). The verb "has become" suggests that he still may be said to be a minister of circumcision, since the result of his work abides. The article is missing with the term "circumcision" in the Greek; therefore, we must render the words "a minister of circumcision." The reference, then, is to the ancient rite, which the Jewish males underwent in becoming a member of the Abrahamic covenant (cf. Gen. 17:1 – 21; cf. Rom. 4:11).

Christ has become a servant of the Abrahamic covenant, of which circumcision was the sign and seal (cf. 4:11 – 12; also Gal. 3:16; 4:4 – 5). The purpose of his ministry of the covenant was "on behalf of God's truth, to confirm the promises made to the patriarchs." The words "on behalf of God's truth" refer to his work as the honoring of the faithfulness of God. God's veracity is extolled in the Son's coming to do what the Father said he would do.

The words "to confirm the promises made to the patriarchs" refer to the establishment of the covenant, which contained promises made to Abraham and confirmed to Isaac and Jacob. God established that covenant, expanded in the Davidic and new covenants, by making it vital, or valid, in Jesus' death, burial, and resurrection. Jesus offered the covenantal sacrifice, necessary for the validity of a covenant, by means of his entire ministry (including his incarnation, death, resurrection, and consequent session at God's right hand). All the promises from "seed of Abraham" to "sun of righteousness" found their fulfillment in him (cf. Gal. 3:16; Mal. 4:2). By virtue of what he did, Israel has all of the benefits mentioned by Paul in an earlier part of this letter (cf. 3:1 – 8; 9:4 – 5).

The ministry, however, involved more than the Jews. Indirectly, the Gentiles were the beneficiaries of the covenant promises. God's divine election comprehended both Jews and Gentiles, and Christ's saving work relates to both of the companies. Paul adds, "so that the Gentiles may glorify God for his mercy."

The Gentiles had no direct covenantal promises from God, but they were included in the promises of the covenants made with Israel (cf. Gen. 12:3; 22:18; et al.). The Lord primarily directed his ministry to Israel, a fact that finds clearest elucidation in his encounter with the Syrophoenician woman (see Matt. 15:21 – 28). As a result of this program, the Jews glorify God for his faithfulness to the promises made to them, and the Gentiles glorify God for the mercy of including them indirectly and secondarily in the covenant blessings.

The Scriptural Confirmation (Romans 15:9b – 12)

The Old Testament Scriptures teach that the blessing of God is for the Gentiles also. In support, Paul refers to several passages, starting with Psalm 18:49, "Therefore I will praise you among the nations [that is, the Gentiles], O LORD; I will sing praises to your name."

The second passage is from Deuteronomy 32:43, a text from the great Song of Moses, in which the past, present, and future of Israel is graphically presented.

The apostle sees the present Gentile salvation as intended ultimately to provoke the Jews to jealousy that they might, after turning from him, return and receive the blessings of the covenantal program. This is the significance of Deuteronomy 32:21, studied in the light of Romans 11:11, 14 (cf. 10:19). Gentiles have no direct covenantal promises, but they do receive blessing through the Jews, preeminently through the Seed of Abraham, the Lord Jesus Christ.

The third text is Psalm 117:1, "Praise the LORD, all you nations; extol him, all you peoples."

The final text is from the well-known messianic chapter, Isaiah 11. From verse 10 Paul cites, "In that day the Root of Jesse will stand as a banner for the peoples; the nations will rally to him, and his place of rest will be glorious." The Lord Jesus is the shoot from David's stock, the royal stock itself having been cut down in unbelief. But life still exists in the tree, for it is from it that the Shoot springs. Paul sees the present Gentile salvation as a fulfillment of the prophecy of Gentile salvation. The fact that the nations will hope in David's Root and Shoot, for he is both (cf. Isa. 11:1, 10), is an additional proof of the deity of Christ.

THE PRAYER FOR ABOUNDING HOPE

13May the God of hope fill you with all joy and peace as you trust in him, so that you may overflow with hope by the power of the Holy Spirit.

The Content of It (Romans 15:13a)

The argument of the entire epistle draws to an end here; with the union of the Jew and the Gentile in Christ, and with the tracing of all the blessings to "joy and peace as you trust in him" (cf. Rom. 1:16, 17; 5:1 – 11; et al.). Paul prays for the joy and peace of the Romans in faith.

The Intent of It (Romans 15:13b)

The intent of the prayer is that they may abound in hope in the power of the Spirit, the power of the Spirit being the element in which and the energy by which we abound. Notice that the prayer begins and ends with accent on the divine agency and resources. We have all in him, and only in him.

CHRIST'S PRIEST TO THE GENTILES

Paul now turns to his personal plans and ministry in the future. The section throws a great deal of light on the nature, extent, and power of ministry. It is critical to remember that what Paul says here is said against the background of a fundamental conception of the doctrine of the Trinity. Listen to John Murray:

> It is noteworthy how in verses 16 – 19a Paul weaves his teaching around the distinctive relations to and functions of the three persons of the Godhead. This shows how Paul's thought was conditioned by the doctrine of the Trinity and particularly by the distinguishing properties and prerogatives of the three persons in the economy of salvation. It is not a case of artificially weaving these persons into his presentation; it is rather that his consciousness is so formed by, and to, faith in the triune God that he cannot but express himself in these terms (cf. vs. 30; Ephesians 4:3 – 6).[6]

The economy of salvation is the work of the Father in electing grace, the work of the Son in atoning grace, and the work of the Spirit in regenerating grace, and the three works are beautifully harmonious and effective. All three persons of the Godhead work together, and they are not, and cannot be, frustrated in their purposes. Ministry is carried on against this comforting background; the servant is assured of the effectiveness of his work according to the divine plan and purpose.

It is a big error to read this section as if Paul is the central figure. The dominant figure is Christ, and it is Christ, through the apostle, who accomplishes effective ministry. As Paul, keeping his eyes on Christ, puts it, "I will not venture to speak of anything except what Christ has accomplished through me in leading the Gentiles to obey God by what I have said and done" (v. 18). The section is full of the emphasis on God's grace working in and through the apostle (cf. vv. 15, 17, 18). Like the undertow on the beaches of the oceans of the world, Paul is caught in the undertow of the divine activity of salvation, for the triune God carries him wherever he willed!

PAUL'S PURPOSE IN WRITING

14I myself am convinced, my brothers, that you yourselves are full of goodness, complete in knowledge and competent to instruct one another. 15I have written you quite boldly on some points, as if to remind you of them again, because of the grace God gave me…

The Qualification of It (Romans 15:14)

Paul began the letter with a section in which personal plans were predominant (1:8 – 17), and now he concludes similarly (15:14 – 33). It is as if the two sections bracket the important doctrinal material of the letter. Paul turns to his purpose in writing the Romans, namely, that he is assured of their ability to handle the problem of Christian liberty, but he still feels it helpful to write and remind them of his ministry and its purpose.

He says that the Romans are "full of goodness, complete in knowledge and competent to instruct one another." Some have sought to have the apostle mean by this that the Romans did not need any further theological information, since they were filled with all knowledge. Why, then, did the apostle write them the most theological of all his letters, in which there is a compendium of the doctrinal teaching of the Bible? What a waste of effort, if they already had such knowledge.

The apostle is not speaking generally; he has in mind the problems he has just finished discussing, the problem of debatable things. The Romans are filled with goodness, he suggests, so much so that it will constrain the strong from despising the weaker brethren in the matter of food, drink, and the observance of days. It will also constrain the weak from judging the strong, when they exercise a freedom with respect to these things that the weak think borders on license. This is the qualification with which he writes of his purpose to remind the Romans of the nature, extent, and power of his ministry.

The Declaration of It (Romans 15:15a-b)

The apostle expresses frankly and directly his purpose in writing: to remind the Romans of the nature of his ministry, a ministry that had as its goal the Gentiles.

The Justification of It (Romans 15:15c)

The clause "because of the grace God gave me" anticipates Paul's description of his position as a minister of the gospel to the Gentiles. Paul refers to that role as a grace given him by God.

GOD'S PURPOSE IN PAUL'S MINISTRY

> [16]to be a minister of Christ Jesus to the Gentiles with the priestly duty of proclaiming the gospel of God, so that the Gentiles might become an offering acceptable to God, sanctified by the Holy Spirit.
>
> [17]Therefore I glory in Christ Jesus in my service to God. [18]I will not venture to speak of anything except what Christ has accomplished through me in leading the Gentiles to obey God by what I have said and done — [19]by the power of signs and miracles, through the power of the Spirit. So from Jerusalem all the way around to Illyricum, I have fully proclaimed the gospel of Christ.

The Declaration of It (Romans 15:16)

In verse 16 the apostle declares God's purpose in his ministry. It is that he minister to the Gentiles as his primary sphere of preaching (cf. Gal. 2:6–10). The remarkable thing here is not so much that fact, but the way in which he expresses that fact. As F. F. Bruce says, Paul speaks in clauses that are full of the "language of worship"[7] of the grace given to him.

Paul says, first, that he is "a minister of Christ Jesus," using a word that suggests priestly service (cf. 13:6; 15:27; Heb. 8:2). Paul conceives of his ministry under the figure of the Old Testament Levite, or priest, persons who ministered in sacred things, authorized by God. This idea is further expounded by the use of the words "the priestly duty of proclaiming the gospel of God." Paul does not mean to suggest that he offer literal sacrifices; rather, Paul serves the gospel as a priest would offer a sacrifice. The sacrifice that removes sin has been offered, the sacrifice of the Son of God for sinners. No further sacrifice is necessary (cf. John 19:30).

In old covenant times, the priests ministered the benefits of that old covenant, which provided a temporary acceptance before the Lord God. The priest was the divinely ordained mediator of the covenant, representing God and humans and keeping the two in fellowship with one another. When a man sinned, he brought the requisite offering to the priest at the door of the tabernacle in order to restore his relationship with the Lord. That offering, to be really effective, had to be brought in faith. When it was, the priest killed the animal, sprinkled the blood before the Lord, and pronounced the fact of forgiveness and restoration.

Now, of course, Paul speaks of the new covenant ministry, for he is a minister of the new covenant (cf. 2 Cor. 3:6). He ministers, via the new covenant, the benefits of the gospel.

In addition, the apostle writes, "so that the Gentiles might become an offering acceptable to God, sanctified by the Holy Spirit." The Old Testament priest offered up a sacrifice brought by sinners to God. Paul conceives of his sacrifice in new covenant ministry being Gentile conversion through the preaching of the gospel of God. His offering, then, is the saints (cf. v. 18; 11:13; Eph. 3:6).

The Eventuation of It (Romans 15:17)

It is not surprising, then, that Paul writes, "Therefore I glory in Christ Jesus in my service to God." Paul limits his glorying and boasting. First of all, he glories only "in Christ Jesus," in order that Christ may have all the glory. It is God who is responsible for all the work of ministry and its effectiveness. Further, he glories, not in all things in general, but specifically "in my service to God."

The Explanation of the Glorying (Romans 15:18–19)

Men and women are made to glorify God. Since this is so, all of God's dealings with people, sinful people, must be in grace. If he dealt with us in justice, we should be lost. Dealing with us in grace, we are saved, but it is he, then, who obtains the glory, for we have and deserve none (cf. Eph. 2:8–9).

He emphatically states that he would not dare to speak of things not done by Christ through him, a negative way of saying that he will speak only of the things that Christ has done through him. And, notice, it is not "what I accomplished through Christ," which might stress his activity too strongly. It is "what God has accomplished through me."

Modern ministers and modern ministries like to lay great stress on numbers, but the apostle would have none of that. To lay great stress on numbers often reflects a departure from the principle of dependence on God for all our resources, as Ray Stedman has pointed out, illustrating the principle from David's numbering of the people.[8]

Paul mentions that the things done through him involved "the power of signs and miracles, through the power of the Spirit" (v. 19). Should we expect to see all the miracles that the early church saw? The fact that a miracle happened in the first century is no evidence, or support, for its happening today. God works in such matters sovereignly. If he wished the miracles to keep happening, they would be happening. The miracles of Paul were signs and wonders associated with his apostolic ministry, confirming and authenticating it. In fact, in Hebrews 2:4, the author of that epistle puts such signs in the past tense, as if to suggest that even in his day they were dying out.

Paul's statement "I have fully proclaimed the gospel of Christ" does not mean that he had preached the gospel to every person; rather, it means that he had completed in representative fashion the preaching of the gospel to the area to which he was sent.

THE PAULINE PRINCIPLE OF MINISTRY

> [20]*It has always been my ambition to preach the gospel where Christ was not known, so that I would not be building on someone else's foundation.* [21]*Rather, as it is written:*
>
> > *"Those who were not told about him will see,*
> > *and those who have not heard will understand."*

The Principle Stated (Romans 15:20)

Paul did not plan to enter the territory assigned by God to others (cf. Gal. 2:6 – 10). He considered his ministry that of founding Gentile churches, or rather, churches in Gentile lands (cf. 1 Cor. 3:7, 10). He did not wish to build on another's foundation.

The Principle Substantiated (Romans 15:21)

The apostle appeals to the Old Testament for substantiation, or perhaps illustration, of his plan of action. The passage, Isaiah 52:15, refers to the ministry of the Servant of the Lord, an Old Testament messianic term, and the worldwide effects on the Gentiles of their future recognition of his person and work, associated with events surrounding his second advent. Paul likens the effects of his recognition to the effects seen in his ministry. He thus identifies the Servant with the Lord Jesus Christ, seeing the salvation of the Gentiles as similar to the worldwide future conversion of them.

THE JERUSALEM OFFERING

In the remainder of the chapter, Paul explains that the occasion of his writing to the Romans lies in his plans for the future, plans that stretch far into the future (cf. vv. 22 – 24), his hope to go on to Spain, and his intention to visit Jerusalem with the gifts from the Greek Christians (cf. vv. 25 – 33).

PAUL'S PLANS TO COME TO ROME

> [22]*This is why I have often been hindered from coming to you.*
> [23]*But now that there is no more place for me to work in these regions, and since I have been longing for many years to see you,* [24]*I plan to do so when I go to Spain. I hope to visit you while passing through and to have you assist me on my journey there, after I have enjoyed your company for a while.*

The Hindrance of Paul's Visit (Romans 15:22)

The opening "This is why" (lit., "wherefore") indicates that Paul's evangelistic ministry is the reason for the delay in coming to Rome. At other times Satan hindered Paul (cf. 1 Thess. 2:18), but here it is simply the work of fulfilling his commission, a work encompassing a territory of 1,400 miles in length (cf. v. 19). The picture given by Paul is of a daily life characterized by planning, which was flexible and persistent, by faithfulness to his responsibilities (cf. Gal. 2:10), and by a continuing trust in the Lord (cf. Rom. 15:29).

The Occasion of Paul's Coming (Romans 15:23)

The apostle feels that he has exhausted his opportunities in the area he has referred to and, furthermore, he has had a longing to visit them. He had not planted the church, but it is obvious that he either knew, or knew of, a large number in the assembly at Rome. While he did not want to follow the plan of building on another man's foundation, still the apostle of the Gentiles wished to see the congregation in the greatest of the Gentile cities of the time.

The Details of Paul's Plans (Romans 15:24)

The apostle did not plan a long stay, and he would make his visit on the way to Spain. He hoped to have a kind of spiritual "fill up" from them, and that they would aid him on his journey to Spain. Later he says he hopes to be "refreshed" by them, a word that refers to one of the aspects of true biblical fellowship, in that it has reference to the sharing of the things of Christ together (cf. 15:32).

PAUL'S JOURNEY TO JERUSALEM

[25]Now, however, I am on my way to Jerusalem in the service of the saints there. [26]For Macedonia and Achaia were pleased to make a contribution for the poor among the saints in Jerusalem. [27]They were pleased to do it, and indeed they owe it to them. For if the Gentiles have shared in the Jews' spiritual blessings, they owe it to the Jews to share with them their material blessings. [28]So after I have completed this task and have made sure that they have received this fruit, I will go to Spain and visit you on the way. [29]I know that when I come to you, I will come in the full measure of the blessing of Christ.

Paul's Plan (Romans 15:25)

This would be Paul's fifth visit to Jerusalem (cf. Acts 9:24 – 30; 11:30; 15:1 – 29; 18:21; and here). He evidently thought the visit was important, because he interrupted his evangelistic work for it. The purpose of the visit was to bear the gifts of the believers of Macedonia and Achaia to the saints at Jerusalem, who were poor believers, probably largely because they were persecuted by the masses there and unable to make the kind of living they had made formerly (cf. Acts 24:17; 1 Cor. 16:3; 2 Cor. 9:1 – 2).

The Reason for Paul's Journey (Romans 15:26 – 27)

Paul must have thought that the sharing of the gifts was a visible illustration of the unity of Jew and Gentile in the one new body of the church. Since that was one of the important truths he proclaimed, he attached a great deal of significance to the successful accomplishment of the undertaking.

He also felt that the Gentiles ought to give to the Jews, since it was from the Jews that they had received the truth about salvation. Those who are blessed by spiritual ministry from others should share with their teachers in the material blessings they have, for the teachers often do not have the time to devote to the building up of material resources that others have (cf. 1 Cor. 9:11). It is a valid principle for today (cf. Gal. 6:6 – 10).[9]

The Sequel: On to Spain (Romans 15:28 – 29)

The apostle here informs the Romans that when he has given the saints in Jerusalem the funds from the Greek Christians, he will come to them and then go on to Spain. Paul is confident that he will come with the divine blessing.

PAUL'S REQUEST FOR PRAYER

> [30]*I urge you, brothers, by our Lord Jesus Christ and by the love of the Spirit, to join me in my struggle by praying to God for me.* [31]*Pray that I may be rescued from the unbelievers in Judea and that my service in Jerusalem may be acceptable to the saints there,* [32]*so that by God's will I may come to you with joy and together with you be refreshed.* [33]*The God of peace be with you all. Amen.*

Paul's Motive (Romans 15:30)

Paul now requests prayer for his impending journey, namely, that he may be delivered from the unbelievers in Judea and that his service may be acceptable to the saints there. He, the apostle of sovereign grace, believes in the efficacy of prayer, which is mysterious in its working but mighty in its power with God. He finds the motive for prayer for him in the believers' union with Christ and in the love for God and for other believers implanted in their hearts by the Holy Spirit (cf. 5:5).

The Object of Paul's Prayer (Romans 15:31)

It is interesting to compare the object of the apostle's request for prayer, the deliverance from the disobedient saints, with the actual things that happened. The facts are that he narrowly escaped death in Jerusalem and was taken into custody by the Romans. He eventually was taken to Caesarea, where he remained in custody for two years. When he appealed to Rome, he was taken as a prisoner of the empire to Rome. Jesus himself had promised Paul that he would testify of him in Rome (cf. Acts 23:11).

Did Paul make it to Spain, as he desired? New Testament scholarship does not give a sure answer to the question. One thing is certain, however. If he did not reach Spain personally, he eventually did by his correspondence. In fact, he has reached the world through the letters he wrote, some of them written while he was detained in Rome. God's promise to him was fulfilled, and Paul's prayers were answered, if not in the precise way in which he framed them.

The Final Aim of Paul's Prayer (Romans 15:32 – 33)

The aim of Paul's petition was spiritual refreshment by and among the Romans (cf. 1:11; 1 Cor. 16:18; 2 Cor. 7:13), or true Christian fellowship. This he did experience (cf. Acts 28:14 – 16, 30 – 31; Phil. 1:12 – 18). A benediction concludes the section, giving another of the descriptions of God found in the chapter (cf. vv. 5, 13).

DISCUSSION QUESTIONS

1. What is genuine Christian fellowship and refreshment? Why is it more than getting together and eating?

2. Paul was thankful for the financial gift of the Philippians, but he never asked them for money for himself (Phil. 4:10 – 19). Why is modern-day evangelicalism so gung-ho for money, using whatever method works? Are subtle suggestions, emotional appeals, sophisticated direct-mail methods, which work due to the gullibility of the simple-hearted genuine saints, anywhere close to the new covenant model of giving? Explain.

3. What does Romans 15 teach us about the Christian doctrine of prayer?

4. Paul, the apostle of divine election, predestination, foreordination, and calling, urges his readers to pray for him. The apostle's strong views on the sovereignty of God did not conflict with urgent appeals for prayer. How can the understanding of divine sovereignty be perfectly harmonious with human prayer?

CHAPTER 26

PAUL'S FRIENDS AND THE STRENGTHENING GOSPEL

ROMANS 16:1–27

Chapter 16 is commonly ignored as simply "a list of names"; nevertheless, it is an intriguing and exciting chapter. Griffith Thomas has called it "a galaxy of saints."[1] It contains that, but much more than that. The large number of believers living in the great city on seven hills by the Tiber River indicates that long before there were any magnificent, imposing ecclesiastical edifices there, the body of Christ was there.

It is encouraging to see from the list that God does care for the individual sinner, saved by redeeming grace. Walter Lüthi comments:

> Here as nowhere else in the Apostle's Letters we are struck by the long list of names that is given. We know nothing at all about many of the people mentioned here, apart from their names, so it is quite reasonable to ask what purpose this list may serve. But in the Bible no name is ever mentioned without good reason ... the Apostle is singling out people who have been redeemed and saved.... Both eastern and western names are mentioned, names that sound Jewish, Latin or Greek.[2]

THE COMMENDATION AND SALUTATIONS OF PAUL

¹I commend to you our sister Phoebe, a servant of the church in Cenchrea. ²I ask you to receive her in the Lord in a way worthy of the saints and to give her any help she may need from you, for she has been a great help to many people, including me.

³*Greet Priscilla and Aquila, my fellow workers in Christ Jesus.* ⁴*They risked their lives for me. Not only I but all the churches of the Gentiles are grateful to them.*

⁵*Greet also the church that meets at their house.*

Greet my dear friend Epenetus, who was the first convert to Christ in the province of Asia.

⁶*Greet Mary, who worked very hard for you.*

⁷*Greet Andronicus and Junias, my relatives who have been in prison with me. They are outstanding among the apostles, and they were in Christ before I was.*

⁸*Greet Ampliatus, whom I love in the Lord.*

⁹*Greet Urbanus, our fellow worker in Christ, and my dear friend Stachys.*

¹⁰*Greet Apelles, tested and approved in Christ.*

Greet those who belong to the household of Aristobulus.

¹¹*Greet Herodion, my relative.*

Greet those in the household of Narcissus who are in the Lord.

¹²*Greet Tryphena and Tryphosa, those women who work hard in the Lord.*

Greet my dear friend Persis, another woman who has worked very hard in the Lord.

¹³*Greet Rufus, chosen in the Lord, and his mother, who has been a mother to me, too.*

¹⁴*Greet Asyncritus, Phlegon, Hermes, Patrobas, Hermas and the brothers with them.*

¹⁵*Greet Philologus, Julia, Nereus and his sister, and Olympas and all the saints with them.*

¹⁶*Greet one another with a holy kiss.*

All the churches of Christ send greetings.

The Commendation of Phoebe (Romans 16:1 – 2)

The chapter opens with a commendation of Phoebe, a member of the church in Cenchrea, one of the ports of the city of Corinth. She evidently is the bearer of the epistle to the Romans to the church in the capital city of the empire. She is called "a servant of the church," which may indicate that she was a deaconess, since the word for "servant" is *diakonos*, a word both feminine and masculine in gender. There is, however, no indication that women served alongside men in their duties.³ They probably served in those ways most suited to the females, such as helpers in baptism or helpers among the sick. Phoebe was an outstanding member of the church. She had assisted Paul and many others, and her name is an honored one in the Scripture. Whoever was able to present a better letter of commendation than the one she presented to the church in Rome?

The Salutations of Paul (Romans 16:3 – 16)

There now follows a long list of names, with some apostolic comments, to whom Paul wishes to extend greetings. We will single out a few for special mention. Heading the list are Priscilla and Aquila, a well-known New Testament couple, seen first at Corinth, then at Ephesus, and now in Rome. The names of Priscilla and Aquila are mentioned about six times in the Word, and four of the times have Pricilla's name first. Two things may be indicated. First, it may suggest that it is she who possessed the better teaching gift (cf. Acts 18:24 – 28). Or, it may indicate that Priscilla was from a higher social stratum. "She may have belonged by birth or manumission to the gens Prisca, a noble Roman family, while he was a Jew from Pontus in Northern Asia Minor," F. F. Bruce points out.[4] One other thing stands out about them. They loved to have the church meet in their house (cf. 1 Cor. 16:19), and the church in Ephesus and a church in Rome did just that (cf. Col. 4:15; Philem. 2).

"Mary the Toiler" is mentioned in verse 6, and the reference is not likely to teaching, but rather to acts of kindness and aid that she performed for the Romans. The apostle also mentions Andronicus and Junias (or Junia; it is really impossible to know whether the second word is masculine or feminine) in verse 7. The phrase "outstanding among the apostles" does not mean they were apostles necessarily, but it may mean simply that they were of note in the estimation of the apostles.

Tryphaena and Tryphosa, names meaning something like Dainty and Delicate, referred to in verse 12, were relatives or sisters, perhaps twins. They are described as "those women who work hard in the Lord," so their work belies their names.

The reference to Rufus in verse 13 is intriguing in the light of Mark 15:21 and Luke 23:26. Simon of Cyrene is described as the father of Alexander and Rufus, and since Mark was written for Rome according to tradition, it is reasonable to identify the Rufus here with the Rufus of Simon. In that case his mother would be the wife of Simon. Thus, from a "chance" encounter of Simon with our Lord, there developed the salvation of the man, his wife, and their children. Paul calls him literally "the elect one in the Lord," words that probably mean the "choice one" in the Lord.

After the mention of a group of men in verse 14, who may have lived together in something like a commune, and another group in verse 15, the apostle concludes with, "Greet one another with a holy kiss. All the churches of Christ send greetings." "The 'kiss of peace,' which plays a part to this day in the liturgy of the Eastern church, is first mentioned as a regular feature of Christian worship in Justin Martyr's First Apology, 65 ('when we have ceased from our prayers, we greet one another with a kiss')" (cf. 1 Cor. 16:20; 2 Cor. 13:12; 1 Thess. 5:26; 1 Peter 5:14).[5] It is the oriental method of salutation, just as handshaking is the occidental.

THE ADMONITION OF PAUL

> [17]*I urge you, brothers, to watch out for those who cause divisions and put obstacles in your way that are contrary to the teaching you have learned. Keep away from them.* [18]*For such people are not serving our Lord Christ, but their own appetites. By smooth talk and flattery they deceive the minds of naive people.* [19]*Everyone has heard about your obedience, so I am full of joy over you; but I want you to be wise about what is good, and innocent about what is evil.*
>
> [20]*The God of peace will soon crush Satan under your feet.*
> *The grace of our Lord Jesus be with you.*

The Avoidance of the False Teachers (Romans 16:17)

The apostle returns to the matter of the believer's duty to God and the church when false doctrine and disorderly people rise up. The heresy in view seems to be a kind of antinomian one, contrary to the apostolic teaching (cf. 6:17). Paul tells them to avoid such heresy, which was contrary to receiving weak Christians (cf. 14:1; 15:7; 16:2). False teachers must never be received.

The Defense of the Admonition (Romans 16:18)

The antinomians would attempt to advance themselves by hypocritical, nice talk and flattery (cf. 2 Cor. 11:13–14). They refused to serve the Lord; rather, they served their bellies (cf. Phil. 3:19). Attempting to advance themselves by smooth and plausible thoughts, they nevertheless indulged the flesh.

The Confidence over the Romans and in God (Romans 16:19–20)

The explanatory "for" (in Greek) introduces reasoning something like this, "I say they will deceive the hearts of the simple, for you, obedient ones, they will not deceive; you are of a different mold." As he warns them of danger, he expresses approval of their faith. Further, he is confident of God's aid. He will bruise Satan under his feet shortly, and that fact gives him confidence of God's activity in their behalf now. The reference to Genesis 3:15 is clear. Paul looks forward to the consummation of the work of the cross in the ultimate consignment of Satan to his final end in the lake of fire. It is striking, as William Shedd points out, that the early heresies were failures. Ebionitism and Gnosticism were soon crushed, and the preservation of primitive Christianity from fatal errors amid heavy attacks from false teachings is a remarkable feature of the history of the church.[6]

THE SALUTATIONS OF PAUL'S COMPANIONS

> [21]*Timothy, my fellow worker, sends his greetings to you, as do Lucius, Jason and Sosipater, my relatives.*
> [22]*I, Tertius, who wrote down this letter, greet you in the Lord.*
> [23]*Gaius, whose hospitality I and the whole church here enjoy, sends you his greetings.*
> *Erastus, who is the city's director of public works, and our brother Quartus send you their greetings.*[7]

The final verses of the section contain greetings from Paul's companions. Gaius's full name was probably Gaius Titius Justus, the Gaius of Acts 18:7, who gave Paul and the church hospitality when they were expelled from the synagogue in Corinth. Erastus is the chamberlain, or the commissioner of public works, of the city (i.e., the city of Corinth) from where Paul wrote this letter.

THE GOD WHO ESTABLISHES

The last paragraph of Paul's most important letter is in the form of a doxology. Its thought is devoted to the importance of being established in God's secret, the mystery of the relation of Jew and Gentile in the body of Christ, the church. The paragraph is one of Paul's most carefully constructed and characteristic benedictions in all of his letters. It is the longest of his doxologies, and it is certainly the most important from a theological standpoint.

> [25]*Now to him who is able to establish you by my gospel and the proclamation of Jesus Christ, according to the revelation of the mystery hidden for long ages past,*

The Power of God (Romans 16:25a)

It is possible that this is Paul's "autographic addition" to the letter. Tertius has just noted that it is he who wrote the epistle, speaking as Paul's amanuensis (cf. v. 22). When Tertius finished, Paul added this final word.[8] The context has gathered around the warning against those who would seduce the Romans by "good words and fair speeches" (v. 18), designed to deceive the innocent. Thus, establishment in the truths of the gospel is needed.

The "now" of verse 25 makes the transition from the weak human author, who can warn and admonish but cannot of himself do the work of strengthening, to the mighty God, who can establish the believer. So, Paul writes, "Now to him who is able to establish you." The power, therefore, is not self-derived; it comes from God in grace. As the Puritan William Gurnall put it, "One Almighty is more than all mighties."[9]

The Work of God (Romans 16:25a)

In Paul's words, the work of God is the establishing of the believer. The Greek word suggests the notion of fixing something firmly, thus to confirm, establish, strengthen. The word seems to mean that Paul is not only interested in their escaping the clutches of the seducers but also in their firmness of inner spiritual life in general, in their obtaining an impregnable spiritual consistency of life. Further, from the words that follow, it is clear that he sees this to be possible only if their faith is settled on the whole body of evangelical doctrine, the "gospel and the proclamation of Jesus Christ."

The Norm of His Work (Romans 16:25a)

The apostle writes, "Now to him who is able to establish you by my gospel and the proclamation of Jesus Christ." As the "by" indicates, the norm of the divine work of strengthening is "my gospel and the proclamation of Jesus Christ."

The phrase "the proclamation of Jesus Christ" means literally "the message about Jesus Christ." It explains the preceding words, "my gospel." It is likely that "my gospel" and the following words are not to be restricted to the simple facts about the death, burial, and resurrection of Christ, but are to include the implications and issues arising from those facts. James Stifler is on the mark when he writes, "A church is 'established' when it reverently believes and says of everything — sin and Satan, Christ, death and life, the past and the future — just what the gospel reveals about these things."[10]

The Hiddenness of It (Romans 16:25b)

The apostle continues his doxology by writing it "according to the revelation of the mystery hidden for long ages past." Speaking biblically, a mystery is not something mysterious. It is a truth, concealed for a time and made known only by divine revelation and illumination. There are aspects of the mystery in other places in the Pauline writings (cf. 11:25; 1 Cor. 15:51; 1 Tim. 3:16), and it is likely that there is a development in the Pauline understanding of the entire teaching, seen in one's progress from Romans to Ephesians. The full statement, it appears, is found in Ephesians 3:3–12 (cf. Col. 1:26–27; 4:3; also Rom. 11:11–32).

The phrase "according to the revelation of the mystery" goes with "the proclamation of Jesus Christ"; that is, the preaching about Jesus Christ is to be according to the mystery. Included in the preaching is the divine purpose in the present age of uniting Gentiles and Jews on an equal basis in the one body of the redeemed. From creation to the coming of Christ a hush rested over the divine program in part. The purpose of God was enwrapped in silence in the past.[11]

THE MYSTERY CONCERNING THE GENTILES

[26]but now revealed and made known through the prophetic writings by the command of the eternal God, so that all nations might believe and obey him—

The Manifestation of It (Romans 16:26a)

That which was hidden in the past has "now" been manifested and disclosed. The reference is to a public manifestation, evident from the apostolic teaching and its historical unfolding, the obvious movement of God among the Gentiles. The mystery does not mean that the gospel was not known in old covenant times; rather, it has to do with the relation of Jews and Gentiles in the body of Christ.

While in old covenant times God worked through Jews among the Gentiles, the Jews were always preeminent in his working. Gentiles came into the covenant community by becoming Jews, that is, by embracing biblical Judaism (cf. Ruth, Naaman, et al.). Now, Paul says, it is different. The Gentiles are "heirs together with Israel, members together of one body, and sharers together in the promise in Christ Jesus" (Eph. 3:6). The mystery, then, is the relation of the Jew and Gentile in the one body, the church, and that relation is one of equality, even though the Jew still has his "advantage" of a great future in the messianic promises (cf. Rom. 3:1 – 8). "The sum of the mystery," Stifler says, "was the union of Jew and Gentile on the same level in Christ 'until the fullness of the Gentiles be come in,' when the Jew should again come to the front and receive his headship."[12]

The Disclosure of It (Romans 16:26b)

The expression "prophetic writings" is equally applicable to Old Testament and New Testament writings. In the light of the absence of the article before "prophetic writings," it is doubtful that the Old Testament is in view. Paul refers to his own writings here.

Paul says it is all "by the command of the eternal God." This is the ultimate cause of the unfolding of the mystery, and the apostle evidently links the words to his own commission to preach to the Gentiles as their apostle (cf. Titus 1:3).

THE GOD ONLY WISE AND GLORIOUS

²⁷to the only wise God be glory forever through Jesus Christ! Amen.

The Wisdom of God (Romans 16:27)

This verse resumes that which has begun at the opening of the doxology. Power was ascribed to God there, which was relevant to the establishing of the Romans in the mystery. Here it is wisdom, which was relevant to the unfolding of his hidden will for Gentiles and Jews in the present age. The broken style reflects the overflowing adoration of the apostle. The Greek text has, "to the only wise God through Jesus Christ," the last phrase reminding the readers that the wisdom of God is found only through him.

The Means of It (Romans 16:27)

It is only in Christ that one may see and understand the wisdom of God in his divine purpose of ages. Jesus Christ and his saving work is the divinely given clue to the meaning of history.

The Eternal Glory of God (Romans 16:27)

While there is some question over the reference of the last clause, I take it to refer to God the Father. It is he to whom Paul ascribes glory unto the ages, but it is through Jesus Christ that he does so.

CONCLUSION

The apostle's doxology is designed to show that God is able to strengthen believers in the truth. May the apostle's doxology be used to aid us in the renewal of our own personal commitment to fulfill the mystery personally by the practical recognition of the indwelling Christ in our lives, and nationally in the evangelism of other Gentile and Jewish friends that we have. In so doing we will be acting in conformity with the purpose of God for this age. Lutheran commentator Johann Bengel added at the conclusion of the apostle's words a wish that we all echo: "And let every believing reader say, 'Amen.'" Amen.[13]

DISCUSSION QUESTIONS

1. How is church unity grounded in a relationship to the common Lord whom Christians serve? How essential is it for believers to be continually focused on the Lord Jesus Christ?

2. What can the church learn today from the saints in Romans 16 who exhibited a great deal of humility, serving primarily as helpers, not leaders?

3. How valuable were the women and their ministries at the church of Rome?

4. How does the gospel establish or strengthen believers?

EPILOGUE

William Tyndale's prologue to Romans also makes a fitting epilogue for this commentary. The famous Bible translator writes:

> First behold thyself diligently in the law of God, and see there thy just damnation. Secondarily turn thine eyes to Christ, and see there the exceeding mercy of thy most kind and loving Father. Thirdly remember that Christ made not this atonement that thou shouldest anger God again: neither cleansed he thee, that thou shouldest return (as a swine) unto thine old puddle again: but that thou shouldest be a new creature and live a new life after the will of God and not of the flesh. And be diligent lest through thine own negligence and unthankfulness thou lose this favour and mercy again.[14]

NOTES

Introduction

1. Some material is adapted from the SLJ Institute, www.sljinstitute.net/about.html; www
.believerschapeldallas.org/OnlineMessages/Speakers/tabid/54/Default.aspx; www.legacy.com
/obituaries/dallasmorningnews/obituary.aspx?pid=1858496; and http://religion.wikia.com
/wiki/S._Lewis_Johnson.
2. Accessed from www.sljinstitute.net/sermons/topical_studies/pages/golgotha5.html.
3. From Fred G. Zaspel, "A Tribute to Dr. S. Lewis Johnson," accessed from www.biblicalstudies
.com/bstudy/events/johnson.htm.
4. Charles Van Doren, *A History of Knowledge: Past, Present, and Future* (New York: Ballantine,
1991), accessed from http://alexpetrov.com/memes/hum/renaissance-man.html.
5. S. Lewis Johnson Jr., *The Old Testament in the New* (Grand Rapids: Zondervan, 1980). As
wonderful as this book is, it was written on a more scholarly level; therefore, it was not a
popular work.
6. Accessed from www.thefreedictionary.com/adapt.
7. S. Lewis Johnson Jr., "The Jesus That Paul Preached," *Bibliotheca Sacra* 128:510 (April 1971);
"The Gospel That Paul Preached," *Bibliotheca Sacra* 128:512 (October 1971); "Paul and the
Knowledge of God," *Bibliotheca Sacra* 129:513 (January 1972); "God Gave Them Up: A
Study in Divine Retribution," *Bibliotheca Sacra* 129:514 (April 1972); "Studies in Romans
Part V: The Judgment of God," *Bibliotheca Sacra* 130:517 (January 1973); "Studies in Ro-
mans Part VI: Rite Versus Righteousness," *Bibliotheca Sacra* 130:518 (April 1973); "Studies in
Romans Part VII: The Jews and the Oracles of God," *Bibliotheca Sacra* 130:519 (July 1973);
"Studies in Romans Part VIII: Divine Faithfulness, Divine Judgment, and the Problem of
Antinomianism," *Bibliotheca Sacra* 130:520 (October 1973); "Studies in Romans Part IX:
The Universality of Sin," *Bibliotheca Sacra* 131:522 (April 1974).

Chapter 1: The Christ Paul Preached

1. Augustine, in *A Select Library of the Nicene and Post-Nicene Fathers of the Christian Church*,
ed. Philip Schaff, Vol. 1, "The Confessions and Letters of St. Augustine, with a Sketch of His
Life and Work" (Buffalo, NY: The Christian Literature Company, 1886), 127.
2. C. H. Dodd, *The Epistle of Paul to the Romans* (New York: Harper and Bros., 1932), xiii.
3. It is fitting that the 1984 edition of the New International Version is utilized throughout the
commentary (unless otherwise noted), since Lewis served on its translation committee.
4. Gk., *doulos*.
5. The apostle's experience on the Damascus road is surely in the background of his thought (cf.
Acts 9:3 – 19; 22:6 – 21; 26:12 – 18).
6. Apostleship is a *gift*, not an *office* (cf. 1 Cor. 12:1, 4, 28, 31; Eph. 4:7, 11). One of the striking
things about New Testament church order is the studied avoidance of the term *office*.
7. The genitive, in light of the phrase in verses 2 – 3, is a subjective genitive.
8. Franz J. Leenhardt, *The Epistle to the Romans*, trans. Harold Knight (London: Lutterworth,
1961), 36.
9. Gerhard von Rad, "Typological Interpretation of the Old Testament," trans. John Bright, in *Essays on Old Testament Hermeneutics*, ed. Claus Westermann (Richmond, VA: Bratcher, 1963),

39. The Lord himself taught the apostles to find the roots of their theology in the Old Testament and to see it fulfilled in his life and ministry (cf. Luke 24:25 – 27, 44 – 47; Acts 1:3).
10. Martin Luther, *Luther: Lectures on Romans*, trans. and ed. Wilhelm Pauck, *The Library of Christian Classics*, vol. 15 (Philadelphia: Muhlenberg, 1961), 12.
11. Otto Kuss, *Der Römerbrief*, 3 vols. (Regensburg: Friedrich Pustet, 1957), 1:4.
12. Literally, "the God man."
13. Charles Hodge, *Commentary on the Epistle to the Romans* (Philadelphia: William and Martin, 1886), 18.
14. Cf. Luke 22:22; Acts 2:23; 10:42; 11:29; 17:26, 31; Heb. 4:7. Most modern commentators and lexicographers agree that *horizō* means "to appoint" in this passage. Cf. Walter Bauer, William F. Arndt, and F. Wilbur Gingrich, *A Greek-English Lexicon of the New Testament and Other Early Christian Literature* (Chicago and Cambridge: University of Chicago Press, 1957), 584.
15. Cf. Rom. 15:12; 2 Tim. 2:8.
16. The ablest defense of the view is that of Benjamin Breckinridge Warfield, "The Christ That Paul Preached," in *The Person and Work of Christ* (Philadelphia: Presbyterian & Reformed, 1950), 73 – 78, 89.
17. Philippians 2:5 – 11 is probably the clearest exposition of the general sense of Rom. 1:3 – 4.
18. R. C. H. Lenski, *The Interpretation of St. Paul's Epistle to the Romans* (Columbus, OH: Wartburg, 1936), 37.
19. Quoted in Horton Davies, *Varieties of English Preaching, 1900 – 1960* (London: SCM, 1963), 54.
20. John Murray, *The Epistle to the Romans*, 2 vols., New International Commentary on the New Testament, F. F. Bruce, gen. ed. (Grand Rapids: Eerdmans, 1959), 1:16.
21. Only one preposition is used, more closely joining the persons together.
22. Cf. Claude Thompson, "Social Reform: An Evangelical Imperative," *Christianity Today* (March 26, 1971), 8 – 12 [588 – 92]. Thompson's misguided article, excellent in some respects, is guilty of the standard error of most attempts to flail evangelicals for their supposed "little social vision and less social action." Now no one, not even the most obtuse Bible-beating, Bible-Belt fundamentalist, will take the position that the teaching of Scripture does not involve the Christian ultimately in social vision and action. But the real issue is one of degree. The primary thrust of the Scriptures is toward the evangelical issue, not the social questions. It is to this issue that evangelicals must apply themselves wholeheartedly and fully. Such evangelism will produce social action and change. The weakness of professing Christianity does not lie in its failure to see and do in the social area, but in the fervor and flame of its commitment to the Christ and the doctrines that Paul preached.
23. C. K. Barrett, *A Commentary on the Epistle to the Romans* (New York: Harper & Row, 1957), 27.
24. The particle is often causal, often simply explanatory. It occurs six times in verses 16 – 20 and provides the perceptive reader with an important key to the progress of Paul's thought in the section.
25. Gk., *euangelion*.
26. Or, "The Dallas Cowboys win!"
27. The genitive, "of God," is subjective. As Charles Hodge says, "The gospel is that in which God works, which he renders efficacious — unto salvation" (Hodge, *Commentary on the Epistle to the Romans*, 28). Cf. 1 Cor. 1:21.
28. Murray, *Epistle to the Romans*, 1:28.
29. The gospel was preached to the Jew first, but this does not mean that that is a pattern to be followed in all ages.
30. Gk., *gar*.
31. The *theou* is most likely a genitive of source.
32. It does not mean the attribute of God's righteousness that was revealed in the law (cf. Ps. 145:17).

33. A full treatment of the word *righteousness* is found in David Hill's excellent work, *Greek Words and Hebrew Meanings* (Cambridge: Cambridge University Press, 1967), 82 – 162. Hill concludes, "Consequently, we may say that the word (*dikaioō*) is primarily and predominantly a forensic term, a word of the law-court, describing a relation to, or a status before God, the judge of all men. It is not a case of God 'making righteous' a person who is not so: he 'puts in the right' the person who is in the relationship of faith (i.e., trust, surrender and identification) with Christ, in whose life and death the righteousness of God in covenant-faithfulness to man has been manifested" (p. 160).

34. Heb., *tsedeq*, ibid., 102. The ideas of right and wrong among the Hebrews were predominantly forensic.

35. Ibid., 109.

36. In this place, as in Rom. 10:3, Paul explicitly says the righteousness is not man's, but God's.

37. E. G. Schwiebert, *Luther and His Times* (St. Louis: Concordia, 1950), 282 – 89.

38. A full discussion of *dikaioō* ("righteousness") may be found in Leon Morris's *The Apostolic Preaching of the Cross* (London: Tyndale, 1955).

39. Quoted in Hugh Martin, *The Atonement* (Louisville: John Knox, 1976), 203.

40. The present tense is frequentative in force. The righteousness is revealed as a saving power at every occurrence of faith.

41. Murray, *Epistle to the Romans*, 1:30.

42. Gk., *ek pisteōs eis pistin.*

43. Barrett, *Commentary on the Epistle to the Romans*, 31. Hodge's view is similar (*Commentary on the Epistle to the Romans*, 32).

44. Gk., *ek.*

45. Gk., *eis.*

46. James M. Stifler, *The Epistle to the Romans* (New York: Revell, 1897), 21 – 22.

47. Similar precise forces are given by Paul to his prepositions in the parallel phrases in 2 Corinthians 2:16, where he uses the phrases "of death" (Gk., *ek thanatou eis thanaton*) and "of life" (Gk., *ek zōēs eis zōēn*).

Chapter 2: The Revelation of God's Wrath

1. Walter Lüthi, *The Letter to the Romans: An Exposition*, trans. Kurt Schoenenberger (Richmond, VA: John Knox, 1961), 22.

2. Frédéric L. Godet, *Commentary on the Epistle to the Romans*, 2 vols., trans. A. Cusin (Edinburgh: T&T Clark, 1881), 1:164. Lightfoot suggests practically the same connection, "A righteousness of God is revealed, being required for the state of mankind; for a wrath of God is revealed and extends to all" (J. B. Lightfoot, *Notes on Epistles of Paul from Unpublished Commentaries* [London: Macmillan, 1904], 251).

3. Gk., *orgē.*

4. G. C. Berkouwer, *Sin*, trans. Philip C. Holtrop (Grand Rapids: Eerdmans, 1971), 384.

5. "Therefore, the wrath of God," Berkouwer writes, "is the answer to ungodliness and wickedness (cf. Romans 1:18) and is roused by the sins of men and the forsaking of his ways. God appears as the 'enemy' of his people: yet his wrath is by no means arbitrary or strange" (ibid., 359).

6. Gk., *apokalyptetai.*

7. Cf. Godet, *Commentary on the Epistle to the Romans*, 1:167 – 68.

8. "Die Weltgeschichte ist das Weltgericht." The words were uttered as Friedrich von Schiller gave his first lecture as professor of history at the University of Jena, Germany, May 26, 1789.

9. Gk., *katechontōn.*

10. Cf. Bauer, Arndt, Gingrich, *A Greek-English Lexicon of the New Testament*, 423.

11. Murray, *Epistle to the Romans*, 1:37.

12. Gk., *dioti.*

13. *Dioti*, of course, may also be connected with the general statement made in v. 18, as Charles Hodge points out. "It may however refer to the general sentiment of ver. 18. God will punish the impiety and unrighteousness of men, because he has made himself known to them. The

former method is to be preferred as more in accordance with the apostle's manner and more consistent with the context, inasmuch as he goes on to prove that the impiety of the heathen is inexcusable" (Hodge, *Commentary on the Epistle to the Romans*, 36).

14. John Calvin, *Commentary on the Epistle of Paul the Apostle to the Romans*, trans. and ed. John Owen (Edinburgh: Calvin Translation Society, 1849), 70.

15. Gk., *kathoratai*.

16. Cf. Wilhelm Michaelis, "ὁράω," et al., *Theological Dictionary of the New Testament*, 10 vols., ed. Gerhard Friedrich, trans. Geoffrey W. Bromiley (Grand Rapids: Eerdmans, 1967), 5:380. Michaelis points out that the Greek *kathoratai* ("made plain") refers to intellectual perception in this instance. He suggests that "what has been made" may refer not only to phenomena noted by sensory perception but also to history, including providences in individual life. The perennial question "Are the heathen lost?" finds its answer here. In Paul's thinking they are without excuse and, thus, lost.

17. Gk., *theiotēs*.

18. Gk., *eis* (with the infinitive).

19. For the application of this to preaching we should consult Calvin's comments on Acts 14 and 17 in his *The Acts of the Apostles*, ed. David W. Torrance and Thomas F. Torrance, trans. John W. Fraser and W. J. G. McDonald, 2 vols. (Grand Rapids: Eerdmans, 1965).

20. Godet, *Commentary on the Epistle to the Romans*, 1:173. The problem is a moral one, as Dodd comments, "Paganism, therefore, in Paul's judgment, has not the excuse of ignorance. The truth is there, but the impiety and wickedness of men hinder it. It is not a case of intellectual error at bottom, but of moral obliquity." Cf. Dodd, *The Epistle of Paul to the Romans*, 25.

21. Gk., *emataiōthēsan*.

22. What has been said of the revelation of God in nature may also be said of the second source of the knowledge of God, the revelation of God in conscience (cf. Rom. 2:15 – 16), by which man is given a native sense of the will of God. It too cannot save sinners. It is, therefore, necessary that man come to the third source of the knowledge of God, the Scriptures. It is in them that God interprets his works. And it is here that God outlines the case history of man, diagnoses his malady, and invites him to partake of the remedy, the blood and cross of Jesus Christ.

23. Lüthi, *The Letter to the Romans*, 19.

24. Gk., *paredōken*.

25. Godet thinks there is a feeling of indignation here. He writes, "The verses have something of that παροξυσμός, that *exasperation of heart*, of which the author of the Acts speaks (xvii.16) when describing Paul's impressions during his stay at Athens" (Godet, *Commentary on the Epistle to the Romans*, 1:177).

26. Godet has put it well, "They sinned, *wherefore* God punished them; they sinned by degrading God, wherefore *also* God degraded them" (ibid., 1:177).

27. Ibid., 1:177 – 78.

28. Schlatter points out that *paredōken* is the usual word for the sentence of a judge (cf. A. Schlatter, *Gottes Gerechtigkeit* [Stuttgart: Calwer Verlag, 1959], 66).

29. Murray, *Epistle to the Romans*, 1:44 – 45.

30. See Friedrich Büchsel, "δίδωμι et al.," *Theological Dictionary of the New Testament*, 2:170. The positive force is present in each occurrence. There is another striking occurrence of the identical form of the verb in Ephesians 4:19, and that passage serves to remind the interpreter that the infliction of punitive justice does not compromise the free agency and responsibility of man. In that passage Paul, speaking of the sin of the Gentiles, writes, "Having lost all sensitivity, they have given themselves over (Gk., *paredōkan*) to sensuality so as to indulge in every kind of impurity, with a continual lust for more."

31. Hodge, *Commentary on the Epistle to the Romans*, 40.

32. Ibid., 45.

33. William G. T. Shedd, *A Critical and Doctrinal Commentary on the Epistle of St. Paul to the Romans* (Grand Rapids: Zondervan, 1967), 27.

34. Hodge, *Commentary on the Epistle to the Romans*, 45.

35. Cf. Barrett, *A Commentary on the Epistle to the Romans*, 38, who writes, "God's judgment has already broken forth; only he has consigned sinners not to hell but to sin — if indeed these be alternatives."

Chapter 3: The Judgment of God

1. R. Govett, *The Righteousness of God, the Salvation of the Believer: or the Argument of the Romans* (Norwich, Great Britain: Fletcher and Son, 1891), 20.
2. God's rectoral justice is the rectitude with which he rules both the good and the evil. Necessary by reason of creation, it includes his institution of moral government in the world, with promises of reward and threats of punishment (cf. Rom. 1:32). God's redemptive justice, which highlights God's just dealing with men, deals with his work of justification.
3. The direct address and the occasional vocative (2:1) are also features of the diatribe.
4. Gk., *dio*.
5. Godet, *Commentary on the Epistle to the Romans*, 1:189.
6. Stifler, *The Epistle to the Romans*, 31.
7. The Greek *sy* is emphatic.
8. Hodge, *Commentary on the Epistle to the Romans*, 48.
9. *Genesis Rabbah*, trans. Jacob Neusner (Atlanta: Scholars Press, 1985), 2:182.
10. Stifler, *Epistle to the Romans*, 36.
11. Schrenk's comment is then correct, "In Paul the legal usage is plain and indisputable." Cf. Gottlob Schrenk, s.v. "δίκη et al.," *Theological Dictionary of the New Testament*, 2:215.
12. Italics added. Since the verb is used of God's justification, it cannot by any stretch of the imagination refer to him as being made just.
13. The alternative option would have Paul using the definite article, "the Gentiles," stressing the particular group of people.
14. The Greek participle refers most likely to the law written in the heart.
15. John Calvin, *Institutes of the Christian Religion*, ed. John T. McNeill, trans. Ford Lewis Battles, vol. 20 of *The Library of Christian Classics*, (Philadelphia: Westminster, 1960), 1:848 (3.19.15).
16. Ibid., 1:368 (2.8.1).
17. Gk., *to thelēma*.
18. Verses 21 – 24, in fact, form the apodosis of v. 17, which begins with *ei de*, "now if."
19. The word *prassēs* means literally *to practice*.
20. The Hebrew word is *yadah*.

Chapter 4: The Jews, the Oracles of God, and the Universality of Sin

1. Lüthi, *The Letter to the Romans*, 39.
2. Bruce Manning Metzger, *The New Testament: Its Background, Growth, and Content* (New York: Abingdon, 1965), 64 – 65.
3. Gk., *poly kata panta tropon*.
4. The word *prōton* (NIV, "first of all") has no secondly following. "The fact that the particular which he is about to mention is first in order," Shedd comments, "implies that it is first in importance" (Shedd, *Commentary on the Epistle of St. Paul to the Romans*, 62).
5. Ibid., 63.
6. The *mē* expects the negative answer.
7. Gk., *mē genoito* (a volitive optative).
8. Paul's language is the language of a court of law. The question concerns one's relationship to law primarily, and one's innate righteousness only secondarily. Shedd agrees, "The forensic meaning here is indisputable. God cannot be made just" (*Commentary on the Epistle of St. Paul to the Romans*, 64).
9. Barrett, *A Commentary on the Epistle to the Romans*, 65.
10. Cf. Shedd, *Commentary on the Epistle of St. Paul to the Romans*, 65.

11. Murray, *The Epistle to the Romans*, 1:99. The genitive, then, is probably subjective. The phrase refers to the righteousness that God dispenses.

12. Paul could not bring himself to even phrase a question that might leave open the question of God's justice. The question expecting the negative answer avoids this. Further, even this form of the question is difficult for the apostle to use, so he adds quickly (lit.), "I speak as a man."

13. Calvin, *Commentary on the Epistle of Paul the Apostle to the Romans*, 119.

14. Murray, *Epistle to the Romans*, 1:99.

15. E. H. Gifford, *The Epistle of St. Paul to the Romans* (London: J. Murray, 1996), 84.

16. Murray, *Epistle to the Romans*, 1:97.

17. Calvin, *Commentary on the Epistle of Paul the Apostle to the Romans*, 123.

18. Cf. *Luther and Erasmus: Free Will and Salvation*, trans. and ed. E. Gordon Rupp, *Library of Christian Classics*, vol. 17 (Philadelphia: Westminster, 1969), 185, 190, 199, 213, 304 – 7.

19. Calvin, *Institutes of the Christian Religion*, 1:355.

20. Cf. Barrett, *Commentary on the Epistle to the Romans*, 69.

21. Otto Michel, *Der Brief an die Römer* (Göttingen: Vandenhoeck, 1957), 84.

22. Dodd, *The Epistle of Paul to the Romans*, 48.

23. Gk., *de*.

24. Barrett, *Commentary on the Epistle to the Romans*, 70.

25. This word is found about twenty-two times in the New Testament and in almost every case it means "because" (see its use in 1:20).

26. Barrett, *Commentary on the Epistle to the Romans*, 71.

Chapter 5: How Should Man Be Just with God?

1. Godet, *Commentary on the Epistle to the Romans*, 1:252.

2. D. M. Lloyd-Jones, *Romans: An Exposition of Chapters 3:20 – 4:25, Atonement and Justification* (London: Banner of Truth, 1970), 149.

3. Ray Stedman, *From Guilt to Glory*, 2 vols. (Waco, TX: Word, 1978), 1:69.

4. The aorist tense is then a constative aorist.

5. Lenski, *The Interpretation of St. Paul's Epistle to the Romans*, 251.

6. Gk., *lytrōsis*.

7. Gk., *apolytrōsis*.

8. Adolf Deissmann, *Light from the Ancient East* (New York: Harper, 1922), 327.

9. Godet, *Commentary on the Epistle to the Romans*, 1:261.

10. Edward Mote, "The Solid Rock," public domain.

11. "Then" represents the Greek inferential particle *oun*.

12. C. E. B. Cranfield, *The Epistle to the Romans*, 2 vols. (Edinburg: T&T Clark, 1975), 1:220.

13. The rendering originated with Origen, not Luther.

14. Barrett, *A Commentary on the Epistle to the Romans*, 82 – 83.

15. Cranfield, *Epistle to the Romans*, 1:222.

16. The Shema is the central statement of Jewish belief.

17. Gk., *ek pisteōs*.

18. Gk., *dia tēs pisteōs*.

Chapter 6: Abraham's Salvation

1. Lüthi, *The Letter to the Romans: An Exposition*, 48.

2. Cranfield, *The Epistle to the Romans*, 1:227.

3. Other translations additionally use "reckoned" and "imputed."

4. Lloyd-Jones, *Romans: An Exposition of Chapters 3:20 – 4:25*, 167.

5. Stifler, *The Epistle to the Romans*, 74.

6. Ibid., 75. Stifler's words are again correct, "Here was the Jew's fatal mistake. He practically took Isaiah in his eight-days-old circumcision for the model of a saved man, and not Abraham in his faith" (p. 76).

7. Cranfield, *Epistle to the Romans*, 1:246.

Chapter 7: Safety, Certainty, and Enjoyment

1. A lengthy discussion of this textual problem could be given, but for our purposes it is not necessary. C. E. B. Cranfield prefers the reading *echomen*, rendered "we have" (cf. Cranfield, *The Epistle to the Romans*, 1:257). He admits the other reading has better attestation, but rightly decides on the basis of internal evidence.
2. Ibid., 1:261.
3. Ibid., 1:265.
4. This type of argument is one that contains a conclusion that follows with even greater logical necessity than another already accepted in the argument.
5. Except insofar as the latter follows from the former.
6. Quoted in W. H. Griffith Thomas, *Grace and Power: Some Aspects of the Spiritual Life* (New York: Revell, 1916), 152.
7. Hodge, *Commentary on the Epistle to the Romans*, 140.

Chapter 8: Imputation and Two Representative Men

1. Cf. S. Lewis Johnson's "Romans 5:12 — 'An Exercise in Exegesis and Theology,'" *New Dimensions in New Testament Study*, ed. Richard N. Longnecker and Merrill C. Tenney (Grand Rapids: Zondervan, 1974), 298 – 316.
2. Gk., *dia touto*.
3. "The master-thought of the whole passage," Gifford writes, "is that unity of the many in the one, which forms the point of comparison between Adam and Christ" (Gifford, *The Epistle of St. Paul to the Romans*, 115).
4. The tree was not the symbol of the sex act, as some have contended, nor was it symbolic of wine.
5. Hodge, *Commentary on the Epistle to the Romans*, 147. Paul wrote, "For since death came through a man, the resurrection of the dead comes also through a man. For as in Adam all die, so in Christ all will be made alive" (1 Cor. 15:21 – 22).
6. Charles Spurgeon, "Lost through One — Saved through One," sermon no. 2744, delivered April 24, 1879, accessed June 12, 2013, www.spurgeongems.org/vols46 – 48/chs2744.pdf.
7. John Murray, *The Imputation of Adam's Sin* (Grand Rapids: Eerdmans, 1959), 21.
8. W. G. T. Shedd, *Dogmatic Theology*, third edition, ed. A. W. Gomes (Phillipsburg, NJ: Presbyterian & Reformed, 2004), 550 – 602.
9. Can we act, in a real sense, before we are? No.
10. Shedd, *A Critical and Doctrinal Commentary on the Epistle of St. Paul to the Romans*, 131.
11. Gk., *kai* (which might be rendered either "even" or "and").
12. Shedd, *Critical and Doctrinal Commentary on the Epistle of St. Paul to the Romans*, 133.
13. Murray, *The Epistle to the Romans*, 1:190.
14. Cranfield, *The Epistle to the Romans*, 1:287.
15. Ibid., 1:288.
16. Ibid., 1:289.
17. Michel, *Der Brief an die Römer*, 85 – 86.
18. Shedd, *A Critical and Doctrinal Commentary on the Epistle of St. Paul to the Romans*, 139.
19. Ibid.
20. Godet, *Commentary on the Epistle to the Romans*, 1:386.
21. Charles Haddon Spurgeon, "Commentary on Romans 5:1," in "Spurgeon's Verse Explanations of the Bible," accessed March 20, 2014, www.studylight.org/com/spe/view.cgi?bk=ro&ch=5.

Chapter 9: "Shall We Continue in Sin?"

1. Shedd, *A Critical and Doctrinal Commentary on the Epistle of St. Paul to the Romans*, 145.
2. Lüthi, *The Letter to the Romans: An Exposition*, 79.
3. J. B. Phillips, *The New Testament in Modern English* (New York: Macmillan, 1947, 1957), 319.
4. Murray, *The Epistle to the Romans*, 1:213.

5. Gifford, *The Epistle of St. Paul to the Romans*, 125.
6. Murray, *Epistle to the Romans*, 1:213.
7. Gk., *ei gar*.
8. John Stott, *Men Made New* (Downers Grove, IL: InterVarsity Press, 1966), 43.

Chapter 10: Only Two Masters

1. Cranfield, *The Epistle to the Romans*, 1:323.
2. Shedd, *A Critical and Doctrinal Commentary on the Epistle of St. Paul to the Romans*, 162.
3. Ibid., 164–65.
4. Cranfield, *Epistle to the Romans*, 1:325.
5. Shedd, *Critical and Doctrinal Commentary on the Epistle of St. Paul to the Romans*, 172.

Chapter 11: Marital Union with Christ

1. Paul then has the husband die so that the woman may be married again to another man, in the case before us, Jesus Christ.
2. Gifford, *The Epistle of St. Paul to the Romans*, 135.
3. Introduced by the consecutive particle "so" (*hōste*).
4. Cranfield, *The Epistle to the Romans*, 1:336.
5. Phillip P. Bliss, "Free from the Law," 1871, (accessed June 12, 2013), www.hymntime.com /tch/htm/f/r/e/freefrom.htm.
6. C. H. Spurgeon, *Flashes of Thought: 1,000 Choice Extracts from the Works of C. H. Spurgeon* (London: Passmore & Alabaster, 1874), 415.
7. Cranfield, *Epistle to the Romans*, 1:351.
8. Ibid.
9. Shedd, *A Critical and Doctrinal Commentary on the Epistle of St. Paul to the Romans*, 185.

Chapter 12: The Struggle

1. This is the view of Luther, Calvin, Melanchthon, Beza, Chemnitz, Gerhard, Owen, Delitzsch, Philippi, Hodge, Shedd, Kuyper, Bavinck, Bruce, and Cranfield.
2. Hodge, *Commentary on the Epistle to the Romans*, 240.
3. Godet, *Commentary on the Epistle to the Romans*, 2:32.
4. Stott, *Men Made New*, 74.
5. F. F. Bruce, *The Epistle of Paul to the Romans*, Tyndale New Testament Commentaries (Grand Rapids: Eerdmans, 1963), 150–51.
6. Stott, *Men Made New*, 77.
7. Gifford, *The Epistle of St. Paul to the Romans*, 140.
8. Cranfield, *The Epistle to the Romans*, 1:358.
9. Alfred Lord Tennyson, "Maud: A Monodrama," pt. 1, sec. 10, stanza 5 (1855).
10. Paul avoids the term *spirit*, although the mind is closely related to the spirit, because there might be a tendency to refer that to the new nature of the believer in conjunction with the Holy Spirit. That is what he wishes to avoid.

Chapter 13: The Delivering Power of the Indwelling Spirit

1. Quoted in Godet, *Commentary on the Epistle to the Romans*, 2:57.
2. Gk., *ara nyn*.
3. The word "law" here probably means something like "principle."
4. Bruce, *The Epistle of Paul to the Romans*, 158.
5. The aorist tense is used, which looks at the action as an event and, here, as a past event.
6. Shedd, *A Critical and Doctrinal Commentary on the Epistle of St. Paul to the Romans*, 227.
7. Ibid., 229.
8. Stifler, *The Epistle to the Romans*, 142.
9. This is the purposive conjunction (*hina*).

10. Bruce, *The Epistle of Paul to the Romans*, 162.
11. Shedd, *Critical and Doctrinal Commentary on the Epistle of St. Paul to the Romans*, 235.

Chapter 14: The Divine Purpose: From Groanings to Glory

1. Cranfield, *The Epistle to the Romans*, 1:408.
2. Lüthi, *The Letter to the Romans: An Exposition*, 113.
3. The Greek includes a connecting "for" in verse 20.
4. Cranfield, *Epistle to the Romans*, 1:414.
5. Some manuscripts of an ancient nature have a conjunction at this point in the text that may be translated either "that," which would introduce the content of the hope, or "because," which would introduce the reason for the preceding statement. It is not an easy decision. I think that the force of "because" is probably correct regardless of the decision concerning the variant reading.
6. Quoted in Murray, *The Epistle to the Romans*, 2:305.
7. C. H. Spurgeon, "Glorious Predestination" (a sermon delivered on March 24, 1872, at Metropolitan Tabernacle), accessed June 18, 2013, www.spurgeon.org/sermons/1043.htm.
8. Cranfield's discussion is one of the most detailed (cf. *Epistle to the Romans*, 1:425 – 29).
9. The 1984 edition of the NIV translates Genesis 4:1, "Adam lay with his wife Eve," while the 2011 edition says, "Adam made love to his wife Eve."
10. In Acts 2:23, due to the construction in the Greek text, there is a strong suggestion that "God's set purpose" is the source of the "foreknowledge" of God and that the two concepts are closely linked together.
11. T. W. Manson, "Romans," *Peake's Commentary on the Bible* (London: Nelson, 1962), 947.
12. Matthew Black, *Romans* (London: Oliphants, 1973), 125.
13. Rudolf Bultmann, "γινώσκω et al.," *TDNT*, 1:715.
14. There are only three answers to the question, "Why did God elect anyone to salvation?" (1) God elected those who did good works. This erroneous view is known as the Pelagian view. (2) God elected those whom, looking down through the years, he foresaw would believe out of their free will, and he then elected them. This view would mean that God gained knowledge by looking down throughout the years. The man who could allegedly respond out of his free will would have something that the man who does not respond does not have. (3) The third possibility has God choosing his elect according to his good pleasure alone. There was not one thing in anyone that God was so enamored with that he decided to choose him or her. Instead, God chooses because of what he was going to make of sinners. The Lord set his love on the elect with all of their flaws, all of their sin, and all of their total depravity. The Bible teaches that election proceeds out of divine love (Eph. 1:4 – 5). Who can explain love? This view is the right option.
15. Cranfield comments, "With this third link of the chain we are in the realm of historical time" (*Epistle to the Romans*, 1:432).
16. Bruce, *The Epistle of Paul to the Romans*, 178.

Chapter 15: God for Us

1. Lüthi, *The Letter to the Romans: An Exposition*, 118 – 19.
2. Speaking grammatically, the condition is a first class condition, a condition of simple supposition, which the context makes clear is one of reality.
3. In the Septuagint, the Greek rendering of the Old Testament on which the New Testament writers so often relied, the same word that Paul uses here occurs.
4. Cranfield, *The Epistle to the Romans*, 1:436.
5. Ibid., 1:437.

Chapter 16: Distinguishing Grace

1. Cf. S. Lewis Johnson Jr., "Evidence from Romans 9 – 11," in *A Case for Premillennialism: A New Consensus*, ed. Donald K. Campbell and Jeffrey L. Townsend (Chicago: Moody Press, 1992), 199 – 223.

2. William Manson, *New Testament Essays in Memory of T. W. Manson,* ed. A. J. B. Higgins (Manchester: Manchester University Press, 1959), 164.
3. Stedman, *From Guilt to Glory,* 2:11.
4. Quoted in Charles B. Cunningham, *Simple Studies in Romans* (Grand Rapids: Baker, 1978), 51.
5. The first announcement of the gospel.
6. There are a few weak manuscripts with variant readings at this point.
7. Barrett, *A Commentary on the Epistle to the Romans,* 180.
8. Nations are simply conglomerations of individual people, so the desire to turn Romans 9 into solely a national election is misguided.
9. Barrett, *Commentary on the Epistle to the Romans,* 182.

Chapter 17: Vessels of Wrath and Vessels of Mercy

1. As S. Lewis Johnson wrote elsewhere, "The mention of the Gentiles in verse 24 is only incidental at this point. It is the sovereign purpose of grace in the salvation of both Israel and the Gentiles that is the point. In other words, the analogy is not a national or ethnic one, it is a soteriological one. It is not so much the *fact* of the calling of the Gentiles now and the future calling of Israel that forms the analogy. Paul, thus, lays stress from Hosea on the electing grace of the calling of both the Gentiles in the present time and the mass of ethnic Israel in the future. This is the point that he finds in Hosea, and it is most appropriate. The use of the verb "to call" supports the point, emphasizing the fact that God's effectual calling in elective grace is true both in the salvation of the Gentiles today and in the salvation of ethnic Israel in the future. Therein lies the resemblance, the analogy, the apostle sees in the present situation and in Hosea's texts. The mention of the salvation of the Gentiles in verse 24 is very appropriate, but their admission into the people of God is itself an act of divine sovereign grace, his theme. In this respect their call is analogical to the call of both Israel's remnant (cf. 11:5) and the future ethnic mass of believers at the time of the Messiah's coming (11:25 – 27)." (Modified from a chapter titled, "Evidence from Romans 9 – 11," by S. Lewis Johnson Jr. in *A Case for Premillennialism: A New Consensus,* 199 – 223.

Chapter 18: Christ, the Law, and Israel's Inexcusable Unbelief

1. Lüthi, *The Letter to the Romans: An Exposition,* 141 – 42.
2. Poem attributed to John Berridge in Charles Spurgeon, *The Salt-Cellars: Being a Collection of Proverbs, Together with Homely Notes Thereon* (London: Passmore and Alabaster, 1889), 200.
3. Barrett, *A Commentary on the Epistle to the Romans,* 200.
4. Charles Haddon Spurgeon, "How Can I Obtain Faith?" in *The Metropolitan Tabernacle Pulpit: Sermons Preached and Revised,* vol. 18 (London: Passmore & Alabaster, 1873), 39.
5. Bruce, *The Epistle of Paul to the Romans,* 209.

Chapter 19: Is Israel's Rejection Total?

1. Lüthi, *The Letter to the Romans: An Exposition,* 151.
2. Arthur S. Way, *The Letters of St. Paul* (London: Macmillan, 1935), 135.
3. John Calvin, *The Epistles of Paul the Apostle to the Romans and to the Thessalonians,* trans. Ross MacKenzie; ed. David W. Torrance and Thomas F. Torrance (Edinburgh and London: Oliver & Boyd, 1961), 255.
4. Murray, *The Epistle to the Romans,* 2:79.
5. Ibid., 2:78.
6. Gifford, *The Epistle of St. Paul to the Romans,* 196.
7. Murray, *The Epistle to the Romans,* 2:96.
8. Ibid., 2:84.
9. Gifford, *The Epistle of St. Paul to the Romans,* 196
10. Cf. Murray, *The Epistle to the Romans,* 2:86; Bruce, *The Epistle of Paul to the Romans,* 217 – 20; Black, *Romans,* 145.
11. Gk., *de.*

12. Shedd, *A Critical and Doctrinal Commentary on the Epistle of St. Paul to the Romans*, 341.
13. Murray, *Epistle to the Romans*, 2:88.
14. William Sanday and Arthur Headlam have "the full completed number" (*Romans*, International Critical Commentary, 5th ed. [Edinburgh: T&T Clark, 2000], 330).
15. Murray, *Epistle to the Romans*, 2:90.
16. It is said that at one time Frederick the Great was having a conversation with his chaplain on the veracity of the Bible. Finally, the king said, "Give me in a word proof that the Bible is the inspired Word of God." The chaplain replied, "I will, your Majesty. It is, 'the Jew.'" Their story is sufficient to show the truthfulness of God and his faithfulness to his promises.

Chapter 20: The Salvation of Israel and God's Agenda for the Nations

1. J. B. Lightfoot, *Saint Paul's Epistles to the Colossians and to Philemon* (London: Macmillan, 1890), 258. Sanday and Headlam have "the full completed number" (*Romans*, 335).
2. Cf. O. Palmer Robertson, "Is There a Distinctive Future for Ethnic Israel in Romans 11?" *Perspectives on Evangelical Theology*, ed. Kenneth S. Kantzer and Stanley N. Gundry (Grand Rapids: Baker, 1979), 219 – 21.
3. Sanday and Headlam, *Romans*, 335.
4. Godet, *Commentary on the Epistle to the Romans*, 2:255 – 56.
5. Calvin, *Commentary on the Epistle of Paul the Apostle to the Romans*, 437.
6. Often cited is the statement from Mishnah *Sanhedrin* 10:1, "all Israel has a portion in the age to come," which is followed by a listing of those kinds of Israelites who do not have a portion in the age to come.
7. Some attempt to prematurely jump to Galatians 6:16 to garner support for a spiritualizing interpretation of "Israel." G. C. Berkouwer admits, "But it is indeed open to question whether Paul, in writing to the Galatians, had in mind the church as the new Israel. The meaning may well be: peace and mercy to those who orient themselves to the rule of the new creation in Christ, and also peace and mercy be upon the Israel of God, that is, upon those *Jews* (italics mine) who have turned to Christ" (*The Return of Christ*, trans. James Van Oosterom, and ed. Marlin J. Van Elderen [Grand Rapids: Eerdmans, 1972], 344. For a fuller treatment of Galatians 6:16 see my "Paul and 'The Israel of God': An Exegetical and Eschatological Case-Study," in *Essays in Honor of J. Dwight Pentecost*, ed. Stanley D. Toussaint and Charles H. Dyer (Chicago: Moody Press, 1986), 181 – 96.
8. Shedd, *A Critical and Doctrinal Commentary on the Epistle of St. Paul to the Romans*, 349.
9. Barrett, *A Commentary on the Epistle to the Romans*, 224.
10. Ibid., 226.
11. Ibid.
12. Way, *The Letters of St. Paul*, 138.
13. Shedd, *Critical and Doctrinal Commentary on the Epistle of St. Paul to the Romans*, 353.
14. Quoted in Charles Swindoll, *The Tale of the Tardy Oxcart* (Nashville: Nelson, 1998), 500.
15. Quoted in Stifler, *The Epistle to the Romans*, 212.
16. Shedd, *Critical and Doctrinal Commentary on the Epistle of St. Paul to the Romans*, 353.
17. Michel, *Der Brief an die Römer*, 253.

Chapter 21: The Mercies of God and Living Sacrifices

1. Roy A. Harrisville, *Augsburg Commentary on the New Testament: Romans* (Minneapolis: Augsburg, 1980), 189.
2. Lüthi, *The Letter to the Romans: An Exposition*, 159.
3. Isaac Watts, "When I Survey the Wondrous Cross," public domain.
4. Richard Francis Weymouth, *The New Testament in Modern Speech* (New York: Harper & Brothers, 1929), 375.
5. Henry Alford, *The New Testament for English Readers in Two Volumes* (London: Deighton, Bell, and Co., 1865), 2:110.

6. Shedd, *A Critical and Doctrinal Commentary on the Epistle of St. Paul to the Romans*, 361.
7. Cranfield, *The Epistle to the Romans*, 2:617.
8. Ibid., 2:619.
9. As someone has said, prophecy is to foretell and to forth-tell.
10. Shedd, *Critical and Doctrinal Commentary on the Epistle of St. Paul to the Romans*, 363–64.
11. We might suppose that most deacons ought to have this gift in order to minister in that office, but that is not specifically stated in Scripture.
12. Cranfield, *Epistle to the Romans*, 2:625.
13. Quoted in J. Oswald Sanders, *Spiritual Leadership* (Chicago: Moody Press, 2007), 72–73.

Chapter 22: Love and Service

1. Thomas Watson, *A Divine Cordial*, online book, www.the-highway.com/Divine_Cordial4 .html.
2. Bruce, *The Epistle of Paul to the Romans*, 228.
3. Alan F. Johnson, *The Freedom Letter* (Chicago: Moody Press, 1974), 183.
4. Alexander Maclaren, *St. Paul's Epistle to the Romans*, vol. 24 (London: Hodder and Stoughton, 1909), 282–83.
5. Chrysostom, quoted in Shedd, *A Critical and Doctrinal Commentary on the Epistle of St. Paul to the Romans*, 369–70.

Chapter 23: The Christian Citizen and the Day

1. Murray, *The Epistle to the Romans*, 2:159.
2. Shedd, *A Critical and Doctrinal Commentary on the Epistle of St. Paul to the Romans*, 381.

Chapter 24: The Christian's Favorite Indoor Sport

1. Bruce, *The Epistle of Paul to the Romans*, 243.
2. Albrecht Beutel, "Luther's Life," trans. Katharina Gustavs, in *The Cambridge Companion to Martin Luther*, ed. Donald K. McKim (New York: Cambridge University Press, 2003), 11.
3. Stedman, *From Guilt to Glory*, 2:139.
4. Shedd, *Critical and Doctrinal Commentary on the Epistle of St. Paul to the Romans*, 387–88; Barrett, *A Commentary on the Epistle to the Romans*, 256.
5. Bruce, *The Epistle of Paul to the Romans*, 244.
6. See Stedman, *From Guilt to Glory*, 2:144.
7. Shedd, *Critical and Doctrinal Commentary on the Epistle of St. Paul to the Romans*, 393.
8. Lüthi, *The Letter to the Romans: An Exposition*, 199.
9. The Son has had judgment delegated to him (cf. Matt. 7:22–23, 25:31; John 5:22; Acts 17:31).
10. Gk., *krinō*.
11. Murray, *The Epistle to the Romans*, 2:192.
12. Murray comments, "It is the contrast between what the extreme sacrifice of Christ exemplified and the paltry demand devolving on us that accentuates the meanness of our attitude when we discard the interests of a weak brother" (ibid., 2:191).
13. Shedd, *Critical and Doctrinal Commentary on the Epistle of St. Paul to the Romans*, 400.
14. Stedman, *From Guilt to Glory*, 2:156–57.

Chapter 25: The Servant of the Nations

1. Mark Twain once quipped, "Few things are harder to put up with than the annoyance of a good example" (Mark Twain, *The Tragedy of Pudd'nhead Wilson*, "Pudd'nhead Wilson's Calendar, ch. 19, 1894. Ebook accessed via www.gutenberg.org/files/102/102-h/102-h.htm) and we shall have to sympathize a bit with him as we observe our Lord's example, for his, of course, is a perfect one.
2. Cf. Barrett, *A Commentary on the Epistle to the Romans*, 269.

3. The psalm has already been cited in the book (cf. Rom. 11:9 – 10).

4. Commentators have taken the last words in two different ways. Some have contended that the words should be translated "the God and Father of our Lord Jesus Christ," making the Father the God of the Lord Jesus. That might seem to suggest a place somewhat less than divine for the Son, but that is not the necessary meaning of the words. Being the God-man, there is an element of truth in the contention that he had a God, with respect to his human nature.

5. I take the sentence to depend on the clause, "Christ has become," rather than on "I say," in verse 8. It seems to me that that clause is the governing one in the verse.

6. Murray, *The Epistle to the Romans*, 2:213.

7. Bruce, *The Epistle of Paul to the Romans*, 260.

8. Stedman, *From Guilt to Glory*, 2:174 – 75.

9. The New Testament teaches grace-giving, that is, giving prompted not by the impulse of the moment, nor by the pressure applied by others, but "in view of God's mercy" (cf. Rom. 12:1), or the "joy" of salvation (cf. 2 Cor. 8:2). All the modern "methods" of inducing giving, such as "matching gifts," "pledge systems," and "faith-promise systems" fall short of the New Testament principles. The important thing to note about the apostle Paul is this: he taught that believers should give and that they should give to others, but he never asked the saints to give to him. The conflict of interest was obvious, and he trusted God to meet his needs.

Chapter 26: Paul's Friends and the Strengthening Gospel

1. Griffith Thomas, quoted in Curtis Vaughan and Bruce Corley, *Romans: A Study Guide Commentary* (Grand Rapids: Zondervan, 1976), 165.

2. Lüthi, *The Letter to the Romans: An Exposition*, 215 – 16.

3. Note also the words of Paul in 1 Timothy 3:11, "In the same way, their wives are to be women worthy of respect," in the midst of words concerning deacons. This is probably to be understood to mean, "Even so must their women," that is, "their women-deacons." This view is unlikely. The preceding context has to do with the male deacons and the following context also has to do with them, and it seems difficult to believe the apostle would interrupt his words concerning deacons to speak of deaconesses and then return to deacons without a specific word in clarifying the matter. I, therefore, incline to the view that the office of deaconess does not exist.

4. Bruce, *The Epistle of Paul to the Romans*, 271.

5. Ibid., 275 – 76.

6. Shedd, *A Critical and Doctrinal Commentary on the Epistle of St. Paul to the Romans*, 433.

7. Verse 24 is probably not genuine, being a repetition of verse 20.

8. Cf. Bruce, *The Epistle of Paul to the Romans*, 282.

9. William Gurnall, *The Christian in Complete Armour: A Treatise of the Saint's War against the Devil* (Google ebook, 2014) accessed at http://books.google.com/books?id=x5phAgA AQBAJ&dq=William+Gurnall+One+Almighty+is+more+than+all+mighties.&source= gbs_navlinks_s.

10. Stifler, *The Epistle to the Romans*, 271 – 72.

11. E. Käsemann, *An die Römer* (Tübingen: Mohr, 1973), 425.

12. Stifler, *Epistle to the Romans*, 272.

13. The reader is encouraged to listen to S. Lewis Johnson's sermons on Romans delivered at Believers Chapel. They can be accessed at www.believerschapeldallas.org/OnlineMessages/Romans/tabid/120/Default.aspx.

14. William Tyndale, *Tyndale's New Testament*, ed. David Daniell (New Haven, CT: Yale University Press, 1995), 224.